The Secret Still Hidden

Christopher A. Ferrara

Good Counsel Publications
Pound Ridge, New York

THE SECRET STILL HIDDEN

First Edition

ISBN: 978-0-9815357-0-8

For all correspondence, contact:

Good Counsel Publications
P.O. Box 203
Pound Ridge, New York 10576-0203
United States of America
1-800-954-8737 • www.secretstillhidden.com

The Secret Still Hidden

An investigation into the Vatican Secretary of State's personal campaign to conceal the words of the Virgin Mary in the Third Secret of Fatima.

Christopher A. Ferrara

Dedication

To the Blessed Virgin Mary,

Mother of the Church, Mother of all humanity,
and Mother of this unworthy son. May this book, in some
small way, serve the cause of the triumph of her Immaculate
Heart, which she foretold and promised at Fatima;

and

To Pope Benedict XVI,

who declared at the beginning of his papacy: "Pray for me,
that I may not flee for fear of the wolves." May the Supreme
Pontiff repel the wolves that surround him, restore the
Church and bring peace to the world by the means Our Lady
provided in the Message of Fatima, whose fulfillment has, for
too long, been impeded by men who think themselves more
prudent than the Virgin Most Prudent.

"As for the Secret, well I happen to be
one of those individuals who thinks
we didn't get the whole thing."

- Mother Angelica

"[T]hat there is a part of the Secret
not revealed and considered unspeakable is
certain. And today — having decided to deny its
existence — the Vatican runs the risk of exposing
itself to very heavy pressure and blackmail."

- Antonio Socci

Abbreviations:

Fourth Secret	Socci, Antonio, *Il Quarto Segreto di Fatima*.
Last Visionary	Bertone, Cardinal Tarcisio, *L'Ultima Veggente di Fatima*.
Message	Congregation for the Doctrine of the Faith, *The Message of Fatima* (English edition).
WTAF, Vol. I	Michel de la Sainte Trinité (Frère), *The Whole Truth About Fatima*, Volume I, *Science and the Facts*.
WTAF, Vol. II	*The Whole Truth About Fatima*, Volume II, *The Secret and the Church*.
WTAF, Vol. III	*The Whole Truth About Fatima*, Volume III, *The Third Secret*.

Table of Contents

Overview

Socci Accuses Bertone

On May 12, 2007, Antonio Socci, one of Italy's most respected Catholic intellectuals, published in his widely read column this astonishing challenge to Cardinal Tarcisio Bertone, the Vatican Secretary of State: "Dear Cardinal Bertone: Who—between you and me—is deliberately lying?"[1] Socci was responding to the Cardinal's suggestion, in a book the Cardinal had published days before, that Socci has misled the Catholic faithful in his own book, *Il Quarto Segreto di Fatima* (*The Fourth Secret of Fatima*).

In *Fourth Secret*, Socci contends that the mysterious vision of "the Bishop dressed in white," published by the Vatican on June 26, 2000, is not the entirety of the Third Secret of Fatima, contrary to what Cardinal Bertone and his Vatican colleagues have asserted. In that vision the white-clad bishop, apparently a future Pope, is executed along with bishops, priests and laity outside a half-ruined city filled with dead bodies, but there are no words of the Virgin to explain how this grim scenario arises. As Socci flatly declares, in agreement with vast numbers of skeptical Catholics, something must be missing: "[T]hat there is a part of the Secret not revealed and considered unspeakable *is certain*. And today—having decided to deny its existence—the Vatican runs the risk of exposing itself to very heavy pressure and blackmail."[2]

A Remarkable Change of Mind

Socci's conclusion is all the more remarkable in that he is a very prominent member of the "mainstream" Catholic establishment in Italy, the host of a popular Italian television show (*Excalibur*), and a personal acquaintance of Cardinal Bertone and the former

---

[1]*Libero*, May 12, 2007 (Via Merano 18, 20187 Milano, Italy); see English translation at http://www.fatima.org/news/newsviews/052907socci.asp.

[2]Antonio Socci, *Il Quarto Segreto di Fatima* (Milano: Rizzoli, 2006), p. 173.

Cardinal Ratzinger, having hosted press conferences for both prelates. Given his position, it is not surprising that Socci was at first determined to demolish the claims of the so-called "Fatimists" that the Vatican is holding something back. Socci once viewed such claims as mere "dietrologies," an Italian idiom for conspiracy theories that look behind (*dietro*) events for hidden plots. He was convinced that the vision of the bishop in white was all there was to the Third Secret, and that in *The Message of Fatima*, the Vatican-published commentary on the vision and the Fatima message in general, Ratzinger and Bertone had laid all questions to rest.

As Socci first believed, "Fatimist" literature casting doubt on the completeness of the Vatican's disclosure originated "from the burning disappointment of a Third Secret that controverted all of their apocalyptic predictions." The "Fatimists" had to be refuted, he thought, because the "polemical arms" in their arsenal were "at the disposal of whoever wanted to launch a heavy attack against the Vatican."[3] But then Socci encountered unexpected strength in the "Fatimist" case, which he had never studied closely. At the same time, his own suspicions were aroused when Cardinal Bertone declined to grant him an interview, despite their friendly relations and Socci's intention to defend Bertone's position. That refusal opened Socci's eyes to the possibility "that there are embarrassing questions and that there is above all something (of gravity) to hide."[4]

As Socci explains: "In the end, I had to surrender.... Here I recount my voyage into the greatest mystery of the 20th century and set forth the result I honestly reached. A result that sincerely contradicts my initial convictions..."[5] What completely changed Socci's mind and made him "surrender" is simply this: overwhelming evidence, which will be surveyed here. The evidence convinced Socci that the "dietrologies" of the "Fatimists"—i.e., loyal Catholics who have reasonable doubts about the official account—were actually correct: there must be a separate but related text of the Secret, not yet revealed, containing "the words of the Madonna [which] preannounce an apocalyptic crisis of the faith in the Church starting from the top." This second text is probably "also an explanation of the vision (revealed on June 26, 2000) where there

---

[3]Ibid., pp. 12, 13.

[4]Ibid., p. 14.

[5]Ibid., p. 14.

appear the Pope, the bishops and martyred faithful, after having traversed a city in ruins."[6] That explanation, writes Socci, would involve "the preannounced assassination of a Pope [the white-clad bishop in the vision] in the context of an immense martyrdom of Christians and of a devastation of the world."[7] Only such an explanation would make sense of the otherwise inexplicable vision.

Motive and Intent: Socci's Hypothesis

It must be noted at the outset that, despite Socci's public challenge to Cardinal Bertone quoted above, *Fourth Secret* does not claim simply that Bertone and his collaborators at the Vatican are a pack of liars and knaves, much less the Popes who have reigned during this controversy. The reality is far more complicated.

As the law recognizes, there is a distinction between motive and intent. For example, from a *motive* of reasonable fear for one's own life, one may have the *intent* to commit bodily harm upon another. Bodily harm intentionally committed for that motive would not be a crime, but rather lawful self-defense. If Socci and the "Fatimists" are correct, then the Third Secret in its entirety— the already published picture and the missing soundtrack, as it were—depict a collapse of faith and discipline in the Church in conjunction with a worldwide catastrophe. That being the case, Vatican officials would have a perfectly human motive to hide the missing part of the Secret, because it would constitute a negative heavenly commentary on their own stewardship of the Church and a warning of global disaster that could cause panic among the faithful. The existence of this *motive*, however, does not necessarily point to *intent* to engage in outright lying about what Socci calls the "part of the Secret not revealed and considered unspeakable."

Rather, Bertone and the other Vatican officials involved may be employing what the moral theologians call a "broad mental reservation," meaning an equivocal statement or statements made with a qualification hidden in the mind of the speaker. An example of this is the statement "Mrs. Smith is not *here*," uttered with the mental reservation "in this room" when Mrs. Smith is in the next room. Suppose Bertone and company have been persuaded—or

---

[6]Ibid., p. 82.

[7]Socci, *Fourth Secret*, pp. 63-64.

have persuaded themselves—that the missing portion of the Secret is "not authentic" but rather something Sister Lucia only thought she had heard from the Virgin Mary. In that case, a broad mental reservation would involve a statement such as: "We have revealed the *authentic* Third Secret," with the mental reservation "but not what we deem the inauthentic words attributed to the Virgin." As we will see, Cardinal Bertone has employed precisely such language in discussing what the Vatican revealed in June of 2000.[8]

It must be noted, however, that a broad mental reservation is not morally justified when the hearer of the statement has a right to know the truth.[9] If, as Socci and others (including this writer) contend, there is a hidden text of the Third Secret, the faithful have a right to know of its existence, even if someone privately deems that text "inauthentic" without a public and authoritative judgment of the Church. Nevertheless, the presence of a mental reservation would allow one to conclude that strictly speaking the prelates in question are not "lying through their teeth," even if they are concealing an element of the truth. Rather, they have convinced themselves they are telling the whole truth so far as the faithful need to know it. They may even think they are doing their duty before God to "protect" the Church from the shock and panic of a "false" revelation. This possible explanation should be kept in view when considering what is presented in the coming pages.

Socci's own hypothesis along these lines, to which we shall return, is that while John Paul II expressed the desire to reveal the entirety of the Third Secret, "a compromise solution was reached." It was decided to reveal the missing portion of the Third Secret *indirectly* through the Pope's sermon at Fatima on May 13, 2000, wherein the Pope (as Sister Lucia did) linked the Secret to apostasy in the Church by pointed references to verses 1, 3 and

---

[8]A "broad" mental reservation, which involves a misleading equivocation from which the truth could still be inferred from the words, is to be distinguished from a "strict" mental reservation, which involves a statement that falsely appears to convey the truth without qualification: e.g., "I did not steal the money," uttered with the mental reservation "with my left hand, but rather with my right hand." As to the Third Secret, a statement involving a "strict" mental reservation would be the unqualified declaration: "We have revealed the entire Third Secret," with the mental reservation "more or less" or "in its essence" or "so far as we consider it authentic." A strict mental reservation is simply a lie, and is never morally permissible. *See* Jone and Adelman, *Moral Theology* (Westminster, Maryland: The Newman Bookshop, 1944), § VIII, Chapter I, LYING, pp. 260-261.

[9]Jone and Adelman, *Moral Theology*, loc. cit.

4 of Chapter 12 of the Book of the Apocalypse. The idea, writes Socci in an allusion to Scripture, is: "He who can understand, let him understand."[10] This indirect revelation of the missing text, combined with publication of the vision, "would have permitted them [the Curia] to be able to say that all of the Third Secret had been revealed, but without an integral explicit publication to avoid—according to their view—a great shock to the Christian people, sensationalistic broadcasts and a reaction of panic."[11]

Thus, the controversy Socci has joined is not simply a question of white hats versus black hats, but a complex clash of human motives with a supernatural event that provokes fear as well as devotion, and has put the faith of certain people to the test by placing them in what they perceive to be an untenable situation.

A Matter of Spiritual and Secular Urgency

And so we enter upon the unprecedented scene of no less than the Cardinal Secretary of State attacking a respected Catholic layman, and that layman, a loyal son of the Church, accusing the Vatican of a cover-up of the very words of the Mother of God. At this moment millions of Catholics around the world are following the Socci-Bertone controversy in newspapers and on the Internet, and it is the talk of cardinals, bishops, and monsignors inside the Vatican walls. So important is this controversy that Cardinal Bertone has felt constrained not only to write a book against Socci, but also to appear for more than an hour on Italy's most popular television talk show, a subsequent radio broadcast, and a second television show he himself produced in an effort to debunk Socci—with Socci himself barred from participating in any of these forums. Yet, as Socci has pointed out, Bertone has failed to address *a single one* of his contentions in *Fourth Secret*, thus conceding Socci's entire case.

Simply at the level of public interest, therefore, this is a sensational story: There is a secret not revealed, and the Vatican, for whatever reason, is hiding it from the world, while the prominent Catholic layman who makes this grave accusation is being attacked, but not answered, by a Vatican prelate of the highest rank. But the contention that the Vatican is concealing part of the Third Secret of Fatima is more than just a sensational news story. If Socci is right,

---

[10]e.g., "He who has ears to hear, let him hear!" (Matt. 11:15).

[11]Socci, *Fourth Secret*, p. 91.

the contents of the hidden text predict catastrophes for the Church and the world which could be averted or at least mitigated if we were given the benefit of the warnings and spiritual correctives the text no doubt contains. The Socci-Bertone controversy revolves, then, around a matter that should concern every man, woman and child on earth, believer and unbeliever alike. We are indeed dealing with "the greatest mystery of the 20th century," a mystery that continues into this century with consequences that could not be more dramatic. That mystery is everyone's concern.

A Word About "Scandal"

Nor should anyone be heard to complain that to air this matter, as Socci has done, "scandalizes" the Church. Such a scandal would be "the scandal of the Pharisees," who attacked the good deeds of Our Lord Himself because they perceived them as threats to their respectability. Besides, as no less than Pope St. Gregory declared, "It is better that scandals arise than that the truth be suppressed." Writing in his own defense against this charge of "scandal," Socci observes: "The Gospel speaks very clearly. Jesus says: 'the truth will make you free.' It does not say: be careful because the truth will create problems.... The Church is not some kind of sect or Mafia gang that demands from us a code of silence. But it is the house of the sons of God, the house of liberty and of truth."[12]

This book, like Socci's, has been written in the spirit of the quest for truth, the truth that makes us free. For the Third Secret of Fatima is not just a mystery one can solve by investigation of the facts, although it is certainly that. As Socci has recognized, the Third Secret is, above all, a vital warning from the Mother of God to the whole Church and all of humanity by which we might avoid the dangers that threaten us and be assisted in our progress toward the final end of man in eternal beatitude.

---

[12]"Bertone nel 'Vespaio' delle Polemiche" ("Bertone in the 'Wasp's Nest' of the Polemics"), *Libero,* June 2, 2007.

Chapter 1

A "Private" Revelation?

In discussing the controversy between Antonio Socci and Cardinal Bertone concerning the Third Secret of Fatima, we must first dispense with the banal objection that the Message of Fatima is "just a private revelation" the faithful can take or leave as they wish. Given the facts and circumstances surrounding the Fatima event, that contention is simply ludicrous.

Like the rest of the Fatima message, the Third Secret was confided by the Blessed Virgin Mary in 1917 to three shepherd children, Lucia dos Santos and her two cousins, Jacinta and Francisco Marto, in a series of apparitions on the 13th of six consecutive months in a field called Cova da Iria near Fatima, Portugal. The apparitions at the Cova culminated with "the Great Secret" the Virgin revealed to the children on July 13, 1917. The "Third Secret" is the popular name for what is really the third part of the "Great Secret," which in turn is popularly referred to as "the Message of Fatima," although there is more to the Fatima message than the Great Secret at its core.[13]

By its very terms the Message is not "private," but rather is addressed to the whole world, even if the Virgin Mary chose to deliver it to three children. Accordingly, Lucia pleaded with "the Lady in white" "to work a miracle so that *everybody* will believe that you are appearing to us," for the local anti-Catholic authorities and other critics were mocking the apparitions and suggesting that the children were liars and fakes. In fact, at one point Lucia and her cousins were literally kidnapped and carted off to jail by the Freemasonic mayor of nearby Ourem, seat of the local judicial district. The children were threatened with torture and death if they did not recant what they had seen and heard in the Cova. All

---

[13]For a complete history of the Fatima-related apparitions in all their detail, see, for example, Frère Michel de la Sainte Trinité, *The Whole Truth About Fatima* (Buffalo, New York: Immaculate Heart Publications, 1989), Vols. I, II and III. *See also* www.fatima.org for a vast amount of information on the Message of Fatima and the history of the Fatima controversies, including the controversy over the Third Secret.

three refused to do so, and the mayor released them after two days of captivity.[14] To silence the critics and persecutors of the children, the Lady promised that on the 13th of October, the date of the last apparition at the Cova, "I will perform a miracle for all to see and believe."[15]

A miracle like no other in history

On October 13, 1917, a crowd of 70,000 people assembled in the rain-drenched Cova to witness the first pre-announced public miracle in the history of the world, and the first miracle Heaven had ever deigned to grant in answer to a challenge by the Church's enemies: the Miracle of the Sun. At precisely the moment pre-announced—noon, solar time—the Miracle began. Over the next twelve minutes the sun danced in the sky, threw off a stunning array of colors that transformed the landscape, and then plunged toward the terrified crowd, instantly drying the muddy field and the clothing of the rain-drenched witnesses before the phenomenon ended with the sun returning to its normal place in the sky. The amount of solar energy involved in that feat would have incinerated everyone present, but not a soul was harmed. Quite the contrary, at the same moment numerous miraculous cures and—hardly surprising!—instantaneous conversions took place among the witnesses.

As the Bishop of Leiria-Fatima, D. Jose Alves Correia da Silva, wrote shortly afterwards: "This phenomenon, which was not registered in any astronomical observatory, and could not, therefore, have been of natural origin, was witnessed by people of every category and class, by believers as well as unbelievers, journalists of the principal daily papers, and even by people kilometers away, a fact which destroys any theory of collective hallucination."[16] One of those remote witnesses was none other than the poet laureate of Portugal, Afonso Lopes Vieira, who, having forgotten about the apparitions at Fatima, was dramatically

---

[14]This incident is abundantly documented in the historical sources, both secular and religious. See e.g., Frère Michel de la Sainte Trinité, *The Whole Truth About Fatima*, Volume I: *Science and the Facts* (Buffalo, New York: Immaculate Heart Publications, 1989) pp. 214-231; and "The Seers Kidnapped (August 13-15, 1917)", at http://fatima.org/essentials/opposed/seerkidn.asp.

[15]In *The Whole Truth About Fatima*, Vol. I, pp. 180-181.

[16]John De Marchi, *Fatima from the Beginning* (Fatima: Edicoes: Missoes Consolata, 1950), p. 140.

reminded of them by the solar phenomenon he observed from his veranda, 25 kilometers distant from the Cova.[17]

There is no place in this short work to give the voluminous testimonies concerning the Miracle of the Sun in the acts of the diocesan investigation that led to ecclesiastical approval of devotion to Our Lady of Fatima and her Message and its spread throughout the entire Catholic Church.[18] Suffice it to say that even Hollywood took notice of the Miracle by producing a very popular movie entitled *The Miracle of Our Lady of Fatima* that still sells quite well today.[19]

What is the "Great Secret" of Fatima?

What is the "Great Secret" the Virgin confided to the three children whose contents continue to cause controversy to this day? As Sister Lucia explained when committing the Great Secret to paper in her Third Memoir (written in 1941): "[T]he secret is made up of *three distinct parts*, two of which I am now going to reveal." Stated otherwise, within the Great Secret there is a First Secret, a Second Secret and a Third Secret. In her Memoir Lucia revealed the First and Second Secrets only. The First Secret is a vision of hell:

> Our Lady showed us a great sea of fire which seemed to be under the earth. Plunged in this fire were demons and souls in human form, like transparent burning embers, all blackened or burnished bronze, floating about in the conflagration, now raised into the air by the flames that issued from within themselves together with great clouds of smoke, now falling back on every side like sparks in a huge fire, without weight or equilibrium, and amid shrieks and groans of pain and despair, which horrified us and made us tremble with fear. The demons could be distinguished by their terrifying and repulsive likeness to frightful and unknown animals, all black and transparent. This vision lasted but an instant. How can we ever be

---

[17]Ibid., p. 142.

[18]The historical record of numerous testimonies concerning cures and conversions resulting from this phenomenon is surveyed in *The Devil's Final Battle* (Terryville, Connecticut: The Missionary Association, 2002), pp. 8-14; see also http://www.devilsfinalbattle.com/ch1.htm.

[19]*The Miracle of Our Lady of Fatima* (Warner Brothers: 1952).

grateful enough to our kind heavenly Mother, who
had already prepared us by promising, in the first
Apparition, to take us to heaven. Otherwise, I think
we would have died of fear and terror.[20]

But the "Lady in white" did not simply leave the children in
fear and terror. She immediately *explained the vision* the children
had just seen—a fact that will be critical to our inquiry into the
Third Secret—and then provided the Second Secret:

> We then looked up at Our Lady, who said to us so
> kindly and so sadly:
>
> "You have seen hell where the souls of poor sinners
> go. To save them, God wishes to establish in the world
> devotion to my Immaculate Heart. If what I say to
> you is done, many souls will be saved and there will
> be peace. The war is going to end: but if people do
> not cease offending God, a worse one will break out
> during the Pontificate [reign] of Pius XI.[21] When you
> see a night illumined by an unknown light, know that
> this is the great sign given you by God that he [sic]
> is about to punish the world for its crimes, by means
> of war, famine, and persecutions of the Church and
> of the Holy Father. To prevent this, I shall come to
> ask for the consecration of Russia to my Immaculate
> Heart, and the Communion of reparation on the First
> Saturdays. If my requests are heeded, Russia will be
> converted, and there will be peace; if not, she will
> spread her errors throughout the world, causing wars
> and persecutions of the Church. The good will be
> martyred; the Holy Father will have much to suffer;
> various nations will be annihilated. In the end, my
> Immaculate Heart will triumph. The Holy Father will
> consecrate Russia to me, and she shall be converted,
> and a period of peace will be granted to the world."[22]

---

[20]Congregation for the Doctrine of the Faith, *The Message of Fatima* (Vatican City:
Libreria Editrice Vaticana, 2000) (*Message*), p. 13; photo-reproducing in its entirety and
quoting from Lucia's handwritten text in her Third Memoir.

[21]As can be seen from the handwritten text photo-reproduced in *Message*, the
Vatican translation of Lucia's original Portuguese arbitrarily substitutes "*Pontificate* of
Pius XI" for Lucia's "*reign* of Pius XI" ("*renado* de Pius XI")—one of many signs of the
"modern" and "ecumenical" attitude that has militated against the authentic Fatima
message since Vatican II, as will be apparent from the rest of this discussion.

[22]*Message*, p. 16.

The content of the first two parts of the Message, conveyed with so few words, is staggering in its scope, theological richness, and implications for the Church and the world: Innumerable souls will be lost for eternity, the world will be punished by war, famine, and persecutions of the Church and the Pope. Yet these calamities can be avoided by establishing in the world devotion to the Immaculate Heart—through the Communion of reparation on the First Saturdays, among other things—and by consecrating Russia to the same Immaculate Heart. And then, nothing less than a terrible ultimatum from Heaven itself: "If my requests are heeded, Russia will be converted, and there will be peace; *if not*, she will spread her errors throughout the world, causing wars and persecutions of the Church. The good will be martyred; the Holy Father will have much to suffer; *various nations will be annihilated.*" Finally, however, a promise of God's mercy:

> "In the end, my Immaculate Heart will triumph. The Holy Father will consecrate Russia to me, and she shall be converted, and a period of peace will be granted to the world."

We know, of course, that every one of the calamities the Virgin predicted in the first two parts of the Great Secret (except the ultimate "annihilation of nations") did in fact happen: World War I ended, World War II ravaged the globe, Russia spread its errors—including international Communism—throughout the world, there were persecutions of the Church, the good were martyred and the Holy Father had much to suffer. The fulfillment of these predictions verifies the authenticity of the Message even more effectively than the Miracle of the Sun, for the very nature of true prophecy is that it unerringly predicts what comes to pass.

A consecration undone?

Jacinta and Francisco died soon after the apparitions, also precisely as the Virgin predicted[23] and long before she returned, as she had promised in 1917, to request from Lucia the First Saturdays devotion (1925) and the Consecration of Russia (1929). While a detailed discussion of these elements of the Fatima message is

---

[23]"I will take Jacinta and Francisco soon." In Frère Michel de la Sainte Trinité, *The Whole Truth About Fatima: Science and the Facts* (Buffalo, New York: Immaculate Heart Publications, 1989) (hereafter *WTAF*), Vol. I, p. 158.

beyond the scope of this work,[24] the Consecration of Russia must be kept in view. Socci, representing a substantial constituency in the Church, maintains that Russia's consecration remains undone, despite the claim that the consecration of Russia was effected by papal ceremonies consecrating the *world* in 1982 and 1984, from which any mention of Russia was *deliberately omitted* to avoid "offending" the Russian Orthodox.[25] Contradicting this claim, John Paul II himself twice stated on March 25 *after* the 1984 consecration of the world that the Virgin was still "awaiting"[26] Russia's consecration, but that he had done all he could "according to our poor human possibilities and the measure of human weakness..."[27]

As Socci notes: "precisely this lack of a specific object (Russia)" is why Sister Lucia "has repeated a thousand times... that there has not been a response to the request of the Virgin."[28] Both before and after the 1982 and 1984 ceremonies Sister Lucia insisted that Our Lady had requested nothing less than the explicit public consecration of Russia by the Pope and the bishops and that, accordingly, a consecration of the world would not comply with

---

[24]On the First Saturdays devotion, see *The Fatima Crusader*, No. 49 (Summer 1995), also at http://www.fatimacrusader.com/cr49/toc49.asp; *see also* "The Five First Saturdays" at http://www.fatima.org/essentials/message/default.asp. On the Consecration of Russia, see Frère Michel de la Sainte Trinité, *The Whole Truth About Fatima*, Vol. II; Father Nicholas Gruner, *World Enslavement or Peace* (Fort Erie, Ontario: The Fatima Crusader, 1989) (also at http://www.worldenslavementorpeace.com); and "Consecration of Russia" at http://www.fatima.org/consecrussia/default.asp.

[25]As one of the Pope's "closest advisors," later identified to this author as Cardinal Tomko, told *Inside the Vatican* magazine, Russia was not mentioned in the 1984 ceremony because "Rome [i.e. certain of the Pope's advisors] fears the Russian Orthodox might regard it as an 'offense' if Rome were to make specific mention of Russia in such a prayer, as if Russia especially is in need of help when the whole world, including the post-Christian West, faces profound problems ..." *Inside the Vatican*, November 2000. Tomko added: "Let us beware of becoming too literal-minded." Evidently, Tomko and his collaborators thought themselves more prudent and less "literal-minded" than the Virgin Mary.

[26]*L'Osservatore Romano*, March 26-27, 1984 Italian edition, pp. 1, 6 (See Appendix V, p. 246): "Illumina specialmente i popoli di cui Tu aspetti la nostra consacrazione e il nostro affidamento." ("Enlighten especially the peoples whose consecration and entrusting *you are awaiting* from us."); *Avvenire*, March 27, 1984, p. 11: "We wished to choose this Sunday, the Third Sunday of Lent, 1984—still within the Holy Year of Redemption—for the act of entrusting and consecration of the world, of the great human family, of all peoples, especially those who have a very great need of this consecration and entrustment, *of those peoples* for whom you yourself *are awaiting* our act of consecration and entrusting." *Avvenire* is the official episcopal newspaper of the Italian Bishops Conference.

[27]*Avvenire*, March 27, 1984, p. 11.

[28]Socci, *Fourth Secret*, pp. 29-30.

the Virgin's request.[29] Cardinal Bertone's contention that during private, unrecorded "interviews" Sister Lucia abruptly changed her testimony on this matter presents an entire controversy unto itself, the details of which cannot be explored here.[30]

At any rate, one would think it beyond debate that a consecration of Russia needs to *mention* Russia. As Dr. David Allen White has put it, attempting to consecrate Russia without mention of Russia is like "publishing a recipe for beef stew that never mentions beef." Consequently, if the Fatima message is taken seriously, as it ought to be, the world remains under the Virgin's ultimatum: consecrate Russia or face the annihilation of nations and the eternal loss of countless souls. As should be apparent from the rise of Vladimir Putin as the militaristic, neo-Stalinist dictator of Russia—a development even the *New York Times* has noticed[31]—there is an integral relationship between what Socci calls the "message-warning" of the Third Secret and Russia's consecration. I shall return to this point in Chapter 12.

The Church gives her highest approval

Lucia, who became a Carmelite in 1948, would live on until February 13, 2005, when she died in the Carmelite convent at Coimbra, Portugal at the age of 97. Since those dramatic days in the Cova, the Message Lucia was given has been treated as worthy of belief by a series of Popes. Pope John Paul II, who attributed his

---

[29]For example, on May 12, 1982, the day before the 1982 consecration of the world, the Vatican's own *L'Osservatore Romano* published an interview of Sister Lucia by Father Umberto Maria Pasquale, a Salesian priest, during which she told Father Umberto that Our Lady had never requested the consecration of the world, but *only* the Consecration of Russia:

> At a certain moment I said to her: "Sister, I should like to ask you a question. If you cannot answer me, let it be. But if you can answer it, I would be most grateful to you ... Has Our Lady ever spoken to you about the consecration of *the world* to Her Immaculate Heart?"
>
> "No, Father Umberto! *Never!* At the Cova da Iria in 1917 Our Lady had promised: *I shall come to ask for the Consecration of Russia* ... In 1929, at Tuy, as she had promised, Our Lady came back to tell me that the moment had come to ask the Holy Father for the consecration of *that country* (Russia)."

[30]*But see, e.g.*, Christopher Ferrara, "A New Fatima for the New Church," *The Fatima Crusader*, No. 75 (Winter 2004), pp. 65ff (also at http://www.fatimacrusader.com/cr75/cr75pg08.asp) for a thorough treatment of this subject.

[31]*See, e.g.*, "With Tight Grip on Ballot, Putin is Forcing Foes out of Parliament," *New York Times*, October 14, 2007 (detailing the moves by which Putin has created an authoritarian one-party regime in Russia like that of "the old days.").

escape from death on May 13, 1981 to the intervention of Our Lady of Fatima (on the very anniversary of the first Fatima apparition), definitively removed the Fatima apparitions from the category of the so-called "private revelation" by a series of papal acts. The Pope beatified Jacinta and Francisco in May 2000, proclaiming February 20th as their feast day, elevated the Feast of Our Lady of Fatima on May 13th to the altars of every church in the world by ordering its inclusion in the Roman Missal, and declared at Fatima in 1982 that "The appeal of Our Lady of Fatima is so deeply rooted in the Gospel and the whole of Tradition that the Church feels herself bound by this message."[32] Moreover, the Fatima prayers ("O my Jesus, etc") have been incorporated into the Rosary, while the First Saturdays devotion is practiced throughout the entire Church.

In view of these facts and circumstances, Socci has best summed up the approach any Catholic should take to the Message of Fatima: "The Fatima event has received on the part of the Church—which in general is very cautious concerning supernatural phenomena—a recognition that has *no equal in Christian history....* It is really impossible—after all this—to continue to speak of a 'private revelation' and of the relative importance of the Message."[33] It is not only impossible but completely irrational to dismiss the Fatima message, and the Third Secret in particular, as a "private revelation." Any reasonable Catholic, and even a non-Catholic inclined to believe in supernatural phenomena, should be prepared to agree that the Message of Fatima is in a category by itself.

The scope of this work does not permit anything like an examination of the fullness of the Fatima message. What I have just presented must suffice for context, for we must focus on the subject at hand: Socci's sensational allegation of a Vatican cover-up of the Third Secret.

---

[32]"Il contenuto dell'appello della Signora di Fatima è così profondamente radicato nel Vangelo e in tutta la Tradizione, che la Chiesa si sente impegnata da questo messaggio." *Sermon at the Sanctuary of the Virgin of Fatima,* May 13, 1982, at http://www.vatican.va/holy_father/john_paul_ii/homilies/1982/documents/hf_jp-ii_hom_19820513_fatima_it.html.

[33]Socci, *Fourth Secret,* p. 17.

Chapter 2

Gateway to the Secret

One cannot appreciate why Socci has reached the conclusion that there is "a part of the Secret not revealed and considered unspeakable" without at least a basic understanding of the evidence he reviewed. That evidence falls into two categories: (a) evidence of the general nature and location of the undisclosed text of the Secret, and (b) evidence of the specific content of this text. This chapter will consider the first category of evidence.

The Secret was too terrible to write

In Chapter 1 I noted that in her Third Memoir Sister Lucia made it clear that at that time (1941) she was going to reveal only the first two parts of the Great Secret of July 13, 1917. But when it came to writing the third part, the Third Secret, the historical record shows that Lucia, who had written freely of something as dire as the annihilation of nations, was subject to a mysterious impediment.

According to the account of Father Joaquin Alonso, the official Fatima archivist, in the summer of 1943, fearing that Lucia would die of pleurisy and take the Secret with her to the grave, Bishop da Silva and Canon José Galamba Oliveira, the Bishop's friend and close advisor, suggested during a conversation in September with the seer that she reveal the Secret if she "wished" to do so. Lucia gave this surprising reply: "Now, if His Grace wants, I can *tell* it to him." When the Bishop objected that he did not want to "meddle" in such a serious matter, Canon Galamba suggested that at least Lucia "write it down on *a piece of paper* and give it to you [the Bishop] in a sealed envelope."[34]

And there the problem arose. Lucia declined this suggestion without a direct formal order from the Bishop, protesting: "It seems

---

[34]Quoted in Frère Michel de la Sainte Trinité, *The Whole Truth About Fatima: The Third Secret* (Buffalo, New York: Immaculate Heart Publications, 2001) (hereafter *WTAF*), Vol. III, p. 40.

to me that to write it down is already, in a way, to disclose it, and I do not yet have Our Lord's permission to do that. In any case, as I am used to seeing the will of God in the wishes of my superiors, I am thinking of obedience and I don't know what to do. I prefer an express command which I can rely on before God, so that I can say in all security, 'They ordered me to do that, Lord'...."[35]

The order was given in mid-October of 1943 by way of a letter from Bishop da Silva. As Lucia recorded: "They have ordered me to write down the part of the Secret that Our Lady revealed in 1917, and which I still keep hidden by command of the Lord. They tell me either to write it in the notebooks in which I've been told to keep my spiritual diary, or if I wish, to write it on a sheet of paper, put it in an envelope, close it and seal it up."[36] Note well Sister Lucia's reference to two different modes of writing the Secret, pointing already to the possible existence of two different but related texts.

Yet despite having received a direct written order from her bishop, Lucia, who had lived a life of holy obedience, could not obey. For more than two months she struggled to write the Secret, but could not bring herself to put pen to paper. In a letter to Archbishop Garcia y Garcia, Lucia confided that this impediment "was not due to natural causes."[37] As Lucia later revealed, it was only after the Blessed Virgin appeared to her in the convent at Tuy on January 2, 1944 to confirm it was indeed God's will, that she was finally able to comply with Bishop da Silva's order.[38]

The inference is inescapable: The contents of the Third Secret must be terrible indeed if this obedient cloistered nun required a special apparition and directive of the Mother of God in order to obey her own bishop's command to write it down. The Secret must involve something even worse than the world wars and the annihilation of nations Sister Lucia had already revealed in the first two parts of the Great Secret. Father Alonso, who spoke from the experience of sixteen years as the official archivist of Fatima and had many conversations with Sister Lucia, aptly observed: "Had it been merely a matter of prophesying new and severe punishments, Sister Lucia would not have experienced difficulties

---

[35]Ibid., p. 42.

[36]Father Joaquin Alonso, *La verdad sobre el Secreto de Fátima* (Madrid: Centro Mariano, 1976), p. 39; quoted in *WTAF*, Vol. III, p. 44.

[37]Alonso, *La verdad sobre el Secreto de Fátima*, p. 41; quoted in *WTAF*, Vol. III, p. 45.

[38]*See WTAF*, Vol. III, pp. 40-48 for a full historical account of this episode.

so great that a special intervention from Heaven was needed to overcome them."[39]

The Secret involves a letter to the Bishop of Fatima

Although the Secret was committed to paper in January 1944, it was not until June 17 of that year that Sister Lucia entrusted it to the Archbishop of Gurza for personal delivery to Bishop da Silva on the evening of the same day. Lucia had placed the Secret in a sealed envelope which was, in turn, placed inside one of the notebooks containing her spiritual notes. As Lucia wrote to Bishop da Silva on January 9, 1944: "I have written what you asked me; God willed to try me a little, but finally, this was indeed His will: it [the Secret] is sealed in an envelope *and it is in the notebooks...*"[40]

That is, in obedience to the order to write down the Third Secret, Lucia had consigned *both* a sealed envelope *and* her notebooks to Bishop da Silva, giving another early indication that, just as Socci has concluded, there are two distinct but related texts of the Third Secret: one written in Sister Lucia's notebook, which would be the vision of the "Bishop dressed in white" that the Vatican revealed in 2000, and a separate text in a sealed envelope, which Socci and millions of other Catholics believe is being concealed. As we will see, that is exactly the case.

Here it must be noted for future reference that when the Bishop of Fatima received the sealed envelope from Lucia, he placed it in a sealed envelope of his own, on which he wrote the following inscription:

> This envelope with its contents shall be entrusted to His Eminence Cardinal D. Manuel [Cerejeira], Patriarch of Lisbon, after my death.
>
> Leiria, December 8, 1945
> † Jose, Bishop of Leiria[41]

As for what was in the sealed envelope that Sister Lucia gave

---

[39] Alonso, *La verdad sobre el Secreto de Fátima*, p. 82.

[40] Joaquin Alonso, *Fátima 50*, October 13, 1967, p. 11; quoted in *WTAF*, Vol. III, pp. 46-47.

[41] Ibid: *Este envelope com o seu conteudo sera entregue a Sua Eminencia O Sr. D. Manuel, Patriarca de Lisboa, depois da minha morte.*
Leiria, 8 Dezembro de 1945
† *Jose, Bispo de Leiria*

her bishop, she described it as *"a letter* to the Bishop of Leiria."[42] Therefore, we know from Sister Lucia herself that the Secret was written in the form of a *letter* to Bishop Jose da Silva. On this point we also have the testimony of Father Hubert Jongen, a Dutch Montfortian, who traveled to Fatima to conduct research in order to defend the authenticity of the Fatima apparitions against attacks by the modernist Dutchman, Fr. Edouard Dhanis. During questioning of Sister Lucia on February 3-4, 1946, Father Jongen had the following exchange with the seer:

> "You have already made known two parts of the Secret. When will the time arrive for the third part?"
> "I communicated the third part *in a letter* to the Bishop of Leiria," she answered.[43]

Thirteen years later Pope John XXIII's diary would note the following, according to the Vatican's official account: "Audiences: Father Philippe, Commissary of the Holy Office, who brought me *the letter* containing the third part of the secrets of Fatima...."[44] A year after this entry, the Vatican's announcement concerning the Third Secret, discussed further below, would refer to *"the letter...* in which Sister Lucia wrote down *the words* which Our Lady confided as a secret to the three little shepherds in the Cova da Iria."

Thus, we know from the historical record that a text of the Secret *in letter form*, revealing the *words* of the Virgin, was contained in an assemblage of *two* envelopes: Sister Lucia's inner sealed envelope, and Bishop da Silva's own outer sealed envelope on which was written his instructions for the disposition of the Secret after his death. This fact will have decisive importance later on, as we shall see in Chapter 8.

The Secret is found in a telltale "etc"

What is in this letter? Sister Lucia herself provided a crucial hint in her Fourth Memoir, written between October and December 1941 at the direction of Bishop da Silva, who wanted a more complete record of the apparitions. In the Fourth Memoir

---

[42]Revue *Mediatrice et Reine*, October 1946, pp. 110-112; *see also WTAF*, Vol. III, p. 470.

[43]Revue *Mediatrice et Reine*, October 1946, pp. 110-112; *see also WTAF*, Vol. III, p. 470.

[44]*The Message of Fatima*, p. 4.

Sister Lucia declared that she would write of everything "With the exception of that part of the Secret which I am not permitted to reveal at present..."[45] But, after restating the first and second parts of the Great Secret as already set forth in her Third Memoir (August 1941), Sister Lucia added to the integral text the words which have, ever since, been at the heart of the Third Secret controversy: "In Portugal, the dogma of the faith will always be preserved etc.[46] *Tell this to no one. Yes, you may tell Francisco."* (Francisco had only seen, but not heard, the Virgin during the apparitions.)

Sister Lucia had added "etc" to Our Lady's words to indicate a discourse by the Virgin that involved a subject clearly different from the first two parts of the Great Secret. Without more—much more—the reference to the preservation of dogma in Portugal would make no sense at all in the context of the first two parts. Yet there it was in the Fourth Memoir, set forth as an integral part of what Our Lady had confided to Lucia, the last surviving visionary of Fatima, for the good of the Church and the world.

Hence it was apparent as early as 1941 that the interrupted *words* of the Virgin were continued in the Third Secret, wherein the Virgin has other things to say besides what she had said in the first two parts of the Great Secret as a whole. And, indeed, when Sister Lucia was asked about the contents of the Third Secret in 1943, she replied: "In a certain way I have already revealed it."[47] That is, she had revealed it with the phrase "In Portugal, the dogma of the Faith will always be preserved etc", which appears in the Fourth, but not the Third, Memoir, and is the only significant difference between the recording of the Great Secret in both memoirs.

The Secret has two parts

That Sister Lucia's "etc" held the place for words of the Virgin which belong to the Third Secret was confirmed in 1952, when an Austrian Jesuit, Father Joseph Schweigl, was sent by Pius XII to interrogate Sister Lucia in her convent at Coimbra. The interrogation took place on September 2nd of that year. While

---

[45]Frère Michel de la Sainte Trinité, *The Whole Truth About Fatima: The Secret and the Church* (Buffalo, New York: Immaculate Heart Publications, 1990) (hereafter *WTAF*), Vol. II, p. 37.

[46]"*Em Portugal se conservera sempre o doguema da fè etc.*"

[47]Father Joaquin Alonso, *La verdad sobre el Secreto de Fátima*, p. 64; see also *WTAF*, Vol. III, p. 684.

bound not to reveal the precise contents of Sister Lucia's statements regarding the Secret, Schweigl did make the following statement: "I may not reveal anything with regard to the Third Secret, but I am able to say that it has two parts: One part concerns the Pope. The other part is the logical continuation—though I may not say anything—of *the words*: 'In Portugal, the dogma of the Faith will always be preserved etc.'"[48]

To this testimony must be added that of Canon Casimir Barthas (a renowned Fatima expert), who interrogated Sister Lucia concerning the Third Secret on October 17-18, 1946. Barthas likewise reported: "The text of *the words of Our Lady* was written by Sister Lucia and enclosed in a sealed envelope."[49] Further, no less than Cardinal Ottaviani, then Secretary of the Holy Office, interrogated Lucia in 1955 concerning the Secret, later revealing that "She wrote on *a sheet* of paper [*folha* in Portuguese] *what Our Lady told her* to tell the Holy Father."[50] Ottaviani read the Secret himself and can hardly have been mistaken in his reference to what Our Lady *told* Lucia to *tell* the Holy Father.

So, it was clear very early on that the Third Secret of Fatima has two parts, one of which presents the *spoken words* of the Virgin Mary embraced within Sister Lucia's "etc".

The Secret is written on a single page

On orders from Rome, the Secret was taken from the custody of the Bishop of Leiria-Fatima and delivered to the papal nuncio, Monsignor Cento, in Lisbon on March 16, 1957, by whom it was delivered to the Vatican in April of that year, along with the accompanying notebooks of Sister Lucia and photocopies of all her writings on file in the chancery of Leiria.[51]

Before the Secret was transmitted to Rome, however, auxiliary Bishop Venancio held Bishop da Silva's outer envelope up to the

---

[48]*WTAF*, Vol. III, p. 710.

[49]Quoted in Laurent Morlier, *The Third Secret of Fatima* (Éditions D.F.T., 2001), p. 196.

[50]Remarks during the Fifth Mariological Conference in the great hall of the Antonianum in Rome, February 11, 1967; quoted in Alonso, *La verdad sobre el Secreto de Fátima*, p. 65. Cardinal Ottaviani's phrase "to tell the Holy Father" appears to be an extrapolation of his, which if anything would highlight the importance of the Secret. In any case, the Cardinal confirms the hard fact that the Secret contains words of the Virgin Mary.

[51]*WTAF*, Vol. III, pp. 479-481.

light and was able to see that it contained Sister Lucia's inner envelope, wherein he could discern "an ordinary sheet of paper" with ¾ centimeter margins on which were written approximately 25 lines.[52] He took the exact measurements of the interior envelope—12 centimeters by 18 centimeters—and recorded this information in a document preserved in the Fatima archives.[53] Cardinal Ottaviani would later affirm that the Secret was indeed written on a single page comprising 25 lines.

The Secret was lodged in the papal apartment

We know that the sealed envelope containing the Secret was lodged, not in the Archives of the Holy Office proper, but rather in the papal bedchamber of Pius XII for personal safekeeping by the Pope himself as a "secret of the Holy Office," of which the Pope was then head. Frère Michel de la Sainte Trinité provides the historical evidence:

> ... we now know that the precious envelope sent to Rome by Msgr. Cento was not placed in the Archives of the Holy Office, but that Pius XII wanted to keep it in his own apartment.
>
> Father Caillon received this information from the mouth of journalist Robert Serrou, who himself got it from Mother Pasqualina, in this way. Robert Serrou was doing a photo story for *Paris-Match* in the apartments of Pius XII. Mother Pasqualina — this woman of great common sense who directed the handful of Sisters acting as the Pope's housekeepers, and who sometimes received his confidences — was present.
>
> Before a little wooden safe placed on a table and bearing the inscription '*Secretum Sancti Officii*' (Secret of the Holy Office), the journalist questioned the Mother:

---

[52]Ibid., p. 81; Frère François de Marie des Anges, *Fatima: Tragedy and Triumph* (Buffalo, New York: Immaculate Heart Publications, 1994), p. 45. Cardinal Ottaviani would later state that the text of the Secret comprised 25 lines, as also revealed by the renowned Mariologist Rene Laurentin (who had spoken to Ottaviani about the Secret). Cardinal Bertone would acknowledge Ottaviani's testimony in his book *The Last Visionary of Fatima* and on national television in Italy on May 31, 2007 (on the *Door to Door* TV program), while claiming to be "amazed" by it.

[53]*See* "Bertone nel 'Vespaio' delle Polemiche" ("Bertone in the 'Wasp's Nest' of the Polemics"), *Libero*, June 2, 2007.

> "Mother, what is in this little safe?" She answered:
> *"The third Secret of Fatima is in there ..."*
>
> The photograph of this safe—which we have
> reproduced here [see photo in photo insert section]—
> was published in *Paris-Match* a year and a half later, in
> two instances, on the occasion of Pius XII's death....[54]

The details of Serrou's testimony were later confirmed in a
letter to Frère Michel on January 10, 1985:

> ... I can confirm for you that I did indeed do a story
> in Pius XII's apartment on May 14, 1957, in the late
> morning, that is a little over a year before the Pope's
> death.... It is exact that Mother Pasqualina did tell me,
> while showing me a little safe bearing a label with the
> mention, "Secret of the Holy Office": "In there is the
> third Secret of Fatima."[55]

In written replies to questions from Father Joaquin Alonso,
the official Fatima archivist, dated July 24, 1977, Archbishop
Loris Capovilla, the personal secretary of Pius XII's successor,
John XXIII, confirmed that Pope John read a text of the Secret on
August 17, 1959. Socci notes Capovilla's contemporaneous written
account that Pope John directed him to write on the outside of "the
envelope" (*plico*) or "wrapping" (*involucro*): "I give no judgment."[56]
Capovilla also recounted that after Pope John read the Secret, he
returned the text to its envelope, which was kept "in the bureau of
his bedroom until his death. Paul VI asked for information about
the envelope shortly after his election."[57]

In a letter dated June 20, 1977, to Fatima scholar Father José
Geraldes Freire, Capovilla likewise confirmed that the Secret
"was kept in the writing table of John XXIII's apartment until his
death."[58] Archbishop Capovilla has further testified that Paul
VI retrieved the envelope containing the Secret from that same
writing desk for reading within days of his election in 1963.[59]

---

[54]*WTAF*, Vol. III, pp. 484-485.

[55]Ibid., pp. 485-486.

[56]Socci, *Fourth Secret*, pp. 143, 165.

[57]*Lampade viventi*, March 1978, pp. 72-74; quoted in *WTAF*, Vol. III, pp. 570-571.

[58]José Geraldes Freire, *O Segredo de Fátima, A Terceira Parte e sobre Portugal?*
(Santuario de Fátima, 1978), pp. 181-182; quoted in *WTAF*, Vol. III, p. 572.

[59]See further discussion in Chapter 6.

Thus, a text of the Secret—recall that the Secret has two parts, per Father Schweigl—was located in the papal apartment, not the Holy Office, during the pontificates of Pius XII, John XXIII and Paul VI. It was most probably still in the papal apartment when Pope John Paul II was elected in 1978 and read the Secret himself in that year—a fact Cardinal Bertone is at pains to evade, as we shall see in Chapter 7.

The Secret contains difficult Portuguese expressions

Archbishop Capovilla has also revealed that when Pope John opened the envelope and tried to read the Portuguese text of the Secret in August of 1959, he was unable to do so because of "difficulty caused by expressions proper to the language,"[60] and "Portuguese dialect expressions,"[61] and that the Pope had to wait for a translation to be prepared by Father Paulo Tavares, a native Portuguese translator attached to the Secretariat of State.[62]

On the other hand, Cardinal Ottaviani testified that Pope John read a text of the Secret in *1960*, that was contained in *another sealed envelope*: "Still sealed, it was taken later, in 1960, to Pope John XXIII. The Pope *broke the seal*, and opened the envelope. Although it was in Portuguese, he told me afterwards *that he understood the text in its entirety*."[63] Here we have another early indication of the existence of two distinct but related texts of the Secret. As Socci concludes: "These two opposed affirmations [by Capovilla and Ottaviani] can be explained by holding that the matter treats of two different readings of two different texts."[64] That is, there are two texts: one read in August 1959, containing especially difficult expressions of the Portuguese language the Pope could not understand without the aid of a translation provided days later; and another text, read in 1960, which the Pope found perfectly comprehensible, evidently because it did *not* contain any such difficult expressions.

As Socci demonstrates in an appendix to *Fourth Secret* prepared by a Portuguese linguist, *there are no difficult idioms or expressions of*

---

[60]*WTAF*, Vol. II, p. 556.

[61]Socci, *Fourth Secret*, p. 150; citing *Perspective in the World*, VI, 1991.

[62]Ibid.

[63]*WTAF*, Vol. III, p. 557.

[64]Socci, *Fourth Secret*, p. 150.

Portuguese dialect in the text of the vision published by the Vatican in June 2000.[65]

The Secret is linked to 1960

Sister Lucia provided yet another early clue to the content of the Secret when she insisted that the Bishop of Fatima promise that the sealed envelope in which she had sent him the Secret "would definitely be opened and read to the world either at her death or in 1960, whichever would come first."[66] On the outside of the envelope Sister Lucia had described as "a letter," she had, accordingly, written: "By express order of Our Lady, this envelope can only be opened in 1960 by the Cardinal Patriarch of Lisbon or the Bishop of Leiria."[67]

Sister Lucia later explained the significance of this date to Cardinal Ottaviani during the 1955 interrogation. As Ottaviani revealed in the aforementioned public address: "The message was not to be opened before 1960. I asked Sister Lucia, 'Why this date?' She answered, 'Because then it will be clearer (*mais claro*).'"[68] In answer to the same question from Canon Barthas in 1946, Lucia replied simply: "Because Our Lady wishes it so."[69]

Thus, Sister Lucia, acting on "the express order of Our Lady," linked the Secret to the year 1960. One can only conclude that there must be some major historical event in close proximity to that year which would make the contents of the Secret "more clear." Only one such event was in view as of 1960: the Second Vatican Council (1962-1965), which John XXIII had announced on January 25, 1959. This date was *the very anniversary of the "night illumined by an unknown light"*, January 25, 1938, which the second part of the Great Secret predicts as the sign of the beginning of World War II

---

[65]*See* linguistic analysis of the text of the vision by Dr. Mariagrazia Russo at Socci, *Fourth Secret*, pp. 241ff.

[66]Quoted in Alonso, *La verdad sobre el Secreto de Fátima*, pp. 46-47. *See* also *WTAF*, Vol. III, p. 470.

[67]"Por ordem expressa de Nossa Senhora este envelope só pode ser aberto em 1960, por Sua Ex.^cia Rev.^ma o Senhor Cardeal Patriarca de Lisboa ou por Sua Ex.^cia Rev.^ma o Senhor Bispo de Leiria." (Envelope shown by Cardinal Bertone on May 31, 2007 on national television in Italy — see photo on p. 126.) The emphasis is mine.

[68]*Documentation Catholique*, March 19, 1967, Col. 542; cited in *WTAF*, Vol. III, p. 725.

[69]Canon Barthas, *Fatima, Merveille du XXe Siècle* (Fatima-Editions, 1952), p. 83.

and the other dire events predicted in the Second Secret.[70]

It can hardly be a mere coincidence that immediately after the Council's conclusion in 1965 the Church suffered the ecclesial equivalent of a world war: a catastrophic decline in every aspect of her life, from the number of religious vocations to Mass attendance to baptisms and conversions.[71] Within a few years of the Council seminaries and convents emptied, while tens of thousands of priests and nuns defected from their vocations. According to the Vatican's own statistics, published in *L'Osservatore Romano* in 2006, in 1965 there were 455,000 Catholic priests in the world, but by 1975 there were only 400,000.[72] That is, 55,000 priests left the priesthood within ten years after the Council. Such a mass defection of priests had never been seen before in the Church's history. To this day the Church has not recovered. There are now only 406,000 priests in the world, 49,000 fewer than there were *42 years ago*, when the Catholic population was much smaller.[73]

The Secret was to be revealed in 1960

Given the "express order of Our Lady," Cardinal Cerejeira, the Patriarch of Portugal, publicly promised that the Secret "will be opened in 1960." Rome at first voiced no objection. Quite the contrary, Vatican Cardinals Ottaviani and Tisserant publicly echoed the promise of Cardinal Cerejeira, as did numerous other Church authorities.[74] There was even an American television show entitled "Zero 1960," which took its theme from the universally expected disclosure of the Secret in that year. Produced by the once-militant Blue Army, the show was so popular it received a "star" rating in *The New York Times*.[75]

---

[70]As the *New York Times* reported the following day: "Aurora borealis startles Europe. People flee, call firemen," January 26, 1938, p. 25.

[71]For a definitive statistical analysis see Kenneth Jones, *Index of Leading Catholic Indicators: The Church Since Vatican II* (Oriens Publishing, 2003).

[72]*L'Osservatore Romano*, April 30, 2006, pp. 8-9, reporting on the publication of the *Annuarium statisticum Ecclesiae 2004* by Libreria Editrice Vaticana.

[73]Ibid.

[74]*WTAF*, Vol. II, p. 528.

[75]Cfr. *WTAF*, Vol. III, pp. 470-478 for a complete review of the historical evidence that, in keeping with the wishes of the Virgin, the Secret was to be disclosed not later than 1960.

The Secret suppressed, but its format confirmed

As the year 1960 began, the world awaited the Vatican's disclosure of the Third Secret. But it was not to be. On February 8, 1960, the faithful received the news that Pope John had decided to bury the Secret. Acting through a Portuguese press agency, anonymous "Vatican sources" let it be known that the Secret would not be disclosed and "would probably remain, forever, under absolute seal." A reading of the full text of the press release confirmed that the Third Secret involved *words* of the Virgin Mary, presented in the form of a *letter* to be opened *in 1960*:

> According to Vatican sources (February 8, 1960), the Secret of Fatima will never be disclosed.
>
> It has just been stated, in very reliable circles of the Vatican, to the representatives of United Press International, that it is most likely that *the letter* will never be opened, in which Sister Lucia wrote down *the words* which Our Lady confided as a secret to the three little shepherds in the Cova da Iria.
>
> As indicated by Sister Lucia, *the letter* can only be opened *during the year 1960*.
>
> Faced with the pressure that has been placed on the Vatican, some wanting the letter to be opened and made known to the world, *others, on the supposition that it may contain alarming prophecies, desiring that its publication be withheld*, the same Vatican circles declare that the Vatican has decided not to make public Sister Lucia's letter, and to continue keeping it *rigorously sealed*.
>
> The decision of the Vatican authorities is based on various reasons: 1. Sister Lucia is still living. 2. The Vatican already knows the contents of *the letter*. 3. Although the Church recognizes the Fatima apparitions, she does not pledge herself to guarantee the veracity of *the words* which the three little shepherds claim to have *heard* from Our Lady.[76]

---

[76]Francisco, of course, heard Our Lady's words indirectly from Lucia, who had been given permission by Our Lady to tell him, as revealed in the Fourth Memoir: "Yes, you may tell Francisco."

> In these circumstances, it is most probable that the
> Secret of Fatima will remain, forever, under absolute
> seal. (A.N.I.)[77]

The Secret must be terrible indeed if the Vatican "sources" had decided to place it *forever* under "absolute seal" and even call into question the veracity of the seers themselves in order to attempt a justification for this otherwise inexplicable action. Whatever the Virgin had said following Sister Lucìa's fateful "etc" must be nothing less than sensational, and it must have some relation to the year 1960, the year immediately following Pope John's announcement to the world of the Second Vatican Council.

Pope John buries the Secret

Socci concludes that the Vatican's action reveals why it had taken possession of the Secret in 1957: "[T]he bishop of Leiria, Monsignor da Silva, and the patriarch of Lisbon, Cardinal Cerejeira, following the indications given by the Madonna through Sister Lucia, had already announced that they would have divulged the Secret in 1960. It was to ward this off that the Holy Office intervened."[78] That is, the Vatican simply did not want the members of the Church or the world at large to know the contents of the Third Secret. Why?

Clearly, the Secret is so explosive that Pope John decided to suppress it despite the "express order" of the Virgin Mary that it was to be opened in 1960. Socci contends that Pope John, who could have read the Secret immediately upon his election to the papacy in October of 1958, deliberately declined to do so because its contents might have impeded his plans for the Council: "[I]t was thought to read the Third Secret immediately, but John XXIII said 'No, wait.' First he wanted to announce the convocation of Vatican Council II, almost as if to put before Heaven a *fait accompli*."[79] Then, once he had read the Secret, Pope John made the decision to suppress it after convincing himself it was "not entirely supernatural," but without having "the courage to give such a judgment solemnly and publicly," because this would involve "almost demolishing all of Fatima."[80] Socci refers to the contemporaneous documentation

---

[77]*WTAF*, Vol. III, pp. 578-579.

[78]Socci, *Fourth Secret*, p. 36.

[79]Ibid., p. 205.

[80]Ibid., p. 164.

of Archbishop Capovilla, who records that Pope John, having read the Secret, stated: "I give no judgment."[81]

Socci does not hold back in his criticism of Pope John's decision to bury the Secret: "[T]hat Message of the Queen of Prophets [not being] to his liking, before the request of the Madonna that she wished her words to be revealed to the world in 1960, Pope Roncalli decided to do exactly the contrary: he decided to hide that message and not give any explanation either to the Church or the world."[82] Pope John's decision, writes Socci, "weighed like a boulder on his successors,"[83] and may account for the "compromise solution" mentioned in the Introduction: to reveal the text of the vision, while revealing the hidden text of Our Lady's own words indirectly in the papal sermon of John Paul II at Fatima in May of 2000.

Pope Paul VI buries the Secret, and disaster follows

As for the other Pope of the Council, Paul VI, he likewise did nothing about the Secret after having read it within days of his election in 1963, but simply put it away in the same desk drawer from which (as we will see) it had been retrieved for his perusal. Yet as early as 1968 Pope Paul was lamenting that "The Church is in a disturbed period of self-criticism, or what could better be called self-demolition."[84] And in 1973 Pope Paul admitted "the opening to the world became a veritable invasion of the Church by worldly thinking. We have perhaps been too weak and imprudent."[85] A year earlier, in perhaps the most astonishing remark ever made by a Roman Pontiff, Paul VI declared that "from somewhere or other the smoke of Satan has entered the temple of God. In the Church too this state of uncertainty reigns. It was believed that after the Council a sunny day in the Church's history would dawn, but instead there came a day of clouds, storms and darkness."[86]

---

[81]Ibid., pp. 164-165.

[82]Ibid., p. 206.

[83]Ibid., p. 164.

[84]Speech to the Lombard College, December 7, 1968.

[85]Speech of November 23, 1973.

[86]Address of June 30, 1972; quoted in Romano Amerio, *Iota Unum* (Kansas City: Sarto House, 1998), p. 6.

Socci is no less candid in his criticism of Pope Paul's decision to keep the Secret buried. Socci relates that Paul VI (per his friend and confidant Jean Guitton) dismissed Sister Lucia as "a simple peasant" for whom he had no time, this attitude being in keeping with his "generic aversion to visionaries." Pope Paul was expecting a "laity animated by the spirit of prophecy" as "fruits of the Council," rather than "by the election (and gift) of heaven, as with the children of Fatima." As Socci remarks acidly: "We are still awaiting the 'prophets' of Vatican II. In compensation, we soon saw the fruits of the Council. Terrible." And while Paul VI came to lament that the smoke of Satan had entered the Church, "he persisted in error: the most devastating of the errors was the traumatic surprise attack of a 'minority revolution' that imposed the liturgical reform (with its thousand abuses), hailed by Paul VI, but clearly not blessed by God.... The mode and contents of this 'surprise attack' have had disastrous effects on the orthodoxy and on the faith of the people while—as the writer Guido Ceronetti has noted—that folly 'pleased communist authorities... they were not stupid, having perceived in their bestial ignorance of the sacred that a crack had been opened.'"[87]

Was disclosure of the Secret in 1960 "optional"?

In response to the objection that disclosure of the Secret by the conciliar Popes was merely optional, it suffices to say that the Mother of God would have had no reason to deliver the Secret in the first place had she intended that it would be kept "forever under absolute seal." The Mother of God would not speak in order to be silenced—even by a Pope. As Pope John Paul II himself declared at Fatima in 1982: "Can the Mother, who with all the force of the love that she fosters in the Holy Spirit and desires the salvation of every man, can she remain silent when she sees the very bases of her children's salvation undermined? No, *she cannot remain silent.*" Nor can even the Pope silence her.[88]

And clearly, as Socci concludes, the Virgin must have had something to say about the terrible and unprecedented developments in the Church after 1960, developments that afflict

---

[87]Socci, *Fourth Secret*, pp. 209-211.

[88]"Può la Madre, la quale con tutta la potenza del suo amore, che nutre nello Spirito Santo, desidera la salvezza di ogni uomo, tacere su ciò *che mina le basi stesse di questa salvezza*? No, non lo può!"

the Church to this day. We shall consider the evidence for that proposition in the next chapter.

Summing up the evidence

To sum up the evidence thus far, as of 1960 it was already clear that the Third Secret involved—

- something so terrible that Sister Lucia could not commit it to paper without a direct intervention of the Virgin Mary in 1944;

- two parts, one of which contains the words of the Virgin that are the "logical continuation" of her statement "In Portugal, the dogma of the Faith will always be preserved etc.";

- a single page of some 25 lines of text;

- a text in the form of a letter to the Bishop of Leiria-Fatima in a sealed envelope;

- a text that was lodged in the papal apartment;

- a text that contains difficult expressions Pope John could not read without a written translation prepared in 1959, unlike the text he read in 1960, which he understood without need of translation;

- a text whose prophecy would become clear in 1960, by which time Vatican II (which would have a disastrous aftermath) had been announced;

The document the Vatican disclosed in the year 2000 does not correspond to *any* of these elements. But there are other aspects of the Secret, also revealed before 2000, which do not correspond to the vision of "the Bishop dressed in white." Let us examine those as well.

Chapter 3

Terrible Words

We have considered briefly the evidence of the general nature and location of the Secret. But what precisely is *in* the Secret if, as Socci has concluded, it is more than simply the vision of the bishop in white?

Over the decades that have elapsed since suppression of the Secret in 1960, the "Fatimist" literature has taken note of numerous testimonies by reliable witnesses who have either read the Secret themselves or received information from Sister Lucia or the Pope indicating its contents. The testimony of all the witnesses converges on the conclusion Socci has reached: that the Secret includes "the words of the Madonna [which] preannounce an apocalyptic crisis of the faith in the Church starting at the top" and "a devastation of the world." [89] Let us survey the testimony.

The future Pius XII – 1931

When he was still Cardinal Pacelli, serving as Vatican Secretary of State under Pope Pius XI, the future Pius XII made this astonishing observation regarding the Message of Fatima:

> I am worried by the Blessed Virgin's messages to little Lucia of Fatima. This persistence of Mary about the dangers which menace the Church is a divine warning against *the suicide of altering the faith, in her liturgy, her theology and her soul....* I hear all around me *innovators* who wish to dismantle the Sacred Chapel, destroy the universal flame of the Church, reject her ornaments and make her feel remorse for her historical past.[90]

The first two parts of the Message of Fatima contain no

---

[89]Socci, *Fourth Secret*, pp. 63, 82.

[90]Msgr. Georges Roche, *Pie XII Devant L'Histoire* (Paris: Editions Robert Laffont, 1972), p. 52.

warning about the "suicide" of alterations in the Church's liturgy, theology and soul. Yet the future Pope linked his prediction of all these events to "the Blessed Virgin's messages to little Lucia of Fatima." It seems probable, then, that in his capacity as Vatican Secretary of State the future Pope had obtained information from Sister Lucia or from the Fatima archives pertaining to the Third Secret, and that this information concerned a coming crisis in the Church of enormous magnitude, amounting even to the "suicide" of the Church itself (relatively speaking, of course).

Father Augustin Fuentes – 1957

On December 26, 1957, Father Augustin Fuentes, the postulator of the causes for beatification of Francisco and Jacinta Marto, met with Sister Lucia at the convent in Coimbra, Portugal. After interviewing Lucia, Father Fuentes published a report on the interview with "every guarantee of authenticity and with due episcopal approval, including that of the Bishop of Fatima."[91]

In speaking with Father Fuentes, Sister Lucia focused on the fast-approaching "deadline" of 1960 and of an even worse chastisement than World War II and the already manifest spread of Communism—a chastisement she reveals *is predicted in the Third Secret*:

> Father, the most Holy Virgin is very sad because no one has paid any attention to her Message, neither the good nor the bad. The good continue on their way, but without giving any importance to her Message. The bad, not seeing the punishment of God actually falling upon them, continue their life of sin without even caring about the Message. But believe me, Father, God will chastise the world and this will be in a terrible manner. The punishment from Heaven is imminent....
>
> *Father, how much time is there before 1960 arrives?* It will be very sad for everyone, not one person will rejoice at all if beforehand the world does not pray and do penance. I am not able to give any other details, because it is still a Secret.... *This is the third part of*

---

[91] Alonso, *La verdad sobre el Secreto de Fátima*, pp. 110-111; quoted in *WTAF*, Vol. III, p. 503. Archbishop Sanchez of Veracruz gave the *imprimatur*. Ibid.

the Message of Our Lady, which will remain secret until 1960.[92]

While Sister Lucia said she could not give "details" of the Third Secret, she did say this to Father Fuentes:

> Tell them, Father, that many times the Most Holy Virgin told my cousins Francisco and Jacinta, as well as myself, that *many nations will disappear from the face of the earth.* She said that Russia will be the instrument of chastisement chosen by Heaven to punish the whole world if we do not beforehand obtain the conversion of that poor nation....
>
> Father, the devil is in the mood for engaging in a decisive battle against the Blessed Virgin. And the devil knows what it is that offends God the most, and which in a short space of time will gain for him the greatest number of souls. *Thus the devil does everything to overcome souls consecrated to God,* because in this way *the devil will succeed in leaving the souls of the faithful abandoned by their leaders,* thereby the more easily will he seize them....
>
> That which afflicts the Immaculate Heart of Mary and the Heart of Jesus is *the fall of religious and priestly souls.* The devil knows that religious and priests who fall away from their beautiful vocation *drag numerous souls to hell....* The devil wishes *to take possession of consecrated souls.* He tries to corrupt them *in order to lull to sleep the souls of laypeople* and thereby lead them to final impenitence....
>
> Father, that is why my mission is not to indicate to the world *the material punishments which are certain to come* if the world does not pray and do penance beforehand. No! My mission is to indicate to everyone the imminent danger we are in of losing our souls for all eternity if we remain obstinate in sin.[93]

There is no reference to a diabolical attack on consecrated souls

---

[92]Ibid., pp. 103-106; quoted in *WTAF,* Vol. III, pp. 504-508; and in Francis Alban and Christopher A. Ferrara, *Fatima Priest* (Pound Ridge, New York: Good Counsel Publications, 1997, Second Edition), pp. 295-298 (also at http://www.fatimapriest. com/Appendix3.htm).

[93]Ibid.

in the first two parts of the Fatima message. Yet Lucia here clearly relates this attack to "the third part of the Message of Our Lady, which will remain secret until 1960." Thus, Sister Lucia all but confirmed that within the "etc" she had placed at the end of Our Lady's reference to the preservation of dogma in Portugal is to be found a heavenly prophecy of apostasy in the Catholic Church.

Notice also that Sister Lucia—*after* World War II and the rise of international Communism—warned of "the material punishments which are certain to come if the world does not pray and do penance beforehand." Thus, Lucia intimates that the Third Secret foretells *parallel chastisements*: spiritual and material. The loss of faith in the Church would be accompanied by temporal punishments of the whole world.

Despite an ecclesiastical campaign to destroy his good name, Father Fuentes would ultimately be rehabilitated. By 1976 the official Fatima archivist, Father Joaquin Alonso (who had been persuaded for a time that the Fuentes interview was faked), had concluded from his review of the Fatima archives that the interview "contains nothing that Sister Lucia has not already said in her numerous published writings."[94] Indeed, it contained nothing that, in substance, Pius XII himself had not long before connected with the Fatima prophecy when he was still Cardinal Pacelli.

Soon after the Father Fuentes interview appeared, Sister Lucia was silenced by order of the Vatican. No more freely given interviews. No more visits from anyone not pre-approved in Rome. Socci notes that from 1960 forward "Sister Lucia could receive in fact only family and those who came authorized by the Vatican." Socci calls this an "inexplicable gagging" of the "only living witness" to the apparitions, and "one of the most incomprehensible paradoxes of Fatima."[95] After 1960 it would be only through her letters and certain limited encounters, approved or by chance, that Lucia would be able to communicate bits and pieces of what concerns us here.

Father Joaquin Alonso – 1965

As the official Fatima archivist, Father Alonso had unrestricted

---

[94]Alonso, *La verdad sobre el Secreto de Fátima*, pp. 112-113, quoted in *WTAF*, Vol. III, pp. 552-553. *See* also "Silencing of the Messengers: Father Fuentes (1959 – 1965)" at http://www.fatima.org/essentials/opposed/frfuentes.asp.

[95]Socci, *Fourth Secret*, p. 112.

access to Sister Lucia and her voluminous writings and was able to conduct innumerable interviews of the seer. Based on what Sister Lucia had said and written, Father Alonso reached these conclusions about what followed the mysterious "etc":

> If 'in Portugal the dogma of the Faith will always be preserved,' ... it can be clearly deduced from this that in other parts of the Church these dogmas are going to become obscure or even lost altogether.

> Thus it is quite possible that in this intermediate period which is in question (after 1960 and before the triumph of the Immaculate Heart of Mary), the text makes concrete references to the crisis of the Faith of the Church and to the negligence of the pastors themselves...[96]

Elsewhere, Father Alonso summed up his conclusions thus: "It is therefore completely probable that the text makes concrete references to the crisis of faith within the Church and to the negligence of the pastors themselves," to "internal struggles in the very bosom of the Church and of grave pastoral negligence by the upper hierarchy," and "deficiencies of the upper hierarchy of the Church."[97]

Sister Lucia – post 1960

Even after she was ordered not to receive any visitors except those approved by the Vatican, Sister Lucia wrote many times to reliable witnesses of a "diabolical disorientation" in the Church and the world of which Our Lady had warned her. For example:

> There is a diabolical disorientation invading the world and misleading souls.... [T]he devil has succeeded in infiltrating evil under the cover of good, and the blind are beginning to guide others.... And the worst is that he has succeeded in leading into error and deceiving souls having a heavy responsibility through the place which they occupy... They are blind men leading other blind men... [They] let

---

[96]Father Joaquin Alonso, *La verdad sobre el Secreto de Fátima*, p. 70; quoted in *WTAF*, Vol. III, p. 687.

[97]Alonso, *La verdad sobre el Secreto de Fátima*, pp. 75, 80-81, quoted in *WTAF*, Vol. III, p. 704.

themselves be dominated by the diabolical wave invading the world....[98]

Even more dramatically, when asked about the content of the Third Secret, Sister Lucia replied simply: "It's in the Gospel and *the Apocalypse*. Read them!"[99] Since the first two parts of the Message of Fatima say nothing of diabolical disorientation in the Church or any connection of the Message to the Book of the Apocalypse, the only reasonable inference is that these matters pertain to the Third Secret.

Cardinal Ottaviani – 1967

During a press conference concerning the Third Secret in 1967, Cardinal Ottaviani, then Pro-Prefect of the Congregation for the Doctrine of the Faith (which had replaced the Holy Office), stated that the Third Secret had not been revealed in order "To avoid that something so delicate, not destined for public consumption, come for whatever reason, even fortuitous, to fall into alien hands."[100]

What could be so "delicate" about the Secret that the Vatican was afraid it would fall into "alien hands"? From the evidence already discussed, we have a good idea of the answer to that question.

Pope Paul VI – 1967

On May 13, 1967, during his trip to Fatima, Paul VI introduced his encyclical letter *Signum Magnum*, whose opening line, in keeping with the revelation of Sister Lucia just mentioned, links the apparitions of Our Lady of Fatima to Chapter 12 of the Book of the Apocalypse: "The great sign which the Apostle John saw in Heaven, 'a woman clothed with the sun,' is interpreted by the sacred Liturgy, not without foundation, as referring to the most blessed Mary, the mother of all men by the grace of Christ the Redeemer."

It cannot have been a mere happenstance that Paul VI chose the occasion of his sermon at Fatima on this date to lament that the

---

[98]Excerpts from letters, quoted in *The Whole Truth About Fatima* (*WTAF*), Vol. III, pp. 758-760.

[99]*WTAF*, Vol. III, p. 763.

[100]*Documentation Catholique*, March 19, 1967, Col. 543.

"renewal" of the Church after Vatican II was going wrong: "What an evil it would be if an arbitrary interpretation, not authorized by the Magisterium, transformed this renewal into *a disquieting disintegration of her traditional structure and constitution...*"

Joining the theme of material chastisement to the spiritual chastisement clearly already in progress, Pope Paul declared: "We say: *the world is in danger.* Therefore, we have come on foot to demand of the Queen of Peace as a gift what only God can give, peace.... Men, think of the gravity and the greatness of this hour, which can decide the history of the present and of future generations."[101] Note well Pope Paul's linkage—*at Fatima*—of the ecclesial crisis with danger to the whole world.

John Paul II – 1980

Thirteen years later, Pope John Paul II made the same linkage. At a meeting with a select group of Catholic intellectuals at Fulda, Germany the Pope was asked: "What about the Third Secret of Fatima? Should it not have already been published by 1960?" The Pope replied:

> Given *the seriousness of the contents,* my predecessors in the Petrine office diplomatically preferred to postpone publication so as not to encourage the world power of Communism to make certain moves.
>
> On the other hand, it should be sufficient for all Christians to know this: *if there is a message in which it is written that the oceans will flood whole areas of the earth, and that from one moment to the next millions of people will perish, truly the publication of such a message is no longer something to be so much desired....*[102]

---

[101] *See* Sermon of Pope Paul VI at Fatima, May 13, 1967, (in Italian) at http://www. vatican.va/holy_father/paul_vi/homilies/1967/documents/hf_p-vi_hom_19670513_ it.html.

[102] *Stimme Des Glaubins* (Voice of Faith), October 1981. This translation was made by Rev. M. Crowdy for *Approaches* magazine, edited by Mr. Hamish Fraser of Scotland. It was translated from an Italian publication by the Roman priest Father Francis Putti, publisher of *Si Si No No.* All three magazines are credible sources. In his 2007 television appearance, which is the subject of Chapter 8, Cardinal Bertone, confronted by the Pope's reported statements at Fulda, avoided any comment, while Giuseppe de Carli, co-author of the Cardinal's book attacking Socci, offered the explanation that Cardinal Ratzinger had offered an "interpretation" of the Pope's remarks that eliminated any apocalyptic reading. No one on the show, however, denied that the Pope had spoken as he did at Fulda. The verbatim transcript of the Pope's remarks in *Stimme Des Glaubins*

The Pope was then asked: "What is going to happen to the Church?" To this question the Pope replied:

> We must prepare ourselves to suffer great trials before long, such as will demand of us a disposition to give up even life, and a total dedication to Christ and for Christ ... With your and my prayer it is possible to mitigate this tribulation, *but it is no longer possible to avert it, because only thus can the Church be effectively renewed.* How many times has the renewal of the Church sprung from blood! This time, too, it will not be otherwise. We must be strong and prepared, and trust in Christ and His Mother, and be very, very assiduous in praying the Rosary. [103]

Thus, in 1980, the Pope warned of *both* a material and a spiritual chastisement in connection with his discussion of the Third Secret.

John Paul II – 1982

On May 13, 1982, during his trip to Fatima after the assassination attempt, Pope John Paul II once again linked the Message of Fatima to apocalyptic developments not mentioned in the first two parts. In his sermon, which I quoted earlier, he revealed that Our Lady of Fatima had issued what Pius XII had called "a divine warning" about an attack on the dogmas of the Faith:

> Can the Mother, who with all the force of the love that she fosters in the Holy Spirit and desires the salvation of every man, can she remain silent when she sees *the very bases of her children's salvation undermined?* No, she cannot remain silent.[104]

These "bases" of salvation must refer to firm adherence to the Catholic faith as found in the dogmatic teachings of the Church

---

matches in all particulars the detailed notes taken by a German priest who attended the same conference. *See* "World War III and Worse?", interview with Father Paul Kramer, *The Fatima Crusader*, No. 82 (Spring 2006), p. 11 (also at http://www.fatimacrusader. com/cr82/cr82pg11.asp).

[103]*Stimme Des Glaubins*, loc. cit.

[104]"Può la Madre, la quale con tutta la potenza del suo amore, che nutre nello Spirito Santo, desidera la salvezza di ogni uomo, tacere su ciò *che mina le basi stesse di questa salvezza*? No, non lo può!"

and in her sacraments, the means by which souls are saved.[105] Thus, albeit in a veiled way, the Pope was linking the Message of Fatima to a threat to dogma and discipline in the Church, just as the future Pius XII did in 1931.[106] But where in the Message is there such a warning? Certainly not in the parts that had already been published as of 1982.

During the same trip to Fatima, John Paul II discussed with Sister Lucia the question why the Third Secret had not yet been revealed. As Sister Lucia informed Cardinal Oddi, while the Cardinal was in Fatima for the annual May 13th celebration of the apparitions in 1985, the Pope told her that the Secret had not been divulged "because it could be badly interpreted."[107] Here the Pope provided a further hint that the Secret would be embarrassing to Church authorities because it concerns a crisis of faith and discipline for which they themselves are responsible.

Bishop do Amaral – 1984

On September 10, 1984 Bishop Alberto Cosme do Amaral, the Bishop of Fatima, emphasized the Secret's prediction of apostasy in the Church. During a question and answer session in the *aula magna* of the Technical University of Vienna, Austria he flatly declared: "Its (the Third Secret's) content concerns only our faith ... The loss of faith of a continent is worse than the annihilation of a nation; and it is true that faith is continually diminishing in Europe."[108]

---

[105]As the opening lines of the St. Athanasius Creed state: *Quicumque vult salvus esse, ante omnia opus est, ut teneat catholicam fidem: Quam nisi quisque integram inviolatamque servaverit, absque dubio in aeternum peribit.* ("Whoever wishes to be saved must before all else adhere to the Catholic faith. He must preserve this faith whole and inviolate; otherwise he shall most certainly perish forever.")

[106]*See,* "Pope John Paul II Has Twice Revealed the Essence of the Secret" and "The Attack is From *Within* the Church", in *The Devil's Final Battle*, Chapter 13, pp. 170, 185 (also at http://www.devilsfinalbattle.com/ch13.htm).

[107]*30 Giorni*, April 1991; cited in Socci, *Fourth Secret*, p. 131. *See* also Lucio Brunelli, "The Third Secret Regards 'Apostasy in the Church'", *The Fatima Crusader*, No. 33 (Summer 1990), pp. 14ff (also at http://www.fatimacrusader.com/cr33/cr33pg14.asp), an interview with Cardinal Oddi originally published on March 17, 1990, in *Il Sabato* magazine, Rome.

[108]Remarks recorded in *Mensagem de Fátima*, February 1985, published by Father Messias Coelho.

Cardinal Ratzinger – 1984

On November 11, 1984, Cardinal Ratzinger, in an interview in *Jesus* magazine, revealed that he had read the Third Secret and that it concerns "dangers *threatening the faith* and the life of the Christian and therefore of the world." There is, of course, no reference in the first two parts of the Message of Fatima to "dangers threatening the *faith*" as distinct from dangers to the Pope and other *believers* in the form of wars and persecutions of the Church by external enemies. The Cardinal further revealed that "the things contained in this 'Third Secret' correspond to what has been announced in Scripture and has been said again and again in *many other Marian apparitions…*"[109]

As to why the Secret had not been published, the Cardinal said: "If it is not published, at least for now, it is to avoid confusing *religious prophecy with sensationalism...*"[110] Apparently contradicting himself, however, the Cardinal added that the Secret had not been revealed "Because, according to the judgment of the Popes, it adds nothing that differs from what a Christian should know from Revelation…" A secret that "adds nothing" to what a Christian should know would not be "sensational"; in fact, it would not even be a secret.[111] Why, then, had the text of the Secret been placed "forever under absolute seal" in 1960? The Cardinal's suggestion that the Secret contains nothing we do not already know hardly comported with the way the Vatican had been handling it for decades.

---

[109]*Jesus* magazine, November 11, 1984, p. 79 (see photo of extract of original Italian article in photo insert section). See also Father Paul Kramer, *The Devil's Final Battle*, pp. 33, 274-276 (also at http://www.devilsfinalbattle.com/ch4.htm, http://www. devilsfinalbattle.com/appendix.htm); "Published Testimony: Cardinal Ratzinger (November 1984)" at http://www.fatima.org/thirdsecret/ratzinger.asp; *WTAF*, Vol. III, pp. 822-823; "Cardinal Ratzinger Speaks on: The Third Secret of Fatima", *The Fatima Crusader*, No. 18 (Oct.-Dec. 1985), pp. S4ff (also at http://www.fatimacrusader.com/ cr18/cr18pgS4.asp); *The Fatima Crusader*, No. 37 (Summer 1991), p. 7 (http://www. fatimacrusader.com/cr37/cr37pg6.asp); and *The Fatima Crusader*, No. 64, (Summer 2000), p. 118 (http://www.fatimacrusader.com/cr64/cr64pg28.asp).

[110]Ibid.

[111]The complete sentence in question reads: "Because, according to the judgment of the Popes, it adds nothing to what a Christian must know from Revelation: i.e., a radical call for conversion; the absolute importance of history; the dangers threatening the faith and the life of the Christian and therefore of the world."

Cardinal Ratzinger and Our Lady of Akita

The Cardinal's linkage of the "religious prophecy" of the Third Secret to "other Marian apparitions" in his 1984 interview was abundantly revealing. The apparition of Our Lady of Akita to Sister Agnes Katsuko Sasagawa, a Japanese nun, on October 13, 1973—the very anniversary of the Miracle of the Sun—was found to be authentic and worthy of belief after an investigation by Bishop Ito of the Diocese of Akita. Here is what Our Lady said to Sister Agnes:

> As I told you, if men do not repent and better themselves, the Father will inflict a terrible punishment on all humanity. It will be a punishment greater than the deluge, such as one will never have seen before. *Fire will fall from the sky and will wipe out a great part of humanity, the good as well as the bad, sparing neither priests nor faithful. The survivors will find themselves so desolate that they will envy the dead.*[112] The only arms which will remain for you will be the Rosary and the Sign left by My Son. Each day recite the prayers of the Rosary. With the Rosary, pray for the Pope, the bishops and priests.
>
> The work of the devil will infiltrate even into the Church in such a way that one will see cardinals opposing cardinals, bishops against bishops. The priests who venerate me will be scorned and opposed by their confreres... churches and altars sacked; the Church will be full of those who accept compromises and the demon will press many priests and consecrated souls to leave the service of the Lord.

Howard Dee, former Philippine ambassador to the Vatican, revealed in a 1998 interview with *Inside the Vatican* that "Bishop Ito was certain Akita was an extension of Fatima, and *Cardinal*

---

[112]It might be asked how the punishment of fire falling from Heaven is consistent with the Pope's remarks at Fulda about the inundation of nations by the oceans and millions of deaths as a result. Both events are consistent with a cometary or asteroidal impact causing tsunamis. The Book of the Apocalypse speaks of how "the second angel sounded the trumpet: and as it were a great *mountain, burning with fire, was cast into the sea*, and the third part of the sea became blood..." (Apoc. 8:8) A prediction of an event of that magnitude would explain why the words of the Virgin were placed "forever under absolute seal" in 1960, and why the Secret has been treated as such a "delicate" matter since then.

Ratzinger personally confirmed to me that these two messages, of Fatima and Akita, are essentially the same."[113]

If the messages of Fatima and Akita are, as Cardinal Ratzinger admitted, "essentially the same"—a great crisis of faith within the Church accompanied by a worldwide chastisement—then it appears we must look to the Third Secret for the content that would make such a comparison apt. The Third Secret, then, as does the Akita prophecy, would make explicit Sister Lucia's own reference to a combined spiritual and material chastisement of the Church much worse than what had already transpired with World War II and the rise of world Communism.

Cardinal Ratzinger - 1985

Adding further to the enigma the Cardinal's own words had created in 1984, the text of this interview, which the Cardinal had reviewed and approved before its publication, was mysteriously revised for republication in the book entitled *Report on the Faith*, which appeared in June 1985. In the *Report* the Cardinal's original reference to "dangers *threatening the faith* and the life of the Christian and therefore of the world" was "sanitized" to read "the dangers threatening humanity." Had the Cardinal said too much? At the same time, however, the reference to the "sensational" content of the Third Secret was made even clearer: "To publish the Third Secret would also signify exposing oneself to the danger of the sensationalistic use of the contents."[114]

Cardinal Oddi – 1990

On March 17, 1990, Cardinal Silvio Oddi, a close personal friend of John XXIII, declared that the Third Secret "has nothing to do with Gorbachev. The Blessed Virgin was alerting us against apostasy in the Church."[115]

---

[113]Reported by *Catholic World News*, October 11, 2001; *See* www.cwnews.com/news/viewstory.cfm?recnum=20583.

[114]Quoted in Socci, *Fourth Secret*, p. 102; see also *WTAF*, Vol. III, pp. 818-840; "Cardinal Ratzinger on the Third Secret", *The Fatima Crusader*, No. 64 (Summer 2000), pp. 35ff (also at http://www.fatimacrusader.com/cr64/cr64pg35.asp).

[115]*Il Sabato*, Rome, March 17, 1990. See also "Apostasy in the Church", *The Fatima Crusader*, No. 33 (Summer 1990), pp. 14-15 (also at http://www.fatimacrusader.com/cr33/cr33pg14.asp).

Cardinal Ciappi – 1995

In 1995 Cardinal Luigi Ciappi, no less than the papal theologian to Popes Pius XII, John XXIII, Paul VI, John Paul I and John Paul II—a span of 40 years—made this revelation concerning the contents of the Secret: "In the Third Secret it is foretold, among other things, that the great apostasy in the Church begins at the top."[116]

Cardinal Ratzinger – 1996

A year later, giving further indications that the Third Secret would cause a sensation, Cardinal Ratzinger said during an interview with a leading Portuguese journalist, Aura Miguel, that "The divulging of the secret should be done only when it will not be able to create one-sidedness and disequilibrium, *concentrating only on its details*; the revelation should be made only when it [the Third Secret] will be able to be understood as an aid to the progress of the faith."[117]

What are these "details" on which we must not "concentrate," lest they cause "disequilibrium" in the Church? From what we have seen thus far, we are dealing with some very precise content that could only involve particular predictions by the Blessed Virgin, as distinct from the unexplained meaning of the wordless vision of the bishop in white.

John Paul II – 2000: the "compromise solution"

Finally, on May 13, 2000 John Paul II renewed the apocalyptic theme of Paul VI at Fatima 33 years earlier, once again linking Our Lady of Fatima to Chapter 12 of the Book of the Apocalypse. In his sermon at the Mass for the beatification of Jacinta and Francisco, John Paul declared:

> According to the divine plan, "a woman clothed with the sun" (Apoc. 12: 1) came down from heaven to this earth to visit the privileged children of the Father. She speaks to them with a mother's voice and

---

[116]Personal communication to Professor Baumgartner in Salzburg, Austria.

[117]Aura Miguel, *Totus Tuus: Il Segreto di Fatima nel Pontificato de Giovanni Paolo II* (Itaca: Castel Bolognese, 2003), p. 137.

heart: she asks them to offer themselves as victims of reparation, saying that she was ready to lead them safely to God…

"Another portent appeared in heaven; behold, a great red dragon" (Apoc. 12: 3). These words from the first reading of the Mass make us think of the great struggle between good and evil, showing how, when man puts God aside, he cannot achieve happiness, but ends up destroying himself….

The Message of Fatima is a call to conversion, alerting humanity to have nothing to do with the "dragon" whose *"tail swept down a third of the stars of heaven, and cast them to the earth"* (Apoc. 12: 4). Man's final goal is heaven, his true home, where the heavenly Father awaits everyone with His merciful love….

In her motherly concern, the Blessed Virgin came here to Fátima to ask men and women "to stop offending God, Our Lord, who is already very offended". It is a mother's sorrow that compels her to speak; *the destiny of her children is at stake….*[118]

Here we encounter the evidence of what Socci has called the "compromise solution" on disclosure of the Third Secret: a papal sermon revealing its apocalyptic content indirectly. As already noted, Sister Lucia also revealed that the Third Secret is related to the Book of the Apocalypse. At Fatima, John Paul II could not have made this more explicit. But, even more important, the Pope's association of the Message of Fatima with "the stars of heaven" being swept down from Heaven by the tail of the dragon who appears in Chapter 12, verses 3 and 4 of the Apocalypse was an unmistakable linkage of the Fatima message to the threat of apostasy in the Church.[119] How do we know this? We know it because the fall of one-third of "the stars of heaven" is traditionally interpreted to mean the fall of *consecrated souls.*

---

[118]*See* www.vatican.va/holy_father/john_paul_ii/travels/documents/hf_jp-ii_hom_20000513_beatification-fatima_en.html.

[119]*See,* "The Secretary of State Targets the Message of Fatima" (in Chapter 8) and "Pope John Paul II Has Twice Revealed the Essence of the Secret" (in Chapter 13) in *The Devil's Final Battle,* pp. 100-101, 170-171 (also at http://www.devilsfinalbattle.com/ch8.htm and http://www.devilsfinalbattle.com/ch13.htm).

Father Herman B. Kramer discusses the traditional exegesis in his commentary on the Apocalypse, *The Book of Destiny*, first published with an *imprimatur*, providentially enough, in 1956, only six years before the opening of Vatican II. As Father Kramer notes, the symbol of one-third of the stars in Heaven signifies "one-third of the clergy," who "shall follow the dragon." By means of these apostate clergy, the devil will probably enforce upon the Church "the acceptance of unchristian morals, false doctrines, *compromise with error*, or obedience to the civil rulers in violation of conscience." Further, "The symbolic meaning of the dragon's tail may reveal that the clergy who are ripe for apostasy will hold the influential positions in the Church, having won preferment by hypocrisy, deceit and flattery." These wayward clergy will include those "who neglected to preach the truth or to admonish the sinner by a good example, but rather sought popularity by being lax and the slaves of human respect," those "who fear for their own interests and will not remonstrate against evil practices in the Church," and bishops "who abhor upright priests who dare to tell the truth."[120]

Surely this scenario sounds familiar to contemporary Catholics, although it would have been viewed with amazement in the 1950s. Pope John Paul cannot have been unaware of the traditional understanding of the apocalyptic passages he had cited at Fatima and linked to the Fatima message. The Pope could only have been evoking the very thing Sister Lucia had confided to Father Fuentes: that the Message of Fatima, in the part that must be kept secret until 1960, warns of a massive defection of priests and religious under the influence of the devil, and consequent apostasy among the faithful who are left without shepherds. To recall Sister Lucia's words: "The devil knows that religious and priests who fall away from their beautiful vocation *drag numerous souls to hell.*"[121]

Again, however, the vision of "the Bishop dressed in white" contains no indication of any such apostasy in the Church. It contains *no words at all* which could explain its content, but only the angel's single word, repeated thrice: Penance! It is reasonable to conclude, therefore, that here the Pope was indirectly revealing the *words* of

---

[120]Father Herman B. Kramer, *The Book of Destiny* (first published 1955, republished by TAN Books and Publishers, Inc., Rockford, Illinois, 1975), pp. 279-284; cited in *The Devil's Final Battle*, pp. 101-102 (also at http://www.devilsfinalbattle.com/ch8.htm).

[121]Alonso, *La verdad sobre el Secreto de Fátima*, pp. 103-106; quoted in *WTAF*, Vol. III, pp. 504-506; and in *Fatima Priest*, pp. 296-297 (also at http://www.fatimapriest.com/Appendix3.htm).

the Virgin explaining the vision as contained in the text of the Secret that has yet to be produced. As Socci notes, that Sister Lucia, Paul VI and John Paul II *all* linked the Third Secret to the Apocalypse "cannot be casual," but must indicate "a strict link between the prophetic book of the Apostle John and the Third Secret."[122]

A summary of the evidence on this point

In sum, before the Vatican's publication of the vision of "the Bishop dressed in white" on June 26, 2000, there was already a large body of evidence that the text of the Third Secret involved—

- a "divine warning" about "suicidal" alterations in the liturgy, theology and soul of the Church (the future Pius XII in 1931);

- a prediction that after 1960 "the devil will succeed in leaving the souls of the faithful abandoned by their leaders," by causing "religious and priests [to] fall away from their beautiful vocation... drag[ging] numerous souls to hell," and that "nations will disappear from the face of the earth" (Sister Lucia to Father Fuentes in 1957);

- contents "so delicate" that they cannot be allowed "for whatever reason, even fortuitous, to fall into alien hands" (Cardinal Ottaviani in 1967);

- a text "diplomatically" withheld because of the "seriousness of its contents" and which predicts, *after 1980*, "great trials" and "tribulation" for the Church which "it is no longer possible to avert" and the destruction of "whole areas of the earth" so that "from one moment to the next millions of people will perish" (John Paul II at Fulda, 1980);

- details that could be "badly interpreted" (John Paul II in 1982);

- a "religious prophecy" of "dangers threatening the faith and the life of the Christian and therefore of the world" (Cardinal Ratzinger in 1984);

- matters which would make for the "sensationalistic

---

[122]Socci, *Fourth Secret*, p. 97.

utilization of its contents" (Cardinal Ratzinger in 1985);

- a prediction of apostasy in the Church that "begins at the top" (Cardinal Ciappi in 1995);

- "details" that would cause "disequilibrium" in the Church (Cardinal Ratzinger in 1996);

- a warning of a material chastisement of the world which accompanies the great apostasy in the Church, like that predicted in the approved apparition of Our Lady of Akita in 1973, whose message is "essentially the same" as the message of Our Lady of Fatima (Cardinal Ratzinger to Howard Dee, as reported in 1998);

- a warning to avoid the "tail of the dragon" (the devil) referred to in the Book of the Apocalypse (12:3-4), which sweeps one-third of "the stars" (priests and other consecrated souls) from Heaven (their vocations) (John Paul II in 2000).

The vision, as we shall see, involves *none* of these elements—a fact that has led Socci and many other Catholics to conclude that there must be a missing text of the Third Secret.

A movement emerges

The body of evidence we have surveyed in this and the preceding chapter is so compelling that it gave rise to a movement in the Church composed of loyal Catholics unjustly derided as "Fatimists"—Catholics who could see that the Secret had been suppressed because its contents were both precise and terrible. Over the decades that followed 1960 this movement grew larger, and the pressure for disclosure of the truth about the Secret, the whole truth, steadily intensified. The issue of the Third Secret would simply not go away; nor could it, given the Secret's heavenly origin and the universal destination of the Message of Fatima as a whole. As Pope John Paul himself declared at Fatima on May 13, 1982: "This Message is addressed to every human being."[123] Thus was the stage set for the Vatican's purported revelation of the Secret in June of 2000.

---

[123]"Questo messaggio è rivolto ad ogni uomo." *Papal Homily at Fatima Sanctuary,* May 13, 1982 at http://www.vatican.va/holy_father/john_paul_ii/homilies/1982/documents/hf_jp-ii_hom_19820513_fatima_it.html.

Chapter 4

Something is Missing

On June 26, 2000, after forty years of growing pressure from the faithful, including such "Fatimist" organizations as Father Nicholas Gruner's Fatima apostolate, the Vatican conducted a press conference to publish what it claimed is the entirety of the Third Secret. Conspicuously absent from the proceedings was the last surviving Fatima visionary. Sister Lucia was not even permitted to watch the internationally televised press conference on television. Sister Maria do Carmo, custodian of Sister Lucia's convent in Coimbra, told *Corriere della Sera* that "We watch TV, but only in exceptional cases. The press conference on the Secret of Fatima is not such." This prompted Socci to ask: "And what are these exceptional cases for the Carmelites of Coimbra? Perhaps the finals of the world soccer championship?"[124]

Some six weeks earlier, then Vatican Secretary of State, Cardinal Angelo Sodano, had announced during the papal Mass for the beatification of Jacinta and Francisco at Fatima that the Secret would be published along with "an appropriate commentary."[125] The text of the purported Secret, spanning four pages and 62 lines, was photostatically reproduced as part of a booklet containing that commentary, entitled *The Message of Fatima* (*Message*). Aside from the commentary, written by Cardinal Ratzinger, then Prefect of the Congregation for the Doctrine of the Faith (CDF), *Message* included an Introduction by then Archbishop Bertone, serving at that time as Secretary for the CDF.

According to *Message*, the Secret that had been suppressed and kept "under absolute seal" since it arrived at the Vatican in 1957 is nothing more than the following:

J.M.J.

The third part of the secret revealed at the Cova da

---

[124]Socci, *Fourth Secret*, p. 34.

[125]Vatican Information Service, May 13, 2000.

Iria-Fatima, on 13 July 1917.

I write in obedience to you, my God, who command me to do so through his Excellency the Bishop of Leiria and through your Most Holy Mother and mine.

After the two parts which I have already explained, at the left of Our Lady and a little above, we saw an Angel with a flaming sword in his left hand; flashing, it gave out flames that looked as though they would set the world on fire; but they died out in contact with the splendour that Our Lady radiated towards him from her right hand: pointing to the earth with his right hand, the Angel cried out in a loud voice: "<u>Penance, Penance, Penance</u>!". And we saw in an immense light that is God; "something similar to how people appear in a mirror when they pass in front of it" a Bishop dressed in White "we had the impression that it was the Holy Father". Other Bishops, Priests, men and women Religious going up a steep mountain, at the top of which there was a big Cross of rough-hewn trunks as of a cork-tree with the bark; before reaching there the Holy Father passed through a big city half in ruins and half trembling with halting step, afflicted with pain and sorrow, he prayed for the souls of the corpses he met on his way; having reached the top of the mountain, on his knees at the foot of the big Cross he was killed by a group of soldiers who fired bullets and arrows at him, and in the same way there died one after another the other Bishops, Priests, men and women Religious, and various lay people of different ranks and positions. Beneath the two arms of the Cross there were two Angels each with a crystal aspersorium in his hand, in which they gathered up the blood of the Martyrs and with it sprinkled the souls that were making their way to God.

Tuy-3-1-1944.[126]

That this vision is *part* of the Third Secret can hardly be doubted. But the worldwide reaction of the Catholic faithful to its disclosure can be summed up with a single incredulous question: "*That's it?*" Yes, the vision is dramatic, but its meaning is far from

---

[126]*The Message of Fatima* (*Message*), p. 21.

clear: An angel with a flaming sword. Flames from the sword threatening to set the world afire, but repelled (temporarily?) by the Virgin. The angel thrice demanding penance from humanity. A "Bishop dressed in White," who seems to be the Pope, hobbling through a half-ruined city filled with corpses (what city? how ruined?). The execution of the Pope by a band of soldiers (who are they?) as he kneels before a rough-hewn cross on a hill outside the city (is it Rome?). And then the martyrdom of countless bishops, priests, religious and laity (who? when? where?), as two other angels gather up the blood of the martyrs to sprinkle on Heaven-bound souls.

What does it all mean? The vision as published does not contain a single word from the Virgin by way of explanation. Yet Our Lady had taken care to confirm for the seers the vision of hell they had clearly understood upon the very sight of it: "You have seen hell, where the souls of poor sinners go." *Message* offered no explanation for the missing words of the Virgin, as if no one should be puzzled by this. But it defied belief that the Virgin had *nothing* to say about the dramatic but ambiguous content of the vision. Doubting questions immediately abounded:

- Where are the *words* of the Virgin which are the "logical continuation" of her statement "In Portugal, the dogma of the Faith will always be preserved etc"?

- What is so terrible about this ambiguous vision that Sister Lucia could not commit it to paper without a direct intervention of the Virgin Mary?

- Where is the letter to the Bishop of Fatima, comprising some 25 lines of text?

- Given that *Message* stated that the text of the vision had been kept in the Holy Office archives,[127] where is the text that was kept in the papal apartment under the Pope's personal custody during the reigns of Pius XII, John XXIII and Paul VI?

- Why is the vision devoid of any reference to a crisis of faith in the Church and dramatic consequences for the world, alluded to by a train of witnesses who had either read the Secret or had indirect knowledge of it?

---

[127]*Message*, p. 5.

There is, on the face of it, no rational explanation for the Vatican's refusal to disclose the text of this vision in 1960 or the rigorous suppression of it for forty years thereafter. Indeed, in his commentary on the Secret in *Message*, the same Cardinal Ratzinger who said in 1984 that the Secret is a "religious prophecy" concerning "dangers to the faith and the life of the Christian and therefore of the world", was now saying that in the Secret "No great mystery is revealed; nor is the future unveiled. We see the Church of the martyrs of the century which has just passed..."[128] If that were true, then why did Cardinal Ratzinger not simply *say so* back in 1984? As Portuguese bishop Januario Torgal declared: "If the Vatican knew it was not apocalyptic, why on earth did it make it public only now?"[129]

What about 1960?

Moreover, on its face the vision has absolutely nothing to do with 1960, the year the Secret was supposed to be revealed because it would be "more clear" then. Evidently in recognition of this problem, Cardinal Bertone claims in *Message* that during an unrecorded "conversation" with Sister Lucia at Coimbra on April 27, 2000, weeks before the press conference, she allegedly told him that the Virgin *had never said anything* about 1960:

> Before giving the sealed envelope containing the third part of the "secret" to the then Bishop of Leiria-Fatima, Sister Lucia wrote on the outside envelope that it could be opened only after 1960, either by the Patriarch of Lisbon or the Bishop of Leiria. Archbishop Bertone therefore asked: "Why only after 1960? Was it Our Lady who fixed that date?" Sister Lucia replied: "*It was not Our Lady.* I fixed the date because I had the intuition that before 1960 it would not be understood, but that only later would it be understood..."[130]

Tellingly, *Message* fails to mention that on the envelope Sister Lucia had written: "*By express order of Our Lady*, this envelope can only be opened in 1960..." Nor does *Message* include a copy

---

[128]Ibid., p. 32.

[129]*The Washington Post*, "Third Secret Spurs More Questions; Fatima Interpretation Departs From Vision," July 1, 2000, quoted in Mark Fellows, *Sister Lucia: Apostle of Mary's Immaculate Heart*, p. 190.

[130]*Message*, p. 29.

of the envelope as part of its supporting documentation. During the telecast of May 31, 2007 Bertone would finally reveal the envelope—or rather, *two* such envelopes, as we will see in Chapter 8. But on June 26, 2000 Bertone had the temerity to claim that Lucia declared to him in private weeks earlier: *"It was not Our Lady. I fixed the date!"* I say temerity, because the Cardinal knew that his representation was flatly contradicted by what Lucia had written on the envelopes he had chosen not to reveal.

One cannot overestimate the significance of what Bertone is claiming here. If the "express order of Our Lady" concerning revelation of the Secret in 1960 was purely Sister Lucia's invention, if she had misled Canon Barthas, Cardinal Ottaviani, the Bishop of Fatima, the Cardinal Patriarch of Portugal, the whole Church and the entire world, why should anyone believe anything she claimed to have heard from the Blessed Virgin? Why should anyone believe a single word of the Message of Fatima?

There are only two alternatives: Either Sister Lucia lied about this crucial matter throughout her life, which is inconceivable, or the words attributed to her by Bertone were not hers. In the latter case, Lucia's purported statement would be either an outright fabrication by Bertone, the product of undue influence upon the seer, or an utterance arising from a loss of mental capacity due to her advanced age. Here, in and of itself, is reason to doubt the entire official account, as Socci does.[131] To quote Socci: "[B]ut Lucia would never have dared to establish herself a date to make it [the Secret] known to everybody: only the Madonna, who had imposed secrecy on the message, could do it."[132]

What about the telltale "etc"?

And what of the famous "etc" in Sister Lucia's Fourth Memoir? To recall again Father Schweigl's testimony, the Third Secret includes

---

[131]By "official account" I do not mean any teaching of the Holy Catholic Church regarding the Third Secret controversy, for there is no such teaching. As will become clear in the course of this discussion, the "official account" means nothing more than the representations of Cardinal Bertone and his collaborators in the Vatican apparatus, who have not been given any papal authority to bind the faithful to their version of the facts or their purported "interpretation" of the vision of the Third Secret. On the contrary, as we will see, the Pope has not intervened in this controversy, and the former Cardinal Ratzinger made it quite clear in 2000 that the commentary on the Secret in *Message* has not been imposed upon the Church. Socci rightly recognizes that the faithful are at liberty to question the "official account."

[132]*Fourth Secret*, p. 38.

the "logical continuation" of the Virgin's discourse following the phrase that ends with Sister Lucia's "etc"—"In Portugal, the dogma of the faith will always be preserved etc." In fact, the attention of Fatima scholars had always been focused on the "etc" as the key to the Third Secret, since it was obvious that the Virgin's words to the seers had not trailed off in the middle of a thought.

Yet, in a maneuver that has undermined all confidence in the official account, *Message* evades any discussion of the "etc" by taking the text of the Message of Fatima from Sister Lucia's *Third Memoir*, where Our Lady's prophecy concerning Portugal does not appear, rather than the more complete Fourth Memoir. Like *Message*'s attack on the credibility of the "express order of Our Lady" regarding 1960, this conspicuous avoidance of the Fourth Memoir could only engender suspicion. Why rely on the Third Memoir when the more complete Fourth Memoir was available? In his Introduction Bertone attempts to explain this curious behavior as follows: "For the account of the first two parts of the 'secret', which have already been published and are therefore known, we have chosen the text written by Sister Lucia in the Third Memoir of 31 August 1941; some *annotations* were added in the Fourth Memoir of 8 December 1941."[133] Significantly, Bertone's Introduction *does not specify* what is contained in these "annotations," which is none other than the very phrase of the Virgin he had to know was at the heart of the entire controversy.

According to *Message*, then, the only difference between the Third and Fourth memoirs is "some annotations" by Sister Lucia, the suggestion being that no one should think it amiss that the drafters of *Message* had "chosen" the former document, which was not cluttered by these "annotations." The suggestion was less than honest, for as we saw in Chapter 2 the Virgin's words concerning the preservation of dogma in Portugal were manifestly not Lucia's "annotations" but *an integral part of the Fatima message*, immediately after which Our Lady herself had said: "Tell this to no one. Yes, you may tell Francisco." Yet Bertone, having characterized the very words of the Virgin as "annotations" buries her words in a footnote that *Message* never mentions again.[134]

Socci calls attention to an evasive but extremely revealing comment by then Archbishop Bertone at the June 26th press

---

[133]*Message*, p. 3.

[134]*Message*, p. 15. The footnote reads: "In the 'Fourth Memoir' Sister Lucia adds: 'In Portugal, the dogma of the faith will always be preserved etc. ...'"

conference. When asked about whether the "etc" is indeed the beginning of the Third Secret, Bertone stated to the press: "It is difficult to say if it [the 'etc'] refers to the second or the third part of the secret [i.e., the Great Secret of July 13, 1917]… it seems to me that it pertains to the second."[135] The implications are astonishing: *Bertone does not deny that the "etc" could in fact be part of the Third Secret*, which would mean that the Third Secret includes the Virgin's *spoken words*. In a curious equivocation, Bertone states it "is difficult to say" whether this is so, and that it "seems" to him that the "etc" pertains to the second part of the Fatima message. It *seems* to him? Why would he not have determined the answer to this crucial question before the momentous Vatican presentation on June 26, given that he had a "conversation" with Sister Lucia concerning the content of the Third Secret only weeks before, on April 27, 2000, as his own Introduction to *Message* reveals?[136]

Furthermore, even if it were the case that, as Bertone suggests, the "etc" pertains only to the Second Secret—i.e., the part of the Great Secret that predicts World War II, the spread of Russia's errors "throughout the world" and so forth—then it follows that the Vatican *has yet to reveal the Second Secret in its entirety*. Thus, no matter how it is viewed, Bertone's comment is a major blow to the credibility of the official account.

Socci asks the pertinent question: "How can one elude that explosive *incipit* [beginning] of the Virgin Mary as if it were a marginal 'annotation'?" There is, writes Socci, "a clear sense of a great embarrassment before a phrase of the Madonna that one cannot succeed in explaining and that one tries to remove silently."[137] Why the embarrassment? Because, as Socci and so many others have concluded, the "etc" is the gateway to the missing words of the Virgin that complete the Third Secret of Fatima. Hence the "etc" must be downplayed and ignored if the gateway is to remain closed.

A telling discrepancy

Bertone's Introduction to *Message* contains another point that would prove to have decisive importance in this controversy.

---

[135]*Fourth Secret*, p. 89; citing Aura Miguel, *Totus Tuus*, p. 141.

[136]*Message*, p. 8.

[137]*Fourth Secret*, pp. 75-76.

According to Bertone, John Paul II did not read the Third Secret until July 18, 1981, a full three years into his papacy, when the text of the Secret was taken from the Holy Office archives and brought to him at Gemelli Hospital, where the Pope was recovering from the assassination attempt.[138] But according to papal spokesman Joaquin Navarro-Valls, as reported by *The Washington Post*, John Paul II read the Third Secret *in 1978, within days of his election.*[139] There is no record, however, of any text of the Secret being brought to John Paul from the Holy Office archives in that year.

Thus, whatever text John Paul read in 1978 must have been located elsewhere—evidently in the papal apartment, as attested by the witnesses and photographs already cited. It is highly significant that *neither Navarro-Valls nor the Pope ever denied the report that the Pope had read the Secret in 1978*, even though (with explosive implications) that report flatly contradicted Bertone's own representations to the press.[140] But it could hardly be the case that John Paul II, the very Pope who evinced a preoccupation with Fatima, would have waited until three years after his election to read the Secret. This major discrepancy between the accounts of Bertone and Navarro-Valls in itself indicates the existence of two distinct but related texts of the Third Secret.

Cardinal Sodano's "preventative interpretation"

The credulity of the faithful was strained past the breaking point by what Socci has called "the preventative interpretation" of the vision launched by Cardinal Sodano in May-June 2000—that is, an interpretation designed to prevent anyone from finding in the Third Secret what Sodano, Bertone and others did not wish them to find. When Sodano announced at Fatima in May 2000 that the Secret would soon be published, he suggested that it was

---

[138]*Message*, p. 5.

[139]Bill Broadway and Sarah Delancy, "3rd Secret Spurs More Questions; Fatima Interpretation Departs From Vision," *The Washington Post*, July 1, 2000: "On May 13, Vatican Spokesman Joaquin Navarro-Valls said the Pope first read the secret within days of assuming the papacy in 1978. On Monday, an aide to Cardinal Joseph Ratzinger [Bertone], Prefect of the Vatican's Congregation for the Doctrine of the Faith, said that the Pope first saw it in the hospital after his attack."

[140]The Associated Press, "Vatican: Fatima Is No Doomsday Prophecy," *The New York Times*, June 26, 2000: "'John Paul II read for the first time the text of the Third Secret of Fatima after the attack,' a top aide to Ratzinger, Monsignor Tarcisio Bertone, told journalists during a news conference to present the document."

nothing more than a prediction of events that had already come to pass, culminating in the 1981 attempt on the life of John Paul II. According to Sodano:

> The vision of Fatima concerns above all the war waged by atheist systems against the Church and Christians, and it describes the immense suffering endured by the witnesses to the faith *in the last century* of the second millennium. It is an interminable Way of the Cross led by the Popes of *the twentieth century.*
>
> According to the interpretation of the "little shepherds," which was also recently confirmed by Sister Lucia, the "bishop dressed in white" who prays for all the faithful is the Pope. As he makes his way with great effort towards the Cross amid the corpses of those who were martyred (bishops, priests, men and women religious and many lay persons), he too falls to the ground, *apparently* dead, under a burst of gunfire.
>
> After the assassination attempt of May 13, 1981, it appeared evident to His Holiness that it was "a motherly hand which guided the bullet's path," enabling the "dying Pope" to halt "at the threshold of death."...
>
> The successive events of 1989 led, both in the Soviet Union and in a number of countries of Eastern Europe, to the fall of the Communist regime which promoted atheism. For this too His Holiness offers heartfelt thanks to the Most Holy Virgin....
>
> *Even if the events to which the third part of the Secret of Fatima refers now seem part of the past,* Our Lady's call to conversion and penance, issued at the beginning of the twentieth century, remains timely and urgent today....[141]

In essence, Cardinal Sodano would reduce the Third Secret to the *Second* Secret—i.e., the second part of the Great Secret of July 13, 1917—which, as we saw in Chapter 1, predicted Word War II, the spread of world Communism and the consequent persecution of

---

[141]Vatican Information Service, May 13, 2000.

the Church, the martyrdom of the faithful and the suffering of the Holy Father. But if the Third Secret merely predicts the very events Our Lady had already predicted in the Second Secret, what is the point of the Third Secret? Why would Sister Lucia have found it so difficult to commit the Third Secret to paper? Why would Our Lady have refrained from directing Sister Lucia to write down the Secret until 1944—*after* World War II and the spread of Communism were already well under way?

As for Sodano's claim that the Pope executed by soldiers outside a half-ruined city filled with bodies was John Paul II, it was manifest that Sodano had misled the public when he declared at Fatima the previous May that the Pope in the vision "falls to the ground, *apparently* dead, under a burst of gunfire." In truth, the Pope in the vision "*was killed* by a group of soldiers who fired bullets and arrows at him" outside the half-ruined city. John Paul II, on the other hand, was *not* killed by a lone assassin during the attempt that took place in a perfectly intact Saint Peter's Square.

Any attempt on the life of a Pope is a grave affair, and John Paul II had suffered greatly at the hands of his would-be assassin. Nevertheless, the Pope had completely recovered from his wounds and resumed an active life that included skiing and hiking in the Italian Alps and swimming in the built-in pool he had installed at Castelgandolfo shortly after his election. His physical condition after recovery was rightly described as "impressive."[142] The Pope's death *a quarter century* after the attempt resulted from the complications of Parkinson's disease, not the shot fired by Ali Agca in 1981. Moreover, why would Our Lady of Fatima give an "express order" (to recall Sister Lucia's writing on the envelope) that the Secret be revealed in 1960, when that year has no relation to the 1981 assassination attempt or to *any other particular* in the vision? In short, the suggestion that John Paul II is the Pope in the vision is not merely a "stretch," it is patently unbelievable. Sodano had blatantly twisted the content of the vision to suit his contrived interpretation.

---

[142]"He has been a terrific sportsman," said George Weigel, author of a biography of John Paul. Weigel said the Pope had a swimming pool built at his summer residence at Castelgandolfo during the first summer of his papacy. "The story goes that he justified it by saying it was cheaper than building a new conclave," he said. "The first 15 years of his pontificate [i.e., until 1993, 12 years after the assassination attempt] he took breaks to go skiing, and the miracle about that was the Italian paparazzi actually left him alone." Quoted in "Pontiff Was Sportsman as Well as Leader," Associated Press, March 4, 2005. After the assassination attempt the Pope "went on to a full recovery, and sported an impressive physical condition throughout the 1980s." *Pope John Paul*, Short Biography at wikipedia.com.

It should go without saying that Catholics are not required to accept Sodano's "interpretation." As Cardinal Ratzinger stated during the June 26th press conference: "*It is not the intention of the Church to impose a single interpretation.*"[143] Ratzinger's own commentary in *Message* would speak only of "attempting" an interpretation. And, ironically enough, *Message*'s own supporting documentation demolishes Sodano's patently unsustainable construction. Bertone's Introduction cites a purported letter from Sister Lucia to John Paul II in 1982 regarding the contents of the Secret. Curiously, both the translation and the photo-reproduction of the original handwriting appended to *Message* present only a fragment of the purported letter, without any address or salutation to the Pope or signature by Sister Lucia. The Pope is not mentioned even glancingly in the fragmentary text, and there is nothing about the fragment to indicate that it was meant for the Pope as opposed to anyone else. But here, in pertinent part, is what the fragment says:

> Since we did not heed this appeal of the Message, we see that it has been fulfilled; Russia has invaded the world with her errors. And if *we have not yet seen the complete fulfillment of the final part of this prophecy*, we are going towards it little by little with great strides.[144]

That is, in *Message*—the very document which argues that the vision of the bishop in white depicts the assassination attempt— Sister Lucia herself is quoted to the effect that, fully a year *after* the attempt, we have *not yet seen* the complete fulfillment of the Third Secret. Furthermore, Lucia makes *no reference whatsoever* to the attempt. As the fragment from the letter shows, the attempt was not even on Sister Lucia's "radar" in 1982, much less at the very center of her understanding of the Secret.

It must be noted that the Portuguese original of this strange epistolary fragment contains a phrase that negates any possibility it was addressed to John Paul II: "The third part of the secret, *that you are so anxious to know*, is a symbolic revelation..." It could not possibly be the case that in 1982 John Paul II was "so anxious to know" the Third Secret, because by all accounts he had already

---

[143]"Vatican releases additional Fatima information," United Press International, June 27, 2000.

[144]*Message*, p. 9.

read it by then. The words "that you are so anxious to know" reveal beyond doubt that the addressee of the purported 1982 letter was someone other than the Pope. But, attention: The English and other translations of the fragment in *Message* all *omit the words* "that you are so anxious to know" so that the phrase reads simply: "The third part of the secret is a symbolic revelation" followed by the remainder of the sentence.[145] No ellipses are used to indicate the omission, as honesty would require. The systematic excision of the key phrase from translation after translation could only be a calculated deception. It would require a Portuguese reader, closely examining the photo-reproduced fragment, to discover the ruse.[146] (*See* Appendix IV.)

Ratzinger follows Sodano – but why?

Despite these enormous problems with Sodano's "preventative interpretation," Cardinal Ratzinger's theological commentary in *Message* adopts it uncritically, albeit while acknowledging that it is only an "attempt" at an interpretation:

> Before attempting an interpretation, the main lines of which can be found in the statement read by Cardinal Sodano on 13 May of this year ...[147]

> For this reason the figurative language of the vision is symbolic. In this regard Cardinal Sodano stated ...[148]

> As is clear from the documentation presented here, the interpretation offered by Cardinal Sodano, in his statement on 13 May...[149]

> First of all we must affirm with Cardinal Sodano...[150]

---

[145]Ibid., p. 8.

[146]From the English translation: "The third part of the secret [deleted: "that you are so anxious to know"] is a symbolic revelation..." The photo-reproduced fragment reads: "A terceira parte do Segredo, *que tanto ansiais por conhecer* [that you are so anxious to know], e uma revelação simbolica ..." *Message*, p. 9.

[147]*The Message of Fatima*, p. 32.

[148]Ibid., p. 38.

[149]Ibid., p. 39.

[150]Ibid., p. 43.

Cardinal Ratzinger's commentary follows Sodano in pronouncing the Third Secret a thing of the past:

> A careful reading of the text of the so-called third 'secret' of Fatima, published here in its entirety long after the fact and by decision of the Holy Father, will probably prove disappointing or surprising after all the speculation it has stirred. No great mystery is revealed; nor is the future unveiled. We see the Church of the martyrs of the century which has just passed represented in a scene described in a language which is symbolic and not easy to decipher.
>
> [W]e must affirm with Cardinal Sodano that "the events to which the third part of the 'secret' of Fatima refers now seem part of the past". Insofar as individual events are described, *they belong to the past*.[151]

These affirmations are plainly impossible to accept, for if the vision reveals "no great mystery" and concerns only 20th Century events, there would have been no reason to keep it under lock and key at the Vatican since 1957, or to declare in 1960 that it would be kept "forever under absolute seal." Nor would there have been any reason for Cardinal Ratzinger to have declared in 1984 that the Secret speaks of "dangers threatening the faith and the life of the Christian and therefore of the world."

There is a mystery here: Cardinal Sodano's competence to "interpret" the Secret is never explained. The Vatican Secretary of State has no doctrinal authority over the Church, and Sodano did not receive any papal authority to undertake his "interpretation," which is presented as a mere "attempt" to explain the vision. Why, then, was Sodano even involved in the matter? This strange situation appears to reflect the ascendancy of the Vatican Secretary of State to the level of a veritable "prime minister" of the Church in keeping with the radical restructuring of the Roman Curia carried out by Cardinal Villot after Vatican II.[152] According to this restructuring the Secretariat of State was elevated above all the Vatican Congregations and Tribunals, the Pontifical Councils, and numerous administrative offices, with the Secretary of State directing and "coordinating" the entire

---

[151]Ibid., pp. 32, 43.

[152]For a detailed discussion of this development see *The Devil's Final Battle*, Chapter 8 (also at http://www.devilsfinalbattle.com/ch8.htm).

ensemble. Thanks to Villot's work, the Secretary of State became nothing less than a kind of *de facto* Pope, even though the divine constitution of the Church does not include this arrangement. In fact, the Vatican Secretariat of State did not even exist until the 15th Century.[153] While the real Pope has retained ultimate authority, in practical terms he has largely been reduced to rubber-stamping the Secretary of State's daily management of Church affairs.

In the postconciliar epoch of "ecumenism," "dialogue" and *aggiornamento* (updating) of the Church, the Message of Fatima has become a matter of ecclesiastical politics over which the Secretariat of State assumed control, and which it stills controls in the person of Sodano's successor, Cardinal Bertone. This explains why Sodano took it upon himself to "interpret" the vision and why even Cardinal Ratzinger, then head of the Congregation for the Doctrine of the Faith, deferred to Sodano when he had no moral or dogmatic obligation to do so.

Did Our Lady give us a cipher?

Sodano's "interpretation" of the Third Secret was said to be necessary because, as Cardinal Ratzinger states in his commentary, the vision is "not easy to decipher." But were the faithful really expected to believe that in 1917 the Blessed Virgin gave the visionaries a *cipher* that would have to be *de*ciphered by—of all people—the Vatican Secretary of State in 2000? That hardly seemed consistent with the clarity and detail of the Second Secret, which, as we have seen, predicted a whole train of clearly specified *future* events: the end of one war and the beginning of another "worse" war following an unknown light in the night sky; the very name of the Pope who would reign in the days leading up to that war; the very name of the nation that would spread its errors throughout the world; precise admonitions concerning war, famine, persecutions of the Church, the martyrdom of the good, the suffering of the Holy Father and the annihilation of various nations; and the ultimate conversion of Russia and the triumph of the Immaculate Heart of Mary.

---

[153]See "Secretariat of State" at www.vatican.va/roman_curia/secretariat_state/ documents/rc_seg-st_12101998_profile_en.html ("The origins of the Secretariat of State go back to the fifteenth century. The Apostolic Constitution *Non Debet Reprehensibile* of 31 December 1487 established the *Secretaria Apostolica...*").

The "not easy to decipher" vision would *not* require deciphering, however, if—as with the first two parts of the Great Secret of Fatima—there are *words* of the Virgin to explain it, as opposed to Vatican prelates "attempting an interpretation, the main lines of which can be found in the statement read by Cardinal Sodano on 13 May of this year ..."[154] The very claim that the Third Secret could not be understood without an "interpretation" suggested by Cardinal Sodano only demonstrated that there must be something more to the Secret than the vision standing alone.

Dispensing with the Consecration of Russia

Although the Consecration of Russia is not the primary focus of this book, the way in which this question was handled in *Message* is indicative of a general intent to sweep inconvenient facts under the rug. Bertone's Introduction purports to enlist Sister Lucia for the proposition that Pope John Paul II's consecration of the world in 1984 sufficed for a consecration of Russia: "Sister Lucia personally confirmed that this solemn and universal act of consecration corresponded to what Our Lady wished.... Hence any further discussion or request [for the Consecration of Russia] is without basis."[155] But how could Sister Lucia "confirm" that the same sort of ceremony that did not suffice during the reigns of Pius XII and Paul VI—a consecration of the world with no mention of Russia and no participation by the world episcopate—was suddenly sufficient?[156]

Curiously, Bertone cites only one solitary piece of evidence in support of his claim: a purported letter from Sister Lucia, identified only as "Letter of 8 November 1989," in which Sister Lucia is alleged to have written: "'Yes it has been done just as Our Lady asked, on 25 March 1984" (*"Sim, està feita, tal como Nossa Senhora a pediu, desde o dia 25 de Março de 1984"*).[157] Even more curious: the addressee of the letter is not identified, nor is a copy of it provided as part of

---

[154]*The Message of Fatima* (*Message*), p. 32.

[155]*Message*, p. 8.

[156]Concerning the consecration of the world by Pius XII and several bishops on October 31, 1942, Sister Lucia wrote: "The Good Lord has already shown me His contentment with the act performed by the Holy Father and several bishops, *although it was incomplete according to His desire*. In return He promises to end the war soon. The conversion of Russia is not for now." Letter to the Bishop of Gurza, February 28, 1943; quoted *WTAF*, Vol. III, pp. 60-61.

[157]*Message*, p. 8.

Message's supporting documentation.

Knowledgeable readers of *Message* knew why: the letter, to a Mr. Noelker, had long since been exposed as a fake. Generated by a computer at the dawn of the personal computer age, the letter contained a blatant error: a statement by "Sister Lucia" that Paul VI consecrated the world to the Immaculate Heart during his visit to Fatima in 1967, when in truth he had consecrated nothing at all on that occasion. Sister Lucia, who was present throughout the Pope's visit, would hardly have made such a mistake. Nor was it credible that an elderly cloistered nun, who had written thousands of letters by hand over her lifetime, would suddenly switch to a word processor at age 80 to peck out a one-page note to a Mr. Noelker, especially when even many business offices in Portugal were without personal computers at that time.[158]

Still more curious: the dubious "letter of 8 November 1989" was the only evidence Bertone cited even though, as *Message* states, Bertone had "conversed" with Sister Lucia on April 27, 2000, only two months earlier, and could have obtained her direct testimony on this question at that time — or indeed at any other time. The failure to cite *any* direct testimony by Lucia, when such testimony was readily obtainable, speaks volumes. And note well: During the April 2000 "conversation" Bertone *did not ask Sister Lucia to authenticate the "Letter of 8 November 1989"*, even though Bertone had to have known of the worldwide circulation of articles decisively debunking the letter.[159] The only reasonable inference is that Lucia was not asked to authenticate the letter because the letter was indeed a fake that could not be authenticated.

To knowledgeable Catholics, it was not surprising that Bertone had been forced to rely *entirely* on a non-authenticated and previously publicly debunked 11-year-old "letter" to an unidentified addressee. That purported letter was the only thing Bertone could pit against a lifetime of contrary testimony by Sister Lucia.[160]

---

[158]Flatly contradicting himself, Bertone would admit seven years later that Sister Lucia "never worked with the computer." *See Last Visionary*, p. 101 ("Sister Lucia never worked with the computer, nor visited any website.") This is one of the many self-contradictions in which the Cardinal has embroiled himself, as Socci has noted.

[159]This letter was published and critiqued on pp. 10-11 of the May 1990 (No. 229) issue of *The Catholic Counter-Reformation* (CRC, English edition, published by Maison Saint-Joseph, F-10260 Saint-Parres-lès-Vaudes). This critique was explicitly referenced in *The Fatima Crusader*, No. 35 (Winter 1990-91), with a circulation of some 500,000 copies, in a story debunking the Noelker letter (on pp. 12ff, or at http://www.fatimacrusader.com/cr35/cr35pg12.asp).

[160]For a detailed presentation of Lucia's testimony from 1946-1987, see *The Devil's*

A funeral for Fatima?

All in all, Sodano's "interpretation" was patently designed to consign the Third Secret in particular and the Fatima message in general to the dustbin of history, evidently in the hope that all questions would cease after June 26, 2000. Following Sodano's lead, Bertone's Introduction goes so far as to declare:

> The decision of His Holiness Pope John Paul II to make public the third part of the 'secret' of Fatima brings to an end a period of history marked by tragic human lust for power and evil, yet pervaded by the merciful love of God and the watchful care of the Mother of Jesus and of the Church.

Not only is the Message of Fatima consigned to the past, but also the very lust for power and evil! But if the Pope had brought an end to the era of the lust for power and evil by publishing the vision of "the Bishop dressed in White" in the year 2000, why had he not ended that same tragic era by publishing the vision much sooner, indeed at the first opportunity? Bertone, however inadvertently, makes a mockery of the Vatican's suppression of the Third Secret for so many years.

Even worse than *Message*'s defense of the "preventative interpretation" is its suggestion that Sister Lucia's entire witness might be suspect. The theological commentary cites one, and only one, "authority" on Fatima: the late Flemish theologian Edouard Dhanis, S.J., whom the commentary identifies as an "eminent scholar" in the field of "private revelations." Cardinal Ratzinger knew, of course, that Dhanis, a modernist Jesuit, made a veritable career out of casting doubt on the Fatima apparitions. Dhanis proposed that everything in the Message of Fatima beyond a call for prayer and penance was cobbled together in the minds of the three children from things they had seen or heard in their own lives. Dhanis thus categorized as "Fatima II" all those things the "eminent scholar" arbitrarily rejected as fabrications—without ever once interviewing Sister Lucia or studying the official Fatima archives. Dhanis, in fact, flatly refused to speak to the seer or study the archives when invited to do so.[161] His intellectual honesty is

---

Final Battle, Chapter 8 (also at http://www.devilsfinalbattle.com/ch8.htm).

[161] See Frère Michel de la Sainte Trinité, "Part II: The Critical Study of Fatima," *The Whole Truth About Fatima: Vol. I, The Science and the Facts*, pp. 381-535.

non-existent when it comes to Fatima.

As Dhanis put it: "All things considered, it is not easy to state precisely what degree of credence is to be given to the accounts of Sister Lucia. Without questioning her sincerity, or the sound judgment she shows in daily life, one may judge it prudent to use her writings only with reservations. ... Let us observe also that a good person can be sincere and prove to have good judgment in everyday life, but have a *propensity for unconscious fabrication* in a certain area, or in any case, a tendency to relate old memories of twenty years ago with embellishments and considerable modifications."[162] In other words, according to Dhanis, Sister Lucia was a very sincere and pious fake.

Yet Dhanis, neo-modernist debunker of the Message of Fatima, is the one and only "eminent scholar" cited by *Message*'s theological commentary on the meaning of the Third Secret and the Fatima message as a whole. The commentary even follows Dhanis' methodology by suggesting that, after all, Sister Lucia may have concocted the vision from things she had seen as a child: "The concluding part of the 'secret' uses images which Lucia may have seen in devotional books and which draw their inspiration from long-standing intuitions of faith."[163] But if that were true of the images in the vision of the bishop in white, it could also be true of any and all aspects of the Fatima apparitions. With a single sentence inserted into the middle of things, the commentary, like Dhanis, undermines the credibility—at least in the minds of a gullible public—not only of the Third Secret proper, but the entirety of the Message of Fatima.

No wonder the headline in the *Los Angeles Times* read: "The Vatican's Top Theologian Gently Debunks a Nun's Account of Her 1917 Vision that Fueled Decades of Speculation."[164] Even the secular press could see what was going on: the attempt at a funeral for Fatima.

Exit Our Lady, enter Gorbachev

The Third Secret having been "gently debunked" on June 26,

---

[162]Dhanis' attack on the veracity of the Fatima message is explained and critiqued in more detail in *WTAF*, Vol. I, Part II, Chapter 1. All quotations of Dhanis are from this source.

[163]*Message*, p. 42.

[164]*Los Angeles Times*, June 27, 2000.

the "prime minister" immediately got down to what he considered the serious business of the Church. The very next day none other than Mikhail Gorbachev was seated as a guest of honor between Cardinals Sodano and Silvestrini at a Vatican press conference. The conference had been called to celebrate one of the key elements of the Church's supposedly new "orientation" after Vatican II, as administered by the Secretary of State: *Ostpolitik*, or the policy of conciliating instead of confronting communist regimes that oppress the Church. Gorbachev had come to the Vatican to help promote the posthumous publication of the memoirs of Cardinal Casaroli, the grand architect of *Ostpolitik* and Cardinal Sodano's predecessor in office.[165] No questions from the press were permitted at this curious press conference—a press conference without questions from the press! Evidently, Sodano wanted to be certain that no one inquired about the Third Secret, or why the Vatican was honoring the likes of Gorbachev, a man who admits he is still a Leninist and whose tax-free foundations are promoting the use of abortion and contraception to eliminate billions of people from the world's population.[166]

What can one conclude from all of this but that the program of "prime minister" Sodano (carried forward by his successor, Cardinal Bertone) is radically inconsistent with the program of Our Lady of Fatima?

Widespread disbelief

For these and many other reasons, reaction to the Vatican's publication of the vision of the bishop in white and Sodano's "interpretation" of it was, quite simply, widespread disbelief. Contrary to what Sodano and company no doubt intended, the

---

[165]"Gorbachev Helps Introduce Casaroli Memoirs," *Catholic World News*, June 27, 2000.

[166]In September 1995, Gorbachev held his "State of the World Forum" in San Francisco. Over 4000 of the world's "elite" paid $5,000 per person to attend the 5-day event. In a closing plenary session of the forum, a philosopher/author named Sam Keen provided a summary and concluding remarks on the conference. It reveals the forum's anti-life, anti-Christian ethos. To the conference participants, Keen said: "There was very strong agreement that religious institutions have to take the primary responsibility for the population explosion. We must speak far more clearly about sexuality, about contraception, about abortion, about the values that control the population, because the ecological crisis, in short, is the population crisis. *Cut the population by 90 percent and there aren't enough people left to do a great deal of ecological damage.*" See "World's Elite Gather to Talk Depopulation," John Henry Western, *The Interim*, April 1996.

June 26th press conference was not the end of the Third Secret controversy, but only a new beginning. On the very day of the press conference, an editor of *Il Giornale* asked René Laurentin, the renowned Mariologist, if he felt the Vatican had now clarified everything regarding the Third Secret. Laurentin replied: "Not at all. There are some things that did not convince me."[167]

Laurentin was putting it mildly; and he was hardly alone in his doubts. As Socci notes, the official account of the Third Secret, especially its "interpretation" by Cardinal Sodano, "leaked water from every part,"[168] and everyone could see it. *La Repubblica*, one of Italy's major newspapers, agreed. Only a day after the press conference an editorial appeared in which the author declared flatly: "The celebrated 'Third Secret' cannot be reconciled with the dramatic events of May 13, 1981. There is no Pope who falls 'apparently dead.' The scene is another. A Pope killed by 'soldiers who fire bullets and arrows at him.' It is no use to invoke the language of symbols and metaphor... [The vision] points somewhere else entirely."[169] But where, Socci asks? "Evidently toward a Pope who has yet to arrive." The words of the Virgin would tell us who that Pope is, but the words of the Virgin were missing.

Less than a year after the *Message* press conference, the worldwide incredulity of the faithful was given voice by Mother Angelica, the foundress of the Eternal Word Television Network, who in May 2001 declared to a television audience of millions:

> As for the Secret, well *I happen to be one of those individuals who thinks we didn't get the whole thing.* I told ya! I mean, you have the right to your own opinion, don't you, Father? There, you know, that's my opinion. *Because I think it's scary...*[170]

Some five years after Mother Angelica expressed her incredulity to the world, Socci would completely change his mind, reject the Vatican's official account and join the growing ranks of Catholics who are convinced the Vatican has withheld from the faithful a text of the Third Secret—a text containing the words of the Mother of God following the telltale "etc" that *Message* so conspicuously avoided. Socci was led to this conclusion by the

[167]Quoted in Socci, *Fourth Secret*, p. 114.

[168]Socci, *Fourth Secret*, p. 62.

[169]Ibid.

[170]"Mother Angelica Live," May 16, 2001.

facts thus far presented. As those facts show, the document the Vatican produced in 2000, while undoubtedly a part of the Third Secret, does not present *any* of the many elements discussed in Chapters 2 and 3. To recapitulate those elements, on its face the vision of "the Bishop dressed in white" is *not*—

1. something so terrible that Sister Lucia would not have been able to write it down without a special intervention of Our Lady;

2. a statement containing the *words* of the Virgin which are "the logical continuation" of "In Portugal, the dogma of the Faith will always be preserved etc." (Father Schweigl);

3. one page and 25 lines in letter form (Sister Lucia, Cardinal Ottaviani, Bishop Venancio) that was lodged in the papal apartment (Archbishop Capovilla, Mother Pasqualina, Robert Serrou);

4. in two parts: one pertaining to the Pope and the other containing the "logical continuation" of the Virgin's words in her opening declaration: "In Portugal the dogma of the faith will always be preserved etc" (Father Schweigl);

5. linked to 1960, the year in which the sealed envelope was to be opened, according to the "express order of Our Lady" inscribed on the envelope (Sister Lucia);

6. a "divine warning" about suicidal changes in the liturgy, theology and soul of the Church (Pius XII);

7. a prediction that after 1960 the devil will decimate the ranks of priests and religious, leaving the faithful without spiritual leaders, and that "nations will disappear from the face of the earth" (Sister Lucia to Father Fuentes in 1957);

8. "so delicate" that it cannot be allowed "for whatever reason, even fortuitous, to fall into alien hands" (Cardinal Ottaviani, 1967);

9. a text that was "diplomatically" withheld because of the "seriousness of its contents," including "great trials" and "tribulation" for the Church which "it is no longer possible to avert," and the destruction of "whole areas of the earth" so that "from one moment to the next millions of people will perish" (John Paul II at Fulda, 1980);

10. a text that—a year *after* the 1981 assassination attempt—
    still could not be revealed because it could be "badly
    interpreted" as of 1982 (John Paul II);

11. a "religious prophecy" of "dangers threatening the faith
    and the life of the Christian and therefore *of the world*"
    (Cardinal Ratzinger, 1984);

12. something that would make for the "sensationalistic
    utilization of its contents" (Cardinal Ratzinger in 1985);

13. a prediction of apostasy in the Church (Cardinal Oddi)
    that "begins at the top" (Cardinal Ciappi) and is "worse
    than the annihilation of a nation" (Bishop do Amaral);

14. a text whose "details" would cause "disequilibrium" in the
    Church as of 1996—a full *fifteen years* after the assassination
    attempt (Cardinal Ratzinger);

15. "essentially the same" as the message of Our Lady of Akita,
    which warns of both a crisis of faith within the Church and
    a planetary catastrophe (Cardinal Ratzinger to Howard
    Dee, former Philippine ambassador to the Vatican, 1998);

16. a warning to avoid the "tail of the dragon" which sweeps
    consecrated souls from their vocations (John Paul II, May
    13, 2000).

The missing key to the vision

While the vision of the bishop in white does not present any
of these elements, it would, however, be *consistent with every one of
them* if there were a separate text—a key to the vision—in which the
Virgin explains the vision along the lines indicated by the many
witnesses already cited. Such an explanation would involve this
scenario: Following a collapse of faith and discipline in the Church
after 1960 the world will suffer a tremendous chastisement, a great
part of humanity will be destroyed, the city of Rome itself will
be reduced to ruins, a hobbling Pope will flee Rome only to be
executed by a band of soldiers on a hill outside the city, and much
of the remnant of the Church will be hunted down and killed after
him. It is worth noting that such a text would also be consistent
with the historically recorded prophetic remarks of Pope St. Pius
X: "I saw one of my successors taking to flight over the bodies of his

brethren. He will take refuge in disguise somewhere; and after a short retirement he will die a cruel death. The present wickedness of the world is only the beginning of sorrows which must take place before the end of the world."[171]

Now, once again, we know from Father Schweigl's testimony that the Third Secret "has *two parts*: One part concerns the Pope…" and the other is the aforesaid "logical continuation" of the words of the Virgin following Lucia's "etc". Therefore, we can conclude, just as Socci has concluded, that the vision of "the Bishop dressed in white" is the part of the Secret that concerns the Pope—i.e., his execution on the hill outside the half-ruined city—and that the second part must explain the events leading to the death of this future Pope. *Only* such a text would convert what Cardinal Ratzinger called a "difficult to decipher" vision into a prophecy as clear as the rest of the Message of Fatima.

Since the Mother of God did not come to Fatima to convey debatable obscurities to mankind, it would become obvious to more and more people that the disclosure of June 26, 2000 was incomplete. Recognizing the growing trend of popular incredulity, Cardinal Bertone would make a move that only increased that incredulity and provided yet another reason for Socci to join the ranks of the "Fatimists."

---

[171]Yves Dupont, *Catholic Prophecy, The Coming Chastisement* (Rockford, Illinois: Tan Books and Publishers, Inc., 1970), p. 22.

Chapter 5

A Disastrous Interview

With the doubts of the faithful continuing to mount, on October 26, 2001—a few weeks after the terrorist attack of September 11, 2001—the story on the Third Secret "broke wide open," as the reporters say. *Inside the Vatican* news service (along with various Italian newspapers) ran an article entitled: "The Secret of Fatima: More to Come?" The article reported: "News has just emerged that Sister Lucia dos Santos, the last surviving Fatima visionary, several weeks ago sent Pope John Paul II a letter reportedly warning him that his life is in danger. *According to Vatican sources*, the letter, claiming that events spoken of in the 'Third Secret' of Fatima had not yet occurred, was delivered sometime after September 11 to John Paul by the bishop emeritus [retired] of Fatima, Alberto Cosme do Amaral."

When asked about the letter, the Bishop of Fatima at the time, Serafim de Sousa Ferreira e Silva, *did not deny that Sister Lucia had sent a letter to the Pope*, but said [drawing a very precise distinction] 'there are no letters from the seer that express fear for the life of the Pope.'" *Inside the Vatican* further revealed that "Sources have also suggested that Sister Lucia's letter encourages the Pope to fully reveal the Third Secret," and that Sister Lucia's letter to the Pope "is said to contain this warning: 'Soon there will be great upheaval and punishment.'"

The *Inside the Vatican* article further reported that an Italian diocesan priest, Father Luigi Bianchi, "claims to have met Sister Lucia dos Santos last week at her cloistered Carmelite convent in Coimbra, Portugal." Echoing the suspicions of Mother Angelica and Catholics everywhere, Father Bianchi "speculated on the possibility that the Vatican *did not reveal the full secret* to avoid creating panic and anxiety in the population; to not scare them."

Concerning Cardinal Sodano's "interpretation" of the Secret as a prophecy of the 1981 attempt on the life of Pope John Paul II, Father Bianchi stated: "The message doesn't speak only about an attempt on the pontiff, but speaks of 'a Bishop dressed in White' who walks amongst the ruins and bodies of murdered men and women ... This means that the Pope will have to suffer greatly, that some nations will disappear, that many people will die, that we must defend the West from becoming Islamicized. That is what is happening in these days."

Inside the Vatican was careful to point out that Sister Lucia *"is not allowed to speak with anyone* who has not received prior permission from the Vatican ..." Accordingly, the magazine hedged its report by stating that "it is not immediately clear whether Bianchi received that approval, circumvented the need for it, or did not actually meet Sister Lucia as he maintains." But no one, including Sister Lucia herself, ever denied that the meeting with Father Bianchi took place.

That at least some of *Inside the Vatican's* sources are within the Curia itself was suggested by Cardinal Ratzinger's response to these developments. The magazine quoted him as having said that the "recent rumors of a letter are only the continuation of 'an old polemic fed by certain people of dubious credibility,' with the objective of *'destabilizing the internal equilibrium of the Roman Curia* and of troubling the people of God.'" Notice, however, that neither did Cardinal Ratzinger actually deny the existence of the letter from Sister Lucia to the Pope.

Cardinal Ratzinger's remark was a window into the effect the "Fatimist" polemic was having on open minds within the Vatican. How could people of "dubious credibility" destabilize the "internal equilibrium of the Roman Curia"? If their credibility were so dubious, the Roman Curia would hardly be destabilized by anything they had to say. And just who were these people of "dubious credibility"? *Inside the Vatican* suggested that Cardinal Ratzinger might have been referring to Father Nicholas Gruner. But where was the evidence that Father Gruner was of "dubious credibility," as opposed to a veritable font of accurate information on the subject, much of which Socci himself has studied in reaching the conclusions he did? And what about René Laurentin? What about Mother Angelica? What about Father Bianchi? What about *Inside the Vatican* itself, whose editor was, if anything, beholden to the Vatican apparatus, as the very name of his magazine suggests? What about the millions of other Catholics who were already harboring the well-founded suspicion that the Vatican had not been entirely forthcoming in its claim that the prophecies of the Message of Fatima, including the Third Secret, "belong to the past," and that its warning of a great chastisement of the Church and the world need no longer concern us? Does any serious Catholic really believe that, given the state of the world today?

Catholics the world over continued to wonder what had happened to the words which follow the Virgin's momentous opening declaration: "In Portugal the dogma of the Faith will always be preserved etc." Why had the collaborators in *Message* run away from this phrase by removing it from the Message of Fatima and consigning it to a footnote? What had happened to the missing words of the Virgin?

What sort of interview is this?

In the face of these and other questions that would not go away, Archbishop Bertone conducted another unrecorded "conversation" with Sister Lucia—like the one of April 27, 2000, in which Lucia had allegedly denied ever hearing of the "express order of Our Lady" she had inscribed on the envelope containing the Secret. This second "conversation" took place on November 17, 2001, but was not revealed for more than a month. On December 21, 2001 *L'Osservatore Romano* published Bertone's brief communiqué concerning the interview, entitled "Meeting of His Excellency Mons. Tarcisio Bertone with Sister Maria Lucia of Jesus and the Immaculate Heart." This was followed by a translation in *L'Osservatore Romano*'s English edition.[172]

The communiqué states that the purported interview was conducted in the presence of Bertone himself and "Rev. Luis Kondor, SVD, Vice-Postulator of the cause of Bl. Francisco and Bl. Jacinta, and of the Prioress of the Carmelite Convent of St. Teresa." That is, Sister Lucia was questioned while being surrounded by authority figures. But no transcript, audiotape or videotape of the two-hour session has been produced, and neither Father Kondor nor the Prioress has ever attested to what was allegedly said by the seer. Although the communiqué claims Bertone and Sister Lucia conversed for "more than two hours," Bertone had provided only his summary of the alleged conversation, sprinkled with a few words attributed to Lucia herself.

---

[172]*See* "Incontro di S.E. Mons. Tarcisio Bertone con Suor Maria Lucia de Jesus e do Coração Imaculado," *L'Osservatore Romano* (Italian edition), December 21, 2001, p. 4; and "Archbishop Bertone met Sr. Maria Lucia: Convent of Coimbra, Portugal, 17 November 2001", *L'Osservatore Romano* (English edition), January 9, 2002, p. 7.

Sister Lucia "agrees" she's a fake

The communiqué immediately undermined its own credibility with the following assertion: "Going on to discuss the problem of the third part of the secret of Fatima, she [Sister Lucia] says that she has read attentively and meditated upon the booklet published by the Congregation for the Doctrine of the Faith [i.e., *Message*], and confirms *everything* it says." For the reasonably skeptical observer, this claim was simply too much to accept. When a Vatican functionary, no matter what his rank, comes out of a locked convent and declares that a 94-year-old nun inside "confirms everything" in a 44-page document he has co-authored (*Message*), reasonable people have the right to expect a bit more by way of corroboration—especially when, as we saw in the previous chapter, that document politely suggests that the nun in question might, more or less, have concocted a pious fable. On these grounds alone one would be justified in suspecting that the latest secret Sister Lucia interview was but another attempt to manipulate a captive and obedient witness, who had yet to be allowed to speak at length to the faithful in her own unfiltered words.

What did Bertone and Sister Lucia discuss for more than two hours, given that the entire communiqué—most of which did not contain *any* alleged words of the seer—could be read aloud in about three minutes? By way of comparison, a one-hour address delivered at a normal rate of speech would require some 14 single-spaced typewritten pages to transcribe; a two-hour address would require about 28 pages, or approximately 14,000 words. Yet Bertone's communiqué concerning an alleged two-hour interview of the seer had provided *a mere 463 words* purportedly from her own mouth, most of which had nothing to do with the matter at issue.[173] These 463 words included *a verbatim quotation of 165 words* from Cardinal Ratzinger's theological commentary, which Sister Lucia had obviously not recited from memory during the alleged "conversation" with Bertone. Yet those 165 words are quoted as if they had been uttered by Sister Lucia herself, indicating that the purported "conversation" was really a cut-and-paste document designed to state a predetermined conclusion.

---

[173]This discussion employs both the *Vatican Information Service* English translation of the communiqué and that provided by the *L'Osservatore Romano* English edition of January 9, 2002, as corrected where errors in translation from the Italian are apparent.

Two hours — nine words!

And what about the burning issue that had supposedly required this special mission to Coimbra to speak with Sister Lucia: the doubts that had been raised about the completeness of the Vatican's disclosure of the Third Secret? Amazingly enough, out of more than two hours of alleged conversation with Lucia, Bertone's communiqué quotes a grand total of *nine words* on the subject, which are as follows: "Everything has been published; there are no more secrets."

The question that allegedly elicited this answer was not provided. Instead, Bertone's communiqué declared: "To whoever imagines that some part of the secret has been hidden she replied: …"—followed by the nine quoted words. Replied to what? What *exactly* was Sister Lucia asked about the Vatican's disclosure of the Third Secret? What was the full context of the question and the answer? And why was Sister Lucia not asked the one question millions of people around the world were asking: *Where are the words of Our Lady* following the phrase "In Portugal the dogma of the Faith will always be preserved etc."? Notice that here, at the very crux of the matter, we are not shown that Sister Lucia was asked even one precise question, such as:

- What are the words of Our Lady following "In Portugal the dogma of the Faith will always be preserved etc."?

- Did the Virgin explain the vision of the "Bishop dressed in white" in her own words at any time?

- Does the Third Secret include a separate text in which the Virgin explains the vision, and if so, where is this text?

- What about the testimony of numerous witnesses (including the Bishop of Fatima and Cardinal Ottaviani) that the Third Secret was written on a single sheet of paper, comprising 25 lines, as distinct from the four sheets on which the vision was written, comprising 62 lines?

All such particulars were studiously avoided. We are not even given the wording of the one question that *was* asked. These omissions could not be more telling. Recall here Bertone's evasive yet highly revealing answer to a query about the "etc" during the press conference in June 2000: "It is difficult to say if it [the "etc"] refers to the second or the third part of the secret… it seems to me that it pertains to the second."[174] Thus Bertone was fully aware of the "etc" issue when he conducted the "interview" in November 2001, yet he failed to ask Sister Lucia herself whether the "etc" pertains to the third or the second part of the Great Secret even though he had a golden opportunity to settle the very question on which the "Fatimists" had focused so effectively. Or, if Bertone did ask Lucia about the matter, he failed to report her answer. This strange behavior is understandable *only* if there is something to hide.

Consider also that the nine words Bertone quoted, allegedly uttered during an unrecorded conversation behind closed doors in November 2001, were literally *the last words "Sister* Lucia" *would ever be allowed to say on the subject before her death.* As *Catholic World News* noted: "Apart from that statement, which was released by the Vatican in December 2001, Sister Lucia maintained her public silence until her death in February 2005."[175] What is to account for the continued "inexplicable gagging" of Sister Lucia even *after* the Third Secret, so Bertone claims, had been totally revealed? If there was nothing to hide, if "everything has been published; there are no more secrets," why was Sister Lucia not free to speak after June 26, 2000?

Does Lucia "confirm" Sodano's "interpretation"?

An additional 14 words are attributed to Sister Lucia concerning Cardinal Sodano's "interpretation" of the vision as a depiction of the 1981 assassination attempt. The purported question and answer are as follows:

> "Is it true that speaking to Rev. Luigi Bianchi and Rev. José dos Santos Valinho, you cast doubt on the interpretation of the third part of the 'secret'?"

> Sr Lucia answered: "That is not true. I fully confirm the interpretation made in the Jubilee Year [2000]."

The faithful could hardly be expected to believe that Lucia had freely and willingly "confirmed" *Message*'s claim that the vision published in 2000 "uses images which Lucia may have

---

[174]Quoted in Socci, *Fourth Secret*, p. 89.

[175]"Fatima Secrets Fully Disclosed, Cardinal Bertone Insists," *Catholic World News*, May 14, 2007 at http://www.cwnews.com/news/viewstory.cfm?recnum=51121.

seen in devotional books and which draw their inspiration from longstanding intuitions of faith."[176]—in other words, that Sister Lucia "confirmed" that she made up the vision in her own head. Nor was it reasonable to believe that Lucia "confirmed" that the vision depicts the 1981 assassination attempt when her own purported letter to the Pope on May 12, 1982, published in *Message*, demolished Sodano's "interpretation" by saying *nothing* about the attempt *a year after it happened*, but rather warned that "we have *not yet seen* the complete fulfillment of the final part of this prophecy."

But even if we assume for the sake of argument that Lucia uttered the suspiciously legalistic phrase "I fully confirm" during the purported interview, we have been deprived of the context of the relevant question and answer as there is no independent record of the encounter. How do we know that Sister Lucia spoke at all as opposed to merely "agreeing" to an answer that had already been written out for her—like the 165 words from Cardinal Ratzinger's theological commentary that Bertone has coming out of Sister Lucia's mouth? How do we know that Lucia was not pressured into giving the answer Bertone wanted? Was she, for instance, asked the same question repeatedly until she gave the "right" answer? Was it suggested to her that the Pope himself expected Lucia to agree with Sodano as a matter of loyalty to the papal office? Was Lucia, a habitually obedient cloistered nun, told that it was her duty to concur with Sodano and "the Pope"? Was she otherwise subjected to subtle or not so subtle pressure that would be apparent if we had a video tape, an audio tape or even a transcript to review?

That we ought to be dubious of Bertone's account is, in the end, shown by Bertone himself. In his book attacking Antonio Socci, published in May 2007, Bertone gives this answer to the question whether Lucia "accepted the interpretation" of the vision by Cardinal Sodano: "Certainly, even if *not in these terms*. She insisted on the force of prayer and on the conviction, like granite, that the Hearts of Jesus and Mary cannot be deaf to our supplications."[177] Now, there is a very great difference between "I fully confirm" (2001 version) and "not in these terms" (2007 version)! The latter phrase means, in fact, simply *no*. For this reason alone, we may reject as unreliable what Bertone claims Lucia told him in November

---

[176]*The Message of Fatima (Message)*, p. 42.

[177]Bertone, Cardinal Tarcisio, *L'Ultima Veggente di Fatima* (Last Visionary of Fatima) (Milano: Rai and Eri Rizzoli, 2007), p. 65 (hereafter "Last Visionary").

2001 concerning Sodano's "interpretation" of the vision or indeed anything else. Moreover, in Chapter 8 I will discuss how, all told, Bertone has given *five different versions* of what he claims Lucia told him concerning Sodano's interpretation, as well as multiple versions of other things he claims Lucia said. No wonder we have never been presented with an independent record of Bertone's interrogation of the seer.

Glaring Omissions

Finally, it appears that during the alleged conversation at Coimbra, Bertone *never asked Sister Lucia about her letter to the Pope* as reported by Father Bianchi and *Inside the Vatican*, nor was she asked about her face-to-face meeting with Father Bianchi, during which they discussed Sodano's "interpretation" of the Secret. Likewise, Bertone once again conspicuously failed to ask Sister Lucia to authenticate the purported "Letter of 8 November 1989," which, as we saw in the previous chapter, was Bertone's *only evidence* for the claim that Sister Lucia "agreed" that the 1984 consecration of the world was a consecration of Russia. Yet Bertone knew that this letter had come under attack as an obvious fake immediately after the press conference of June 26, 2000. These glaring omissions only further undermined the credibility of the "interview."

Moreover, as Socci notes, Sister Lucia's 303-page book on the Message of Fatima, *The Appeals of the Message of Fatima*, published a month before the purported interview, says nothing about the widespread doubts which had arisen concerning disclosure of the Third Secret, even though Lucia states she had written the book as "an answer and a clarification of *doubts and questions* addressed to me," and the preface, by the Bishop of Leiria-Fatima at the time, likewise observes that Sister Lucia had asked the Holy See's permission to write a book in order to "answer *multiple questions* in a global manner, not being able to answer every person individually." Sister Lucia's failure to address the one Fatima-related question uppermost in people's minds—has the whole Third Secret been disclosed?—spoke volumes. As Socci observes: "It is inevitable to conclude that this heavy silence is very eloquent, because it is a precise choice: she did not want to affirm that which was attributed to her."[178]

---

[178]Socci, *Fourth Secret*, p. 126.

Socci's assessment: a disaster

This was the sum total of what Bertone attributed to Sister Lucia concerning the controversy he had gone all the way to Coimbra to address during a two-hour conversation of which no independent record had been made. Socci states the only reasonable conclusion: "The few words attributed to her... are such as to not have objective credibility."[179] In his elegant Italian way, Socci summarizes the impact of the purported interview of November 17, 2001: "The sensation that arises from this 'management' of the last witness of Fatima, this ecclesiastical self-contradiction, is of a certain brazenness, and of seasonal and colorful versions of the truth. Almost as if public opinion, the mass media and the faithful did not know how to reason critically and to catch contradictions and evasive answers."[180] In sum, the purported interview was, as Socci puts it, "disastrous," because "once it was decided to do it... it was necessary to respond totally and seriously to the objections and questions, not eluding them or giving clearly inconsistent answers. It was necessary to do it in a convincing way, incontestable, verifiable by anyone and above all suspicion. Otherwise, there would result the opposite of what was wished: it would furnish definitive proof that something grave was being hidden..."[181]

And that is exactly what happened. The "meeting with Sister Lucia" in November 2001 had backfired even more loudly than the press conference in June 2000. The "disastrous" interview would, in fact, be a major reason for Antonio Socci's "conversion" to the cause of the "Fatimists" in 2006, when public incredulity was cresting to a new high. Another reason was the testimony of a living eyewitness who would come forward in that year to confirm that there are indeed two different but related texts comprising the Third Secret of Fatima—testimony Socci would bring to the attention of the entire world.

---

[179]Ibid., p. 156.

[180]Ibid., p. 127.

[181]Ibid., p. 116.

Chapter 6

Two Texts,
Two Envelopes

From all the evidence we have surveyed thus far, it was readily apparent to Catholics around the world that the vision published by the Vatican in 2000 must be only one of two texts comprising the entire Third Secret. In *Fourth Secret* Antonio Socci would give wide publicity to the testimony of a witness who, in a stunning development, says exactly that: Archbishop Loris F. Capovilla, no less than the personal secretary to Pope John XXIII.

Socci relates how Archbishop Capovilla, now age 92 and residing in Sotto il Monte, Italy, granted an interview to "a young Catholic intellectual," Solideo Paolini, on July 5, 2006 in connection with Paolini's research for his own book on the Third Secret controversy. In response to Paolini's query whether there is an unpublished text of the Secret, the Archbishop replied: "*Nulla so!*" — literally, "nothing I know," which in the Sicilian dialect means: "I must say nothing." That answer puzzled Paolini, who expected that the Archbishop, "among the few who know the Secret, would have been able to respond to me that this is a completely impracticable idea and that everything had already been revealed in 2000." Instead, the Archbishop had used "An expression that I imagined he wished ironically to evoke a certain *omertá* [code of silence]."[182] That impression was confirmed by subsequent events.

After the interview, Paolini received from Capovilla in the mail a package of papers from his files, along with a perplexing cover letter advising him to obtain a copy of *Message*, which Capovilla must have known Paolini, a student of Fatima, would already have. Was this not, thought Paolini, "an invitation to read something in particular in that publication in relation to the documents sent by the same Archbishop?" That intuition was correct. Among the documents Capovilla had sent was a stamped "confidential note" by Capovilla, dated May 17, 1967, in which the

---

[182]Socci, *Fourth Secret*, p. 140.

Archbishop had recorded the precise circumstances of the reading of the Third Secret by Pope Paul VI.[183] According to the note, Paul VI read the Secret on June 27, 1963, only six days after his election to the papacy and before he had even been seated officially at the coronation Mass (which took place on June 29). But according to Bertone's representation in *Message*, Paul VI did not read the Secret until nearly two years later: "Paul VI read the contents with the Substitute[184] Archbishop Angelo Dell'Acqua, on 27 March 1965, and returned the envelope to the Archives of the Holy Office, deciding not to publish the text."[185]

Capovilla's confidential note had revealed a telling omission: Why had Bertone and his collaborators failed to mention a reading of the Secret by Paul VI nearly two years before the date given in the official account? There was no reason not to mention such an important historical event... *unless* it was an event they wished to hide.

There are two envelopes!

The huge discrepancy between the date recorded by Capovilla and that mentioned by Bertone prompted Paolini to telephone Capovilla at precisely 7:45 p.m. on the same day he received the documents from the Archbishop. During this conversation, Paolini asked the Archbishop to explain the discrepancy, and Capovilla protested: "Ah, but I spoke the truth. Look I am still lucid!" When Paolini politely insisted that, still, there was an unexplained discrepancy, Capovilla first offered explanations that suggested "eventual lapse of memory, interpretations of what he had intended to say," whereupon Paolini reminded the Archbishop his own stamped, "confidential note" had recorded the year Paul VI read the Secret: 1963, not 1965 as the Vatican's account claimed. Capovilla then gave this reply: "But I am right, because perhaps *the Bertone envelope is not the same as the Capovilla envelope.*"

---

[183]The document is reproduced here, in both the Italian original and the English translation, at Appendix I. *See also*, "Some Certified Notes of Archbishop Capovilla Re: the Third Secret" at http://www.fatima.org/news/newsviews/092707capovilla. asp; for the original document in Italian, see http://www.fatima.org/it/news/itnote_ capovilla.asp.

[184]Shorthand for the title Substitute of the Secretary of State, to which Dell'Acqua had been appointed in 1954.

[185]Socci, *Fourth Secret*, p. 141, and citing *The Message of Fatima*, p. 15 (English print edition).

Stunned, Paolini then asked the question that began a whole new stage in the Third Secret controversy: "Therefore, both dates are true, because there are two texts of the Third Secret?" After a brief pause, the Archbishop gave the explosive answer: "Exactly so! (*Per l'appunto!*)."[186] Pope John's own personal secretary had just confirmed the existence of a missing envelope and a missing text of the Third Secret of Fatima.

"It is in the right-hand drawer"

Capovilla's "confidential note" corroborates his testimony in detail. According to the note, on the date Pope Paul read the Secret (June 27, 1963), Monsignor Angelo Dell'Acqua—the same "Substitute" referred to in *Message*—telephoned Capovilla to ask: "I am looking for the Fatima envelope. Do you know where it is kept?"[187] The note records that Capovilla replied: "It is in the right-hand drawer of the writing desk called Barbarigo, *in the bedroom.*" That is, the envelope was in the former bedroom of John XXIII, which was now the bedroom of Paul VI; it was *not* in the Holy Office archives. The note further records that the "Fatima envelope" *was found in that desk*: "An hour later, Dell'Acqua telephoned me again. Everything is fine. The envelope has been retrieved." Finally, the note records that in an audience the next day Paul VI asked Capovilla directly: "Why is your name on the envelope?" Capovilla replied: "John XXIII asked me to inscribe a note concerning the manner of arrival of the envelope in his [Pope John's] hands and the names of all those to whom he considered it necessary to make it known."[188]

Thus, Capovilla verifies what we already knew: that a text of the Third Secret was kept in the papal bedchamber, where it remained during the pontificates of Pius XII, Pope John and Paul VI. But Capovilla also confirms something else: that a text of the

---

[186]Socci, *Fourth Secret*, p. 142. For more documented evidence to prove the existence of a missing text of the Third Secret, see also "Does the Third Secret Consist of Two Distinct Texts?", *The Devil's Final Battle*, Chapter 12 (also at http://www.devilsfinalbattle.com/ch12.htm).

[187]Notice Dell'Acqua evidently presumed that the envelope was somewhere in the papal apartment, not in the Holy Office archive, of which Capovilla was not the custodian. Otherwise, Dell'Acqua would have asked the custodian of the archive, Cardinal Ottaviani, where the "Fatima envelope" was, rather than Capovilla, Pope John's former personal secretary. The confidential note is reproduced at Appendix I.

[188]Socci, *Fourth Secret*, p. 142.

Secret is contained in an envelope on which Capovilla had noted his name and the names of others at the instruction of Pope John XXIII. He also confirms, as already mentioned, that Pope John directed him to write on the same envelope, at the Pope's dictation, "I give no judgment."

Here it must be noted that Capovilla's "confidential note" refers to both "envelope" (*plico*) and "wrapping" (*involucro*) as the place where Capovilla made the notations at John XXIII's direction. Thus, rather than making the notations on the Third Secret envelope proper, Capovilla could well have made them on an outer envelope or official folder that held the envelope containing the Secret. This point needs to be clarified by further testimony from the Archbishop. The ambiguity on this point, however, does not affect Capovilla's testimony concerning the existence of an *inner* envelope containing the Third Secret in the desk drawer in Pope Paul's bedroom, where Pope John had left it. The Vatican has never produced that envelope, nor any outer envelope or wrapping bearing the notations attested to by Capovilla. In fact, the envelope or wrapping with Capovilla's notations has never even been *mentioned* in the official account—a very conspicuous omission that would be inexplicable unless that envelope or wrapping contains something we have not been allowed to see.

There would be further developments concerning Capovilla's testimony by way of attempts to obtain a retraction of his revelations to Solideo Paolini. As we will see in Chapters 9 and 10, the attempts not only failed, but actually resulted in the confirmation of Capovilla's testimony and additional revelations pointing to the existence of a hidden text of the Secret.

But there would emerge another piece of evidence even more important than what Capovilla has provided: During his television appearance in late May 2007, *Bertone himself would reveal the existence of two identically prepared Third Secret envelopes*, after having failed to mention the second envelope during the previous seven years. I will consider that sensational development in Chapter 8. First, however, I will consider Cardinal Bertone's book in answer to Socci—a book that, as Socci observes, is another "disaster" for the Vatican's position.

Chapter 7

The Cardinal Defaults

By the closing months of 2006 the former Archbishop Bertone, Secretary of the CDF, had become Cardinal Bertone, successor to Cardinal Sodano as Vatican Secretary of State under Pope Benedict XVI. During the previous year Sister Lucia had passed on to her eternal reward at the age of 97, to be followed shortly by Pope John Paul II. But the controversy over the Third Secret had not only failed to abate, it had reached a higher intensity than ever before. Antonio Socci's *Fourth Secret* (published in November 2006) had shifted to the Vatican a heavy new burden of proof. The evidence Socci had given such wide publicity, including the testimony of Archbishop Capovilla, made it incumbent on the Vatican to demonstrate clearly and convincingly that it was not in fact engaged in what could only be called a conspiracy to conceal the words of the Virgin Mary indicated by Lucia's momentous "etc" and set forth in a text once located in the papal apartment, in the right-hand drawer of the writing desk called "Barbarigo."

The Risk of Default

This was an unprecedented development in the history of the Church: a nationally prominent lay Catholic and television celebrity had, in essence, publicly accused the Vatican Secretary of State and his collaborators of deceiving the Church and the world in a matter of grave spiritual and temporal importance. This time, the accusation could not be handled with a dismissive reference to "Fatimists." Socci obviously could not be considered biased since he had been in *agreement* with Bertone's position before he began to examine the evidence. But as more and more members of the faithful, including Socci, were coming to recognize, the "Fatimists" were nothing more or less than faithful Catholics who were dead right in their contentions. Thanks to Socci's book, which gave voice to the concerns of these Catholics, the Vatican apparatus responsible for the handling of the Third Secret had been well and truly indicted in the court of public opinion. Now there was no choice but to answer the indictment; for not to answer it would be to concede that it was true.

On the other hand, to answer Socci would be a perilous undertaking. If his (and the "Fatimists'") allegations were indeed true, then denying them would require further deception and the grave risk of further contradiction by the known facts. On the other hand, to join issue with Socci but then fail to address his allegations on their merits would be even worse than not answering him at all; it would amount to a total default by Bertone and the Vatican. Given the danger, if the allegations were true there could be no "official" Vatican response, and certainly no response from the Pope (who has always remained aloof from the controversy). And, in fact, as of this writing there has been no official Vatican response at all to *Fourth Secret* or the case it presents. Socci, then, would have to be answered "unofficially" so as to preclude Vatican accountability for any unfavorable outcome. The failure of whoever answered Socci would be *his* failure, not the Vatican's. That, at least, appears to be the reasoning behind the means by which Socci was answered.

A book that answers nothing

In May of 2007, Rizzoli, the same publisher that had published *Fourth Secret*, rushed into print a book by Cardinal Bertone entitled *L'Ultima Veggente di Fatima* ("The Last Visionary of Fatima") (*Last Visionary*).[189] *Last Visionary*, which appeared in bookstores a mere six months after *Fourth Secret*, is essentially a 100-page interview of the Cardinal concerning various subjects, followed by another 50 pages of appendices. This mass of verbiage surrounds a mere nine pages of comment in response to the claims of Socci and the "Fatimists" (including Father Gruner, whose name is also mentioned by the Cardinal). The interviewer was a layman, Giuseppe De Carli, a *vaticanista* (reporter on the Vatican beat) and ardent admirer of the Cardinal, whose fawning questions not only posed no real challenge to the Cardinal, but actually assisted him in promoting what Socci had called "the official reconstruction" of the Third Secret.

The book is subtitled "My meetings with Sister Lucia." These

---

[189]Bertone, Cardinal Tarcisio, *The Last Visionary of Fatima* (Milano: Rai and Eri Rizzoli, 2007). All English translations are mine.

were the purported meetings the Vatican had sent Bertone to conduct in preparation for "revelation" of the Third Secret in June 2000 and to defend his position after publication of the vision and *Message* were met with widespread incredulity. *Last Visionary* states that there were three meetings in all: April 27, 2000 (the one in which Sister Lucia supposedly denied ever receiving an "express order of Our Lady" regarding disclosure of the Third Secret in 1960), November 17, 2001 (the "disastrous" interview discussed in Chapter 5), and a never previously mentioned meeting on December 9, 2003, whose contents are not explicitly cited. Bertone says these three encounters lasted "at least ten hours" in total.[190] In view of what has already been presented here, it should hardly be surprising that not even one minute of those ten hours was transcribed or recorded on audio or videotape. Instead, the Cardinal "took notes" of which he later made "syntheses."[191]

In an entirely new revelation, however, the Cardinal claims that he drew up "edited minutes (*verbali redatti*)" of the meetings which Sister Lucia "signed with full conviction..."[192] These allegedly signed "edited minutes" have never been published and were never mentioned before *Last Visionary*. Nor, quite tellingly, does the Cardinal provide copies of either the "edited minutes" or his "notes" as appendices to *Last Visionary*. And none of the purported witnesses to these interviews has ever attested to the accuracy of Bertone's "notes," "syntheses" and "edited minutes."[193]

Incredibly enough, in *Last Visionary* Bertone reveals that he did not even draft a list of specific questions in preparation for his three important missions from the Vatican to interrogate Sister Lucia.[194]

---

[190]Ibid., p. 39.

[191]Ibid., pp. 39, 48.

[192]Ibid., p. 100.

[193]*Last Visionary* states that during the meeting of April 27, 2000 the then Bishop of Fatima, Serafim de Sousa Ferreira e Silva, was also present (p. 42). I have already noted that during the purported meeting of November 17, 2001, Rev. Luis Kondor, SVD, Vice-Postulator of the cause of Bl. Francisco and Bl. Jacinta, and the prioress of the Carmelite Convent of St. Teresa in Coimbra were said to be present. To my knowledge, none of these witnesses has come forward to authenticate Bertone's accounts of what Sister Lucia allegedly said to him, with one exception: Bishop Serafim appeared on television in September 2007 to confirm what he pointedly noted was "*only one fact*": that he saw Sister Lucia authenticate the text of the vision of the bishop in white during Bertone's meeting with the seer on April 27, 2000. See discussion in Chapter 10. Of course, no one disputes the authenticity of this text.

[194]Bertone, *Last Visionary*, pp. 49-50.

Yet De Carli himself notes that when he went to interview Bertone for the book he was "armed with neat pages of questions and a tape recorder."[195] That is the usual procedure for conducting a reliable interview of an important subject for the historical record. But all such safeguards were dispensed with here. Today, there is no way of verifying independently what Sister Lucia is alleged to have said to Bertone during ten hours of conversation. We have only Bertone's alleged "notes," "syntheses" and "edited minutes," but even these are not provided. And that, obviously, is exactly the way the Cardinal wants it.

Avoiding every issue

In undertaking to answer Socci, Cardinal Bertone was obliged to address at least these major points of Socci's presentation in *Fourth Secret*:

- the testimony of Archbishop Capovilla that there are two texts and two envelopes comprising the Third Secret;

- the testimony of Bishop Venancio and Cardinal Ottaviani that there is a text of the Secret one page and 25 lines in length, as opposed to the four pages and 62 lines of the vision of "the Bishop dressed in white";

- the words of the Virgin following Sister Lucia's "etc" in the Fourth Memoir;

- the evidence for the lodging of a text of the Secret in the papal apartment, as distinct from the text in the Holy Office archives;

- the reading of texts of the Secret by two Popes (Paul VI and John Paul II) on dates *years earlier* than the dates in the official account in *Message*, strongly evidencing the existence of a text other than the text of the vision produced in 2000;

- the Virgin's "express order" linking the Secret to 1960, the year following the calling of the Second Vatican Council by John XXIII;

- the abundant testimony that the Secret refers to a grave

---

[195]Ibid., p. 31.

crisis in the Church after 1960 in conjunction with a planetary catastrophe.

Although he has written an entire book to answer Socci, Bertone ducks *every one* of these points in *Last Visionary*, with one exception: linkage of the Secret to 1960. On this issue, Bertone offers an explanation that is patently incredible, as we shall see. Let us examine briefly *Last Visionary*'s attempt—or rather, *failure* to attempt—an answer to Socci.

Conceding Capovilla's testimony

First of all, in *Last Visionary* Bertone silently concedes Archbishop Capovilla's testimony that there are indeed two envelopes and two texts pertaining to the Third Secret. On this decisive point it is crucial to note that De Carli *specifically invites* Bertone to comment on the claim that there are "Two texts of the Third Secret. One made known in 2000, the other remains in the papal apartment where it was put by Pius XII, consulted by John XXIII and by Paul VI. The so-called 'Capovilla envelope', for the name of Monsignor Loris F. Capovilla, secretary of Pope Roncalli."[196]

And the Cardinal's reply? *He simply ignores the reference to Capovilla.* Instead, he issues an indignant and irrelevant protest:

> You know what they who use the magnifying glass of prejudice cling to? They cling to the fact that in the 'Secret' revealed there is not one word of the Virgin addressed to the shepherds…. The words of the Virgin would have been temerariously censored, because they are considered devastating. And on what stands the apodictic certainty that the "envelope" always remained in the "apartment", even in a drawer of the bedside table of the Pope?[197]

Attention, first of all, to the tacit admission (under the appearance of a denial) that there *was* a text in the papal apartment! Bertone has subtly recast the issue to be whether that text *"always remained"* there. Bertone then asks to know the basis for the claim that the text "always remained there"—as if he doesn't know! Yet, Bertone is perfectly aware of Archbishop Capovilla's testimony—

---

[196]Ibid., p. 78.

[197]Ibid.

put before him a moment earlier by De Carli—that there are two envelopes and two texts of the Third Secret, one of which was lodged in the papal apartment.

Bertone's stupendous evasion leads to these alternative conclusions, all fatal to the "official reconstruction": (a) Bertone, whose very mission is to defend the "official reconstruction," declined to speak with Archbishop Capovilla about his "explosive" testimony because he knows or suspects that testimony is true and does not wish to have it confirmed to him directly by Capovilla; (b) Bertone attempted to remonstrate with Capovilla concerning his testimony, was unable to obtain a retraction, and Capovilla has stood by that testimony despite pressure from the Vatican Secretary of State; or (c) under the mental reservation I have already discussed, Bertone is mentally operating as if the missing text does not "exist" because it has been deemed "inauthentic," so that Capovilla's testimony concerning it can likewise be treated as "non-existent."[198]

Apart from the testimony of Capovilla, which he fails disastrously to address, Bertone also ignores the testimony of other witnesses concerning the lodging of a text in the papal apartment (Mother Pasqualina and Robert Serrou), and the photograph in *Paris-Match* magazine. Nevertheless, as we will see in Chapter 10, Bertone would finally be forced to admit that there was indeed a text in the papal apartment, despite his evasions and apparent denials over the previous seven years.

There is also a glaring omission here. Despite being aware for many years of the issue of the text in the papal apartment, and certainly since 2000 when *Message* was published, Bertone does not state in *Last Visionary*, and has never stated elsewhere, that he simply *asked* John Paul II, Cardinal Ratzinger, Stanislaw Dziwisz (the Pope's beloved personal secretary and now the Archbishop of Krakow), or any number of other people who would know the answer, whether in fact there was a text of the Third Secret in the papal apartment during the reign of John Paul II or any of his predecessors. It would have been a simple matter to line up witnesses, including the late Pope himself while he was still alive,

---

[198] Any possible sudden "retraction" by Capovilla in the future would obviously be suspect, and would contradict his own document recording the location of the Third Secret in the desk drawer of the writing desk in the papal bedchamber. I will discuss in Chapters 9 and 10 Bertone's failed attempts to obtain a "retraction" from Capovilla, who has not only retracted nothing he said to Paolini, but has actually made further revelations damaging to the official account.

to testify that there was never any such text—if such were really the case. But not even one witness is presented on this crucial point from a host of people who have knowledge of the matter.

Only three conclusions are possible: (a) Bertone never asked the question because he does not wish to know the answer, or (b) he knows the answer but is concealing it dishonestly, or (c) under the mental reservation the document in the papal apartment does not "exist" because it is deemed "not authentic." No matter which conclusion is accepted, Bertone's failure to contest or even to *mention* Capovilla's testimony means that the case is over: Bertone has defaulted.

Conceding Cardinal Ottaviani's testimony

In *Last Visionary* De Carli himself summarizes some of the evidence, including the key testimony of Cardinal Ottaviani, that "the 'Secret' was written on a single piece of paper. *Twenty, twenty-five lines in total*," whereas the document published by the Vatican in 2000 "was of 62 lines. Four pages, exactly." Then De Carli inquires of Bertone demurely: "Could not the first document contain the words of the Madonna and the second the description of the vision?" Bertone's reply begins with another blatant evasion:

> The first document does not exist. It has never existed *in the Archive of the Holy Office*. To arrive at the documents of the *archive* three keys are necessary. Then [the 1950s] there was not the figure of the Congregation [for the Doctrine of the Faith, successor to the Holy Office], the Pope himself was head of the Holy Office. *I do not know what the words of Cardinal Ottaviani refer to.*[199]

Notice that Bertone is careful to qualify his denial: the posited missing document "never existed *in the Archive of the Holy Office*," which of course is not the same as saying that it never existed at all. Bertone knows quite well that the claim before him is precisely that the missing document was *not* in the Archive, but rather in the papal apartment. This is the very claim Bertone has already conceded by failing and refusing to address the testimony of Archbishop Capovilla, or indeed any of the other evidence placing the document in the papal apartment.

---

[199]Bertone, *Last Visionary*, p. 76.

As for Bertone's evasion that he does not know what Cardinal Ottaviani was talking about regarding a one-page text of 25 lines, here we see again a very curious lack of effort to investigate and refute a key piece of evidence that demolishes the "official reconstruction." If the report of Cardinal Ottaviani's testimony were false, Bertone had access to still-living witnesses and Vatican records that could have demonstrated this. Yet Bertone does not even try to deny that Ottaviani said what he is reported to have said. He merely claims *not to know* what document Ottaviani was referring to. The testimony of Cardinal Ottaviani is thus conceded just as completely as the testimony of Archbishop Capovilla.

Again, Bertone has defaulted. In fact, as we shall see in Chapter 8, during his television appearance a few weeks later, Bertone, reversing his claim that he had no idea what Ottaviani was talking about, would *positively admit* that Ottaviani had testified that the Secret was written on a single page with 25 lines of text—an admission that contributed to the total collapse of the "official reconstruction" during Bertone's appearance.

Evading the testimony of Joaquin Navarro-Valls

Bertone's next evasion concerns the crucial evidence of the statement by papal spokesman Joaquin Navarro-Valls, reported by *The Washington Post*, that John Paul II read a text of the Third Secret in 1978, only days after his election. As noted in Chapter 4, the text John Paul II read after the assassination attempt in 1981 was brought to him from the Holy Office archives, whereas there is no record of any text of the Secret being brought to him from those same archives in 1978. Therefore, it follows that what the Pope read in 1978 must have been a *different* text located in the papal apartment, where indeed a text of the Secret was lodged during the pontificates of John XXIII and Paul VI, as Archbishop Capovilla and other witnesses have testified *without contradiction* by Bertone.

Here De Carli was at least persistent, but his persistence was rewarded with a series of clearly calculated dodges. First, De Carli asks: "According to you, John Paul II first had the 'Third Secret' brought to him in Gemelli Polyclinic in July of 1981. Had he already read the text?" Bertone's astounding reply: "I am convinced he had not read it."[200] He is *convinced*? Bertone was the key man responsible for managing the Third Secret controversy from 2000 going forward, yet he never simply *asked* the Pope before he died in 2005 when His Holiness first read the Third Secret? He never asked Navarro-Valls, who is *still alive*?

Pressing further, De Carli asks: "You are convinced of it or you are sure of it?" In reply, the Cardinal dodges again: "I am sure. I base myself on the documentation of the Archive of the Congregation for the Doctrine of the Faith, documentation that I compared with the results of the Archive of the Secretary of State."[201] Amazingly, Bertone, who could have simply asked the Pope—and can still ask Navarro-Valls—when the Pope first read the Third Secret, has failed to do so but instead tells us that he "bases" himself on a comparison of two sets of documents that would tell us nothing about the matter!

Pressing still further (even as he moves into the next chapter of *Last Visionary*), De Carli asks: "A Pope who feels devotion to Mary in his spiritual DNA, knows that the Secret exists and *does not read it as soon as elected*?"[202] Indeed, it is impossible to believe that John Paul II had no interest in reading the Third Secret until he was in the hospital in July 1981, nearly three years into his pontificate, especially when one considers that his predecessor Paul VI read the Secret within *six days* of his election, even before he had been installed as Pope. Here is Bertone's evasive answer—his third on this point: "*In my opinion*, no. It depends on the sensibility, on the particular circumstances. Just elected, John Paul II had put himself to the objective of re-evangelizing the world."[203]

In his *opinion*? When all he had to do was ask the Pope? When all he has to do today is ask Navarro-Valls to confirm or deny the report in *The Washington Post*? When, for that matter, he could ask anyone else who would know, such as Pope Benedict XVI or Archbishop Dziwisz? And John Paul II, we are asked to believe, had no time to read the Third Secret *during the first three years of his pontificate* because he was too busy re-evangelizing the world? But what could have been more helpful in that endeavor than the contents of the Secret, containing precious advice from the very

---

[200]Ibid., p. 57.

[201]Ibid., p. 58.

[202]Ibid., p. 59.

[203]Ibid., p. 59.

Mother of God to whom the Pope was devoted, as Bertone is at pains to remind us?

What is to account for Bertone resolutely confining himself to an "opinion" (or a pointless document comparison) on a matter of fact he could have verified instantly with an inquiry of the Pope, Navarro-Valls, Archbishop Dziwisz and who knows how many others who would be able to answer the simple question whether the Pope read a text of the Secret in 1978? Once again, only three conclusions are possible: (a) Bertone does not wish to know the answer so that he can appear to deny (without actually denying) that the Pope read the Secret in 1978; (b) he already knows the Pope did so and is hiding the truth because it shows the existence of another text; or (c) under the mental reservation, whatever text John Paul II read in 1978 is "not authentic" and thus does not "exist."

In any case, Bertone's evident aversion to admitting that the Pope read a text of the Secret in 1978 (just as Navarro-Valls reported) is understandable: Again, if the Pope read the Secret in 1978, then the document he read was not brought to him from the Holy Office archives, which has no record of any such transaction. Since it was not in the archives, it must have been in the papal apartment—precisely where Archbishop Capovilla places it in testimony Bertone refuses to address *even when he is asked about it directly* by a friendly questioner.

Moreover, Bertone had nothing to say about the testimony of Archbishop Capovilla that Pope Paul VI likewise read a text of the Third Secret *years before* the official account says he did: in 1963, versus 1965, as the official account claims. Still another resounding silence in the face of powerful evidence that there is a text of the Secret we have yet to see.

Post-mortem "surprise" testimony from Sister Lucia

In the remainder of his discussion of the issue of a text of the Secret in the papal apartment, Bertone offers another evasion combined with a surprising new statement posthumously attributed to Sister Lucia:

> Two things I know: that in the memory of those who have managed *the archive* there has never existed two envelopes, but only one envelope. The other is the word, on the contrary, the official recognition of

> Sister Lucia: "This is the 'Third Secret' and it is the
> only text?" "Yes, this is the Third Secret, and I have
> never written other." The most hardened Fatimists,
> I am thinking of those who revolve around Father
> Nicholas Gruner, remain disappointed.[204]

Before we discuss Bertone's newly introduced "quotation" of Sister Lucia, which appears nowhere in the previous seven years of the "official" account, we must pause to consider the careful wording of his repeated evasion that in the Holy Office *archive* there was only one envelope in "the memory" (the memory of who, exactly?) of those who have managed it. Once again, Bertone knows full well that the text in the Holy Office archive is beside the point, but notice the qualifier that precedes his statement: "Two things *I know...*" followed by the "two things" Bertone "knows." That is, Bertone does *not* "know"—because he *chooses* not to "know"—whether there is (or was) another text of the secret in an envelope stored in the papal apartment rather than the archive. He does not "know" this because *he did not ask.* Or, even worse, he did ask and will not —at least not yet—tell us the answer.

But, as I will discuss further in Chapter 8, it will be *Bertone himself* who finally reveals the existence of the second envelope as if it had always been part of what was in the archive, suggesting that Lucia had for some reason redundantly employed two identical sealed envelopes to hold one text, even though he had never even hinted at the existence of a second envelope before. And, as we will see in Chapter 10, Bertone, via De Carli, would finally acknowledge during his own television broadcast in September 2007 that there is yet *another* envelope pertaining to the Secret, bearing the dictation of John XXIII and the names of those who had read the text of the Secret, which envelope Bertone has *never produced* even though his own broadcast concedes that this envelope *was indeed kept in the papal apartment.*

What, then, is one to make of Bertone's above-quoted declaration in *Last Visionary* that in "the memory of those who have managed *the archive* there has never existed two envelopes, but *only one envelope"*? Clearly, if there was only one envelope in the archive, the second, never-before-mentioned envelope must have come from somewhere else: i.e., the papal apartment.

---

[204]Ibid., p. 76.

Now to the posthumous "surprise" testimony of Sister Lucia. In the above-quoted passage Bertone suddenly introduces—for the first time ever in this controversy—a purported statement by Lucia he somehow has failed to mention before: "Yes, this is the Third Secret, and I have never written other," in response to the purported question: "This is the 'Third Secret' and it is the only text?" Where did this alleged statement come from? When does Bertone claim it was uttered? Was it during any of his three unrecorded interviews of Lucia? If so, was it the interview in 2000, 2001 or 2003? Who claims to have witnessed this previously unheard-of statement besides Bertone himself?

As Socci asks: "Why did Bertone never report such an important phrase in his official publication [*Message*]?" To which I would add: Why does the purported statement not also appear in Bertone's communiqué concerning the "disastrous" post-*Message* interview of Sister Lucia on November 17, 2001? Both *Message* in 2000 and the communiqué in 2001 were published for the very purpose of quashing all further speculation about the Third Secret. Yet we are asked to believe that a purported statement by Lucia bearing directly on the question of a missing text was somehow inadvertently omitted not only from these "official" documents, but from any other statement by Bertone or other Vatican officials *over the next seven years*, only to jump out of the top hat during an interview with Giuseppe De Carli—conveniently enough, at the very moment a living eyewitness (Capovilla) has just confirmed the existence of the missing text.

It seems Bertone's mysterious "notes," "syntheses" and "edited minutes" of his private encounters with the late Sister Lucia rather conveniently yield just what he needs, just when he needs it—and not a moment sooner. And we are asked to believe this posthumously revealed statement by the same man who has already claimed that Sister Lucia, who wrote on the Third Secret envelope "By express order of Our Lady...", told him that she had never received an express order of Our Lady. Further, as Socci observes, we are asked to believe a "new statement that now—and only now that the seer is already dead—the prelate attributes to her."[205]

Furthermore, it is difficult to see why we should believe the

---

[205]Antonio Socci, "Dear Cardinal Bertone: Who—Between You and Me—is Deliberately Lying?", *Libero*, May 12, 2007; English translation at http://www.fatima.org/news/newsviews/052907socci.asp. See also *The Fatima Crusader*, No. 86 (Summer 2007), pp. 35-42.

Cardinal's claim regarding this suddenly introduced statement when, as the Cardinal himself will reveal on television in a few weeks, his claim that there is "only one envelope" pertaining to the Secret is false.

Ducking the "etc" – again

But not even the suddenly revealed "saving" statement of "Sister Lucia" clearly and unequivocally addresses the question Bertone resolutely refuses to answer or even to acknowledge when it is put to him directly: Whether Lucia wrote down anywhere the words of Our Lady concluding the discourse whose ominous beginning she recorded in her Fourth Memoir: "'In Portugal the dogma of the faith will always be preserved etc." Or this question: Whether Lucia ever wrote down any words of the Virgin *at all* explaining the vision of the bishop in white. That, apparently, is something else Bertone can say he does not "know."

Socci asks how, absent a motive to conceal, the question of the remainder of the Virgin's discourse interrupted by "etc" could have been overlooked by Bertone in his multiple interrogations of Sister Lucia: "Can one perhaps accept that a phrase of such capital importance had been distractedly forgotten? What better occasion to clarify the sense of that dramatic word remaining in suspense? But nothing, unfortunately, that Bertone wished to ask the seer (had he perhaps a fear of the answer?).... A choice that unfortunately credits the idea of an insurmountable embarrassment concerning that phrase of the Madonna and worsens the suspicion that there is something grave to hide..."[206]

In *Last Visionary* Bertone continues to avoid like the plague any discussion of the "etc" issue even though he *states the issue himself* in answering Socci's claim that a withheld text of the Secret mentions terrible events for the Church after 1960:

> One returns to the hashed and rehashed thesis that the attempt on the Pope of May 13, 1981 is not the content of the Third Secret.[207] The 'Third Secret' would be instead the sequel of the phrase 'In Portugal the dogma of the faith will always be preserved etc...'

---

[206]Socci, *Fourth Secret*, p. 90.

[207]Notice the attempt to pass off Cardinal Sodano's nonsensical and widely rejected "interpretation" of the vision of "the bishop dressed in white" as if it were self-evidently "*the* content of the Third Secret."

that, according to the Fatimists, would be explosive. After that "etc" *there is* [N.B.: a revealing slip of the tongue?] there would be, other text.[208]

Having stated the "Fatimist" claim accurately enough, Bertone then fails to make the least attempt to refute it. He simply mocks it as a "hashed and rehashed thesis." As if it were beyond the pale to point out that "etc" means the following words have been omitted! As if Father Schweigl, who was certainly no "Fatimist" but rather the emissary of Pius XII in 1952 had not testified (without contradiction by anyone) that the *second part* of the Third Secret "is the logical continuation—though I may not say anything—of the *words*: 'In Portugal, the dogma of the Faith will always be preserved etc.'"[209] As if no one should be suspicious that, despite the Vatican knowing of this burning issue for many years, Bertone never bothered to ask Sister Lucia what follows the "etc" and where she had written it down, or, if he did ask her, has hidden the answer. As if there were nothing amiss in Bertone and his collaborators using Sister Lucia's Third Memoir instead of the more complete Fourth, which contains the words of the Virgin ending with Lucia's "etc", so that *Message* could pretend those words are not part of the Message of Fatima, but rather Lucia's later-added "annotations" which could be relegated to a footnote and conveniently ignored.[210]

Taking up the very issue Bertone had just raised only to duck it, De Carli, while offering a soothing comment about how unfair it is that Bertone has been "put on the griddle," makes this statement:

> That 'etc', according to Socci and others… would allude to the text that the Vatican has not wished to reveal. It is not revealed because it is a boomerang against the Church. The prediction of a planetary apostasy on the part of the Church. An "Apocalypse Now" for Rome. Rome will lose the faith and become the seat of the Antichrist. The smell in the air of the smoke of Satan…"

---

[208]Bertone, *Last Visionary*, p. 77.

[209]*The Whole Truth About Fatima* (*WTAF*), Vol. III, p. 710.

[210]Although Bertone and company shunned the Fourth Memoir in their attempt to "interpret" the Third Secret as a mere depiction of past events in *The Message of Fatima*, in *Last Visionary* Bertone suddenly discovers its merits, citing it as "the more extensive" document, and quoting it concerning Sister Lucia's explanation that the content of the apparitions was indelibly imprinted on her soul and "almost impossible to forget… God himself [sic] doesn't want it to be forgotten." Bertone, *Last Visionary*, p. 80.

And the Cardinal's reply? He *once again* completely ignores the "etc", uttering an indignant protest while waving a red herring:

> They are pure ravings. Excuse me, you wish that the prophecy of Fatima concerns the apostasy of the Church of Rome? Rome the place of the Antichrist?[211] With the love the Madonna has for the Pope and the Pope for the Madonna? All the Popes of the 20th century, including Pope Ratzinger? Books can be written... which denounce the presence of a conspiracy, a warped plot, to not speak the truth but to transmit it in code. And he who can understand, let him understand. No, it is a reconstruction, an inquest... I am amazed that journalists and writers who proclaim themselves Catholic lend themselves to this game.[212]

Nowhere amidst the indignation is there an answer to the charge that Bertone and his collaborators have deliberately evaded the telltale "etc" because they know it is the continuation of a missing part of the Message of Fatima. Here Bertone continues to evade the issue, even though De Carli has just brought it to his attention! Instead, Bertone rather demagogically defends the honor of the conciliar and postconciliar popes, when no one, including Socci, has contended that Our Lady prophesied that *the Popes* will lose the faith.[213] Quite the contrary, the Message of Fatima prophesies that the Pope "will have much to suffer," and that suffering includes what the Third Secret (in the missing explanatory words of the Virgin) predicts: apostasy in the Church, which, after all, is predicted by Sacred Scripture itself.[214]

---

[211] A clear reference to the approved apparition of Our Lady of La Salette, who warned in 1846 that "Rome will lose the Faith and become the seat of the Antichrist," but not that Popes would apostatize. Curiously, Bertone cites the reported words of Our Lady as if they were the "ravings" of "Fatimists," without mentioning that they pertain to an apparition of the Virgin decisively approved as authentic by the Bishop of Grenoble, who established devotion to Our Lady of La Salette. *See* CATHOLIC ENCYCLOPEDIA (1917), *La Salette*. The precise content of the Secret that Our Lady of La Salette conveyed to the seer Melanie Calvat is beyond the scope of this book. The content of the apparition is in no way necessary to my presentation.

[212] Bertone, *Last Visionary*, p. 78.

[213] Notice also that Bertone has read Socci's book attentively enough to have caught Socci's phrase "he who can understand, let him understand" apropos his hypothesis that the Third Secret has been revealed indirectly via the apocalyptic sermons of John Paul II at Fatima in order to make it possible for the Vatican to claim that "everything" has been revealed. Socci, *Fourth Secret*, p. 91.

[214] E.g. "Let no man deceive you, for it [the Last Times] will not come unless the

Ignoring a train of witnesses

As for Bertone's remark that Socci and the "Fatimists" promote "pure ravings" unworthy of true Catholics by contending that the Secret predicts an apostasy in the Church, Socci points out that it is not he, but rather unimpeachable witnesses who link the Third Secret to apostasy:

> In his book [Bertone] adds an attack on me, because I would have suggested that the Secret foresees the "apostasy of the Church of Rome", and of the upper hierarchy. First of all: Bertone should carefully read again what Jesus said to Sister Lucia in His apparition in August 1931.[215] Furthermore, it's not I who talked about apostasy, but Cardinal Ottaviani and Cardinal Ciappi ("In the Third Secret, it is foretold, among other things, that the great apostasy in the Church will begin *at the top*").[216] An analogous concept appears in Sister Lucia's words to Father Fuentes and in two statements by Cardinal Ratzinger....[217]

Yet in *Last Visionary* Bertone has not one word to say about the testimony of the parade of witnesses already discussed here, including cardinals, popes and Sister Lucia herself, who establish that the Third Secret involves more than a wordless and ambiguous vision of a "Bishop dressed in white."

What we have just discussed represents Cardinal Bertone's entire attempt in *Last Visionary* to answer the case Socci had presented in *Fourth Secret*. As we can see, Bertone effectively concedes Socci's entire case, thereby inflicting major damage on the official account. Bertone gives the mere appearance of answering Socci, when in truth the Cardinal has defaulted on

---

apostasy comes first, and the man of lawlessness is revealed, the son of perdition" (II Thess. 2:3).

[215]"Make it known to My ministers that given they follow the example of the King of France in delaying the execution of My request, they will follow him into misfortune..." *WTAF*, Vol. II, pp. 543-544.

[216]See Fr. Gerard Mura, "The Third Secret of Fatima: Has It Been Completely Revealed?", the periodical *Catholic* (published by the Transalpine Redemptorists, Orkney Isles, Scotland, Great Britain), March 2002.

[217]Socci, "Dear Cardinal Bertone...", loc. cit. (at http://www.fatima.org/news/newsviews/052907socci.asp); see also *The Fatima Crusader*, No. 86 (Summer 2007), pp. 35-42. Socci is here referring to Father Fuentes' interview of Sister Lucia in 1957 and the statements of Cardinal Ratzinger in 1984 and 1985, which were discussed in Chapter 3.

every count of Socci's meticulously pleaded indictment. As Socci notes: "The problem is that this book doesn't give even a single answer to the questions I raised. On the contrary it causes further problems. I felt totally embarrassed while reading such a bungled and self-wounding response."[218] But the damage to the "official reconstruction" caused by *Last Visionary* does not end there.

A new version of Sister Lucia's "confession"

In *Last Visionary*, Bertone presents an entirely new version of the claim he first made in *Message*: that during an unrecorded interview of Sister Lucia she told him that the Virgin never gave her an "express order" that the Secret "can only be opened *in 1960*" by the Patriarch of Lisbon or the Bishop of Leiria. For the reasons already discussed, Bertone and his collaborators were clearly intent on negating the very idea that the Virgin Mary herself linked the Third Secret to 1960, the year after the calling of Vatican II by Pope John XXIII. In *Last Visionary* the attack on the "express order of Our Lady" continues.

Addressing this issue, De Carli comments that "On the envelope of the Congregation [the one allegedly containing the vision] was written '1960'. It was necessary to open it in that year.... It was a precise wish of Sister Lucia." That framing of the question already steers us away from the truth: Sister Lucia wrote much more than '1960' on the envelope, and what she wrote was much more than *her* wish. But De Carli has set up Bertone's reply:

> At the approach of that date someone thought that in that year something extraordinary should happen. I asked Sister Lucia: "Was it the Madonna who suggested that date, to indicate a deadline so precise?" She responded: "*It was a decision of mine* because I felt that 1960 would be a date very far from the writing of the 'Secret' in 1944 and because I had thought that I would be dead in that year, therefore the last obstacle to the interpretation and to the disclosure of the secret would have been taken away. *The Madonna did not communicate anything to me* in that regard."... It was

---

[218]Socci, "Dear Cardinal Bertone: Who—Between You and Me—is Deliberately Lying?", loc. cit. (at http://www.fatima.org/news/newsviews/052907socci.asp); see also *The Fatima Crusader*, No. 86 (Summer 2007), pp. 35-42.

a *fictitious date* and Lucia *confessed it* with disarming candor.[219]

Amazingly, Bertone once again publicly accuses Sister Lucia of being a confessed liar—the chosen seer of God who, at age 10, would not lie under a threat of torture and death by the Mayor of Ourem, as we saw in Chapter 1. Just as amazingly, Bertone suggests that God chose a messenger who would simply invent orders from the Blessed Virgin that had never been given. Bertone's new account of Sister Lucia's alleged "confession" that she simply invented an express order of the Mother of God—an order she obediently inscribed on the outside of the *two* envelopes Bertone will show the world on television only weeks later—is unbelievable on its face. Before examining this incredible "confession," however, it will be helpful to place it side-by-side with the original "confession," published seven years earlier in *Message*.

TABLE 1

BERTONE'S TWO VERSIONS OF SISTER LUCIA'S ALLEGED
"CONFESSION" REGARDING THE "EXPRESS ORDER OF OUR LADY."

June 26, 2000 (Message)[220]	May 10, 2007 (Last Visionary)[221]
Bertone: "Why only after 1960? Was it Our Lady who fixed that date?"	Bertone: "Was it the Madonna who suggested that date, to indicate a deadline so precise?"
"Lucia": "It was not Our Lady. I fixed the date because I had the intuition that before 1960 it would not be understood, but that only later would it be understood."	"Lucia": "It was a decision of mine because I felt that 1960 would be a date very far from the writing of the 'Secret' in 1944 and because I had thought that I would be dead in that year, therefore the last obstacle to the interpretation and to the disclosure of the secret would have been taken away. The Madonna did not communicate anything to me in that regard."

---

[219]*Last Visionary*, p. 92.

[220]*The Message of Fatima*, p. 29.

[221]Bertone, *L'Ultima Veggente di Fatima* (Last Visionary), p. 92.

We see, to begin with, an alarming "liquidity" in Bertone's quotations of Sister Lucia, allegedly drawn from his never-produced "notes." The wording and content of the two purported quotations are entirely different, and Bertone mysteriously fails to indicate during which of his three unrecorded interviews of the seer (April 2000, November 2001, December 2003) he allegedly obtained the 2007 version of her "confession." Nor does he provide any contemporaneous record of the alleged "confession."

An examination of Bertone's "notes" would be quite interesting since, as between the 2000 version and the 2007 version of the "confession," there is a drastic alteration of Lucia's alleged rationale for "choosing" the date 1960. In the 2000 version Lucia is quoted as having chosen the date because of an "intuition" that it would not be understood before 1960, but would be understood after that year. In the 2007 version, however, the "intuition" regarding 1960 has disappeared, to be replaced by a mere "decision" based on totally different reasons: 1960 was "very far" from 1944, Sister Lucia thought she would be dead by 1960, and with her death the *last obstacle* to revealing and "interpreting" the Secret would be removed.

The 2000 version of the "confession" was merely incredible, for the reasons already discussed in Chapter 4. The 2007 version—another posthumous "surprise" Bertone had never mentioned before—is not only incredible, but filled with nonsense that could not possibly have been uttered by Sister Lucia unless it was the product of undue influence upon the seer. At least six objections present themselves:

- *First*, Sister Lucia would never, on her own, make a "decision" when to reveal the Secret Our Lady had ordered her to "tell no one" except Francisco. The very idea is laughable.

- *Second*, 1960 was not "very far" from 1944. And even if it were, that a date was "very far" from 1944 was not a logical reason for Lucia to "decide" that *this* date, of all dates, would be a good time to reveal the Secret she was under heavenly orders *not* to reveal.

- *Third*, what would give Sister Lucia the idea that she would be dead in 1960 when she lived to the advanced age of 97? Nowhere in any of her writings do we find the least suggestion that she anticipated dying before her 53rd birthday.

- *Fourth*, why, of all the years that elapsed between 1944 and her death in 2005, would Sister Lucia "choose" 1960 as the year to reveal the Secret? Why *sixteen* years from 1944, rather than a round number like ten or twenty years?

- *Fifth*, what would make Sister Lucia think that she, the very recipient of the Third Secret, the chosen seer of God, was an *obstacle* to its disclosure and "interpretation," such that only her death would remove "the last obstacle to the interpretation and to the disclosure of the secret"? And even if she had expressed this absurd idea, why would she view herself as the *last* obstacle?

- *Sixth*, in *Last Visionary* Bertone claims that he was sent to Coimbra to interview Lucia in April 2000, just before publication of the vision and the commentary in *Message*, because the Pope "had need of a definitive interpretation on the part of the religious."[222] Yet, in the same book, Bertone asks us to believe that Sister Lucia viewed her very existence on earth as "the last *obstacle*" to the Secret's interpretation!

Having announced the latest version of Sister Lucia's "confession"—unmentioned during the previous seven years, and revealed only after her death—Bertone says it is a "plausible explanation, but I think that it cannot be completely satisfactory. [To say the least!] The arc of time from 1944 to 1960, probably, signified for her a remote horizon, a sufficiently wide temporal arc for the comprehension of the sense of the vision."[223]

Bertone apparently fails to recognize the monumental absurdity of this declaration: that Sister Lucia, the chosen seer of God, was so deprived of any sense of the vision God Himself had deigned to give her, and so abandoned by Our Lady of Fatima in the aftermath, that she had to construct her own "temporal arc" for assessing the vision's meaning, including the arbitrary selection of the year 1960 as the end point of this "arc." This, we are asked to believe, was the disordered state of affairs the Mother of God left behind for Cardinals Sodano and Bertone to tidy up with their "interpretation" of the Third Secret in 2000, some 83 years after the Fatima apparitions.

---

[222] Bertone, *Last Visionary*, p. 39.

[223] Ibid., p.92.

Why so much concern over 1960?

One might wonder why Cardinal Bertone would devote so much attention to discrediting Sister Lucia's testimony that the Virgin had linked disclosure of the Third Secret of Fatima to the year 1960. What does it matter to Bertone and his collaborators that Our Lady had temporally connected that particular year to the Secret? Why are they apparently so unwilling to let that connection stand? And why, as if to make it easier to convict Lucia of inventing the date, did they keep from the public the envelope (or, as it would turn out, *two* envelopes) confirming precisely that connection by an "express order of Our Lady"? There are two reasons that would explain these actions as anything other than pointless and irrational.

First, as I have already suggested, if the very Queen of Heaven had expressly linked the events prophesied in the Secret to the year 1960, this fact alone would destroy the "preventative interpretation," which demands that the vision of the "Bishop dressed in white" depict the 1981 assassination attempt, which has no connection whatever to 1960—or, for that matter, to what is plainly depicted in the vision itself: a Pope being executed by soldiers, followed by the killing of bishops, priests, religious and members of the laity on a hill outside a ruined city.

Second, the authors of *Message* know that Our Lady's directive to delay disclosure of the Secret until 1960 points unmistakably to the conclusion that the vision, which has no apparent connection to that year, must be only one part of the Third Secret, whose connection to 1960 (and events following) could be made clear *only by another text* wherein the Virgin explains the vision's historical context and meaning. I recall here once again Father Schweigl's revelation that the Third Secret "has *two* parts," one of which is "the logical continuation... of the words: 'In Portugal, the dogma of the Faith will always be preserved etc.'"[224]

So, the "express order of Our Lady" had to go. Only by eliminating the Virgin's temporal connection of the Third Secret to the year 1960 could Bertone succeed in re-linking the Secret to 1981, in keeping with his "interpretation" of the vision, while directing attention away from the fact that the vision standing alone cannot possibly be complete, as there is nothing about it

---

[224]*WTAF*, Vol. III, p. 710.

which would, to recall Sister Lucia's words to Cardinal Ottavinai, "be more clear" (*mais claro*) in 1960 as opposed to, say, 1950. Thus, to defend Bertone's account it would be essential to claim that Sister Lucia had invented the Virgin's directive. Conveniently enough, Lucia is unable to contradict Bertone today.

But Catholics must ask themselves: *Who is more likely to be guilty of an invention here: the chosen seer of God or a prelate intent on defending his personal position?* It is opportune to repeat Socci's observation about Bertone's unrecorded and selectively reported interviews of the seer: "The sensation that arises from this 'management' of the last witness of Fatima, this ecclesiastical self-contradiction, is of a certain brazenness, and of seasonal and colorful versions of the truth. Almost as if public opinion, the mass media and the faithful did not know how to reason critically and to catch contradictions and evasive answers."[225]

A new version of Lucia's "agreement"
with the "preventative interpretation"

But there is still more "management" of Sister Lucia to consider. Offering another posthumously revealed statement, in *Last Visionary* Bertone suggests, but does not actually say, that in the end Sister Lucia explicitly agreed with Cardinal Sodano's justly ridiculed interpretation of the vision of the executed bishop in white as a depiction of the failed attempt on the life of John Paul II. As Bertone now reports for the first time in this seven-year controversy: "I asked her [Lucia]… if she had connected the reference to the 'Bishop dressed in white' with the attack on John Paul II, if the 'Third Secret' regards not only the Popes, but in a quite particular way, Pope Wojtyla." De Carli asks Bertone what Sister Lucia answered, and Bertone replies: "That she had immediately connected, as soon as it came to her knowledge, the 'Third Secret' with the attempt to assassinate the Pope."[226]

Here, however, neither the alleged question nor the alleged answer is quoted, but only Bertone's characterization of what he claims was said seven years ago. And what Sister Lucia is alleged to have said—revealed only after her death—is a distinct "improvement" on the version that appeared in *Message*:

---

[225]*Fourth Secret*, p. 127.

[226]*Last Visionary*, p. 62.

As regards the passage about the Bishop dressed in white, that is, the Holy Father—as the children immediately realized during the "vision"—who is struck dead and falls to the ground, Sister Lucia was in full agreement with the Pope's claim that "it was a mother's hand that guided the bullet's path and in his throes the Pope halted at the threshold of death" (Pope John Paul II, *Meditation from the Policlinico Gemelli to the Italian Bishops*, 13 May 1994).[227]

In 2000 Bertone asserted in *Message* that Lucia told him she "was in full agreement" that the Virgin guided Ali Agca's bullet into a non-fatal trajectory, *not* that the bishop in white was in fact John Paul II. In *Messsage* it was *Bertone*, not Sister Lucia, who referred to the "passage about the Bishop dressed in white," whereas Lucia referred only to the trajectory of the bullet. By juxtaposing the two unconnected statements, Bertone had created an impression—and that is all it ever was—that Sister Lucia agreed with Cardinal Sodano's interpretation of the vision. But now, seven years later, Bertone suddenly announces that Sister Lucia "immediately connected, as soon as it came to her knowledge, the 'Third Secret' with the attempt to assassinate the Pope." Yet this news appears nowhere in Bertone's more contemporaneous account in *Message*, his communiqué concerning the alleged post-*Message* interview in November 2001, or in any other statement by Bertone before publication of *Last Visionary*.

But wait: After Bertone scoffs at "the Fatimists" for maintaining that a vision of the Pope being killed by soldiers signifies that a Pope is killed by soldiers, De Carli takes the bull by the horns and asks Bertone outright: "All of this you explained to Sister Lucia and she accepted the interpretation?" Bertone's answer: "Certainly, *even if not in these terms*. She insisted on the force of prayer and on the conviction, like granite, that the Hearts of Jesus and Mary cannot be deaf to our supplications."[228]

In other words: No! When asked a direct question, Bertone was forced to concede that Sister Lucia did *not* actually agree that the Pope in the vision is John Paul II. And if she did not agree, then she could not have believed that the Third Secret relates entirely to 20th Century events culminating in the 1981 assassination attempt.

---

[227]*Message*, p. 29.

[228]*Last Visionary*, p. 65.

Yet another disaster

I could go on for many more pages, but it is time to stop, for the point has been made: *Last Visionary* is another disaster for Bertone and the Vatican. What Bertone seriously maintains was "an operation of transparency"[229] in May-June 2000 is shown by his own book to be what Socci had already proven it to be: a cover-up. The worst case scenario has unfolded for the Vatican: Bertone joined issue with Antonio Socci but failed to answer him on the merits, thereby conceding Socci's case—and, still worse, embroiling himself in even more contradictions and implausible contentions than before. As Socci rightly concludes in his reply to *Last Visionary*, this is bad news not only for Bertone and the Vatican, but for the Catholic Church as a whole:

> For any author, being personally attacked by the Vatican Secretary of State without a scrap of evidence would be a coup. But for me it is a disaster, because I consider myself first of all a Catholic before a journalist. I would have preferred to be dead wrong and to be confuted. Or I hoped that the Holy See would finally decide to reveal the entire truth about the Third Secret of Fatima, by publishing—as Our Lady requested—the still concealed part. Otherwise, I would have preferred to be ignored, snubbed, boycotted. But the only mistake, the only thing to avoid, is exactly what Bertone did: presenting himself publicly, without answering anything and, rather, adding disastrous new revelations. For him and for the Vatican.[230]

Yet Bertone had refused to admit the slightest problem with the "official reconstruction" he so indignantly defended in *Last Visionary*, a reconstruction that "leaks water from every part." Instead, Bertone complains of those (such as Socci) who refuse to accept, as Bertone would have it, that "the prophecy is not open to the future, it is consigned to the past."[231] Bertone accuses his

---

[229]Ibid., p. 57.

[230]Socci, "Dear Cardinal Bertone: Who—Between You and Me—is Deliberately Lying?", loc. cit. (at http://www.fatima.org/news/newsviews/052907socci.asp); see also *The Fatima Crusader*, No. 86 (Summer 2007), pp. 35-42.

[231]*Last Visionary*, p. 79.

critics of "not wanting to surrender to the evidence"[232]—what evidence?—even as he tellingly ignores a mountain of evidence that negates the official account.

Papal praise for both Bertone and Socci?

I cannot conclude this chapter without noting that Bertone's book boasts a letter of "presentation" from Pope Benedict, in which His Holiness very conspicuously avoids even the smallest detail of the controversy. In this letter, as Socci notes, the Pope "confines himself to generalities" that have nothing to do with Socci's contentions. But, in a thickening of the plot, Socci reveals that *he* has a letter from the Pope "concerning my book, thanking me for 'the sentiments which have suggested it.'" Socci says that the Pope's words are "comforting before the insults and coarse accusations" Bertone has hurled at him.[233]

While Socci is understandably comforted by the Pope's letter, it raises enormously troubling questions: Why would the Pope thank Socci for a book that accuses the Vatican of a veritable conspiracy to conceal the very words of the Mother of God, while at the same time appearing to lend support to his Secretary of State in an attack on Socci, filled with evasions that only confirm the suspicions of the faithful? If what Bertone says is true and what Socci says is false, then why did the Pope's letter to Socci apparently contain not a word of rebuke or correction? And why has neither the Pope nor the Vatican issued *any* official criticism of *Fourth Secret*, which launches into the worldwide public forum the gravest possible accusations against Vatican officials, and even Popes John XXIII and Paul VI?

Here we must return to our provisional hypothesis. Perhaps, as Socci suggests, Pope Benedict himself labors under the mental reservation first put into play by John XXIII's private decision that he could not (or rather would not) determine the unpublished text to be authentic. Just as Pope John privately (but without any authoritative judgment) deemed the Secret inapplicable "to the years of my pontificate," evidently because it warns of an ecclesial and planetary catastrophe he regarded as inconceivable and at odds with his personal optimism, so also certain members of the

---

[232]Ibid.

[233]Socci, "Dear Cardinal Bertone...", loc. cit.

Vatican apparatus since then have privately concluded that the missing text is "not authentic" because it constitutes a profoundly negative heavenly commentary on the state of the Church and the world on their watch. To recall Socci's observation, Pope John's initial dismissal of the Secret "weighed like a boulder on his successors."[234] Benedict and the Vatican apparatus, then, would have inherited a veritable legacy of privately regarding the unpublished text as impossible to accept and thus, conveniently enough, consider the text to be the mere "thoughts" or "annotations" of Lucia rather than authentic words of the Blessed Virgin. From which premise it would be easy for them to rationalize the unpublished part of the Secret as "non-existent."

Yet, Pope Benedict knows that Socci is correct in his investigations into the existence of this "non-existent" text. Thus, the Pope, under the posited mental reservation—to which he had committed himself as Cardinal Ratzinger, co-author of *Message*—would be able to lend his name informally to Bertone's denials (which are not really denials) while also acknowledging the validity of Socci's work. And in the process of lending his name to Bertone's work while also expressing gratitude to Socci for *his* work, the Pope would not himself be admitting or denying anything, unlike Bertone and his collaborators. It is hard to see another explanation for the Pope's personal letter of appreciation to Socci regarding a book that indicts Vatican prelates for covering up part of the Third Secret of Fatima!

What a mystery there is before us! As Socci says, it is "the greatest mystery of the 20th century."[235] A mystery that has only intensified during the first seven years of this century. A mystery that, only a few weeks after the publication of Bertone's *Last Visionary*, could not have been more intense, as Bertone made an unprecedented television appearance in an effort to shore up the crumbling official account.

---

[234]Socci, *Fourth Secret*, p. 164.

[235]Ibid., p. 14.

Chapter 8

The Cover-up Collapses

Porta a Porta ("Door to Door"), on the *Rai Uno* channel, is one of Italy's most popular television shows. Hosted by Bruno Vespa, Italy's equivalent of Phil Donahue, the show has provided a forum for both Italian and world celebrities of all stripes. On May 31, 2007 the show would provide a forum for the Vatican Secretary of State in his continuing effort to answer Antonio Socci without really answering him. The publicity for the broadcast had promised that it would include the on-camera display of the "authentic" Third Secret. For this reason alone, millions of Italians were tuned in.

This was another unprecedented development in the Third Secret controversy: Seated in a gilded chair at the Apostolic Palace, the Vatican Secretary of State was appearing by remote feed on national television in response to the stunning, and thus far entirely conceded, accusations of a prominent lay Catholic who is himself a television celebrity. Surrounded by the trappings of authority, Bertone would not actually impose anything he was about to say on the faithful, nor would he have any message from the Pope concerning the controversy. Despite the trappings, he was appearing like any other guest involved in a controversial current event.

An open net, but no goal

That this episode of *Door to Door* would be anything but a fair debate between Socci and Bertone was evident from the very title of the program: "The Fourth Secret of Fatima Does Not Exist"—a direct attack on the title of Socci's book, projected in huge letters on the right-hand side of the stage set. That the program would not, in fact, be a debate at all was evident from Vespa's astounding failure to invite Socci to defend his own book. As Socci states in his comment on this travesty: "The title shot explicitly at my book [yet] Vespa called only Cardinal Bertone and not the undersigned, who is the target, but not invited.... Thus Cardinal Bertone was offered, on a silver platter, the possibility of attacking me without any contradiction…."[236]

Yet, as Socci observes, Bertone did on television precisely what he did in *Last Visionary*: "avoided all of my contentions: he did not give even one answer. On the contrary, he did more: He offered the proof that I am right." Not only did Bertone fail to kick a goal into the empty net on Socci's side of the field, he "scored the most sensational goal against himself: he demonstrated (involuntarily) that as a matter of fact the explosive part of the 'Third Secret of Fatima' exists yet is well hidden…. For this service to the truth (although indirect) it is necessary to thank the Cardinal. And to encourage him now to tell everything because—as the Gospel explains—'the truth will make you free.'" The Cardinal's seemingly smooth but actually disastrous performance on *Door to Door* showed that Socci is not boasting but, if anything, is understating the magnitude of what took place before millions of viewers.

A ludicrous opening

The debacle began with Bertone offering the ludicrous contention that "the two Popes [John XXIII and Paul VI] decided not to publish it because they did not hold so significant, probably, for the life of the Church, the publication of the Third Secret."[237] If the Secret was "not so significant" for the life of the Church, then why had the Vatican placed it "forever under absolute seal" in 1960, an action that only fueled speculation and worry about its "not so significant" contents? Why had Cardinal Ottaviani described it as "so delicate" that it could not be allowed to fall "even accidentally, into alien hands"? Why had Cardinal Ratzinger told us the Third Secret warns of "dangers threatening the faith and the life of the Christian and therefore of the world" and clearly explosive "details" that could cause "disequilibrium" in the Church? And why did John Paul II say that the Secret had not been revealed because it could be "badly interpreted," as he put it to Sister

---

[236]Antonio Socci, "Bertone in the 'Wasp's Nest' of the Polemics," *Libero*, June 2, 2007.

[237]All quotations from the telecast are based on an Italian transcript prepared for this author by Alessandro Fuligni, a professional translator in Rome, compared with my own repeated viewing of the Italian video, and my own translation of the key statements during the telecast. The nuances of the Italian language and even the loose oral syntax of the Cardinal's remarks have been fully respected.

Lucia during their conversation in 1982? Here again we see the blatantly self-contradictory theme of the "official reconstruction": the Secret that is "so delicate," but "not very significant"; the secret that is a "prophecy," but "adds nothing" to what we already know and depicts events we have already seen; the Secret that must not be allowed to lead to "sensationalism," but "reveals no great mystery."

A devastating slip of the tongue?

Moving on to the old saw that Fatima is just a "private revelation," Bertone made a very revealing, if not devastating, choice of words. He said that while we are dealing with a "private revelation," there are elements of the apparitions Sister Lucia would always remember, so that, regarding the Third Secret, "the perception of *the words* from 1917 to 1944 — because she wrote the Secret in 1944 — she therefore memorized and registered indelibly in her memory, this perception and this *interior locution*."

What *words*? What "interior *locution*"? Interior locution is a theological term for spoken *words* from an external source that register in the mind and are directed specifically to the hearer, as in the Second part of the Great Secret, in which Our Lady speaks directly to Lucia and Jacinta.[238] The only spoken words in the Third Secret vision are the angel's admonition: "Penance, Penance, Penance!," which is actually one word repeated three times, and this one word is *not* directed to the seers specifically; that is, the angel is not conversing with them, as Our Lady does in the second part of the Fatima message. Lucia hardly needed supernatural assistance to remember one word repeated thrice by the angel, whereas the rest of the vision consists entirely of Sister Lucia's *own* words describing what she saw, not words she heard from the Virgin.

Was this not an inadvertent disclosure by Bertone that the Third Secret involves a discourse by the Virgin whose precise verbal content was indelibly engraved in Sister Lucia's memory?

---

[238]Locution means "word, phrase, or expression." *American Heritage Dictionary.* An *interior* locution, in Catholic theological parlance, means literally a voice speaking internally and directly to the subject, *not* a mere vision the subject sees, such as the vision of the "bishop dressed in white."

Avoiding Socci's evidence

The show continued with a voiceover asking: "Has the text of the [Third] Secret of Fatima been published entirely? Or has a part of it been omitted?" In a slight departure from the usual demagoguery (no doubt thanks to Socci's breakthrough book) the voiceover acknowledges: "Such doubts seem to be advanced not only by the Lefebvrists and the Fatimists but also some [!] orthodox Catholics, who suspect that there has been concealed part of the Secret in which is announced internal struggle and apostasy in the Church. Antonio Socci has given voice to these doubts, through a complex investigation in a recently published book entitled *The Fourth Secret [of Fatima]*."

What followed in the voiceover was only a partial statement of Socci's thesis: that there is a missing text of the Secret that concerns a crisis of faith and apostasy in the Church, a battle between the devil and the Virgin as seen in St. John's Apocalypse; that John XXIII and Paul VI decided not to publish the text in order to "avoid furnishing arguments to the critics of Vatican II"; and that John Paul II and then Cardinal Ratzinger "arrived at a compromise" by which the essential contents of the text would be revealed indirectly in John Paul II's sermon at Fatima on May 13, 2000, which links the Message of Fatima to Chapter 12, verses 3 and 4 of the Apocalypse. This compromise, the voiceover concludes, would permit the Vatican "to say to the Church that the Third Secret was revealed, but without an integral publication that would have caused a great shock in the Christian community."

That was the extent of the program's presentation of what the voiceover itself described as Socci's "complex investigation." Missing from the voiceover's superficial summary, of course, were the following crucial matters, among others:

- the decisive testimony of Archbishop Capovilla (already conceded by Bertone's silence in *Last Visionary*) on the existence of two envelopes containing two different texts pertaining to the Secret—the "Capovilla envelope" and the "Bertone envelope";

- the evidence (including the testimony of Capovilla, Mother Pasqualina, Robert Serrou, and photographs in *Paris-Match* magazine) for the location of "the Capovilla envelope" in the papal apartment during the pontificates of Pius XII, John XXIII, Paul VI and probably John Paul II;

- the evidence that John Paul II, Paul VI and John XXIII each read two different texts of the Secret on two different dates, years apart, including a 1978 reading by John Paul II of a text that did not come from the Holy Office archives — *three years* before the Vatican claims the Pope first read the text of the vision of the bishop in white, brought to him from the archives;

- the testimony of papal emissary Father Schweigl that the Third Secret "has two parts: One part concerns the Pope. *The other part* is the logical continuation — though I may not say anything — of *the words*: 'In Portugal, the dogma of the Faith will always be preserved etc.'";

- the Vatican's suspicious and systematic refusal to address the mysterious "etc," which interrupts words of the Virgin that are logically the beginning of the Third Secret;

- the numerous references to the content of the Secret by the Vatican itself (in the 1960 press release), Father Schweigl, Cardinal Ratzinger, Father Alonso, Father Fuentes, Cardinal Ciappi, Cardinal Oddi, John Paul II and Sister Lucia, among others, which show beyond doubt that the Secret must contain *words of the Virgin* and disturbing "details" concerning a crisis in the Church, and consequently the world, of apocalyptic proportions, related to the Book of the Apocalypse pointedly cited by John Paul II in his sermon at Fatima in 2000.

If Bertone had any answers to these points, this was his grand opportunity to provide them without fear of contradiction on camera. Instead, he avoided every point. And so did Vespa and the other guests on the show: Marco Politi, the renowned Vaticanist and biographer of John Paul II; Giulio Andreotti, the former Prime Minister of Italy; Paola Rivetta, a Roman journalist; and a positively sycophantic Giuseppe De Carli, who was there to heap praise on the Cardinal and defend his own role in the Cardinal's attack on Socci in *Last Visionary*.

Pretending Capovilla does not exist

The first point Bertone had to address was the testimony of

Archbishop Capovilla, which the Cardinal had ducked in *Last Visionary*. Again, failure to address the testimony of this living eyewitness that there are two envelopes and two texts comprising the totality of the Third Secret would be to concede that the testimony is true. Not only did Bertone once again fail to address the testimony, there was an evident tacit agreement of all the participants in the show that they would act as if Archbishop Capovilla did not exist! The failure of any participant even to *mention* Capovilla during the 100-minute telecast was not only a concession to the truth of his testimony, but also evidence of a veritable conspiracy of silence designed to protect Bertone and the crumbling official account.

For this reason alone Bertone's appearance had only served to vindicate Socci and the "Fatimists" completely. But there was much more to come by way of vindication. Practically every statement by Bertone for the remainder of the broadcast represented a setback for the official account.

A curiously weak "denial"

Bertone's few comments concerning the voiceover that had selectively summarized Socci's case were strangely tentative and elusive. Concerning Socci's claim that the Vatican is holding back an explosive text of the words of the Virgin under the mental reservation that the Secret has "essentially" been revealed by John Paul II in his sermon at Fatima in 2000, Bertone issued no firm denial, but rather stated only "it seems to me a phantasmagorical reconstruction..."[239]

It *seems* to him? Wouldn't he know this for certain if it were really the case? Further on Bertone employed the phrase "a little problematic." *Problematic*? How about libelous and outrageous, if Bertone really thought Socci's grave public accusations were utterly false and without foundation?

"I don't want to enter into polemics," said Bertone. But entering into the polemic on the Third Secret is precisely what he had done by appearing on *Door to Door*. Yet Bertone continued to concede

---

[239]By his choice of word Bertone evidently meant to connote something surreal or unrealistic. "Phantasmagorical: fantastic sequence of haphazardly associative imagery, as seen in dreams or fever." *The American Heritage® Dictionary of the English Language*, Fourth Edition.

Socci's most telling points by failing and refusing to address them.

A curious new emphasis on an "authentic" text

Further commenting on the voiceover, Bertone introduced the idea of an "authentic" text of the Third Secret, as if there were an inauthentic text at issue. "John XXIII and Paul VI," said Bertone, "had read the text of the Secret, the *integral, authentic* text and the only text written by Sister Lucia..."—the only "authentic" text, that is. Leaving no doubt that he was signaling a new emphasis on an "integral" and "authentic" text, Bertone made this major revelation: "When John Paul II made the decision to publish the Secret—I was present at the time of the meeting—he decided to publish *all that actually existed in the archives of the Holy Office...*"

The choice of words was very careful: Bertone did not say simply that the Pope decided to publish the Third Secret. Qualifying his statement in a very strange way, he said only that the Pope decided to publish "all that actually existed *in the archives.*" Bertone knew full well of Socci's allegation and Capovilla's testimony that there is (or was) another text pertaining to the Secret in the papal apartment. Hence, in the context of the developing controversy, Bertone's sudden emphasis on "all that actually existed *in the archives*" clearly implied the existence of a document related to the Secret that was *not* in the archives: the text Capovilla and other witnesses had located in the papal apartment; the text that John Paul II evidently read in 1978 (contrary to the official account in *Message*); the text that Paul VI read in 1963 (contrary to the official account). What about *that* text? For now, at least, Bertone continued to observe a studious silence in the face of overwhelming evidence that the text in the papal apartment exists—evidence he could easily have refuted before millions of viewers if the evidence were false. His continued silence on this burning issue spoke volumes to viewers with any knowledge of the matter.

Bertone's new emphasis on an "authentic text" "that actually existed in the archives" could only have been a response to the enormous pressure Socci's book had brought to bear on the Vatican apparatus. Given Socci's wide publication of Archbishop Capovilla's testimony—testimony Bertone was not prepared to mention, much less deny on camera—it was understandable that Bertone was forced to retreat to the affirmation that the Vatican had produced an *authentic* text from the *archives*, as opposed to whatever text Capovilla was talking about. This subtle rhetorical retreat, however, was little short of a concession that Socci had discovered the truth.

As Socci points out in his post-broadcast reply to Bertone, the theme of the "authentic" text of the Third Secret—the text that "actually existed in the archives"—is a road to the truth that was first opened by the currently reigning Pope himself: "In the end, the Pope, in the letter published by Bertone, opens the road to the truth when he says that in 2000 there were published 'the authentic words of the third part of the Secret.' Suggesting clearly that there exist words of the secret held 'not authentic.' Courage then: publish everything. 'The truth will make you free.'"[240]

In the course of the broadcast Bertone also revealed inadvertently why he and his collaborators would view a text of the words of Our Lady concerning apostasy in the Church as "not authentic." Bertone seems to think that apostasy in the Church is impossible: "[T]here is an obstinacy in this expectation of a prophecy of apostasy in the Church. It seems to me a little problematical, this expectation, almost an aspiration that there exists a prophecy of the Madonna, Mother of the Church, she who extends her maternal hand over the life of the Church, the Auxiliatrix, who accompanies the Church on her road in time, that there exists a prophecy of apostasy in the Church."

But while Bertone might find it impossible to see how the Mother of God could warn of apostasy in the Church, that is exactly what she did in other recognized Marian apparitions, including Akita—which, to recall the former Cardinal Ratzinger's statement to the Philippine ambassador to the Vatican, is "essentially the same" as the Message of Fatima. Socci rightly observes that Fatima is part of a "tragic escalation" of Christian history as foretold in a "prophetic cycle" of Marian apparitions.[241] Moreover, as I have already noted, Scripture itself predicts precisely such an apostasy, which must take place before the Last Times.[242]

Thus, it is precisely *in* her capacity as Mother of the Church that Our Lady would give such a warning—and *has* given it before and after Fatima. But it seems that Bertone has *a priori* excluded

---

[240]"Bertone in the 'Wasp's Nest' of the Polemics," loc. cit.

[241]Socci, *Fourth Secret*, p. 67.

[242]*See, e.g.* "Let no man deceive you, for it [the Last Times] will not come unless the apostasy comes first, and the man of lawlessness is revealed, the son of perdition" (II Thess. 2:3).

The window of the jail where the Mayor of Ourem imprisoned the three children.

Arturo de Oliveira Santos, the Mayor of Ourem, who had the Fatima seers kidnapped and imprisoned in August 1917, threatening the children with execution if they did not reveal the Secret the Virgin Mary told them. They refused to give in to the threat and were finally released.

The front page of the anti-clerical paper *O Seculo*, a major Portuguese newspaper, reporting in great detail the Miracle of the Sun. Even this anti-Catholic newspaper was forced to acknowledge "how the sun danced in the sky at mid-day in Fatima."

A crowd of 70,000 people assembled in the rain-soaked Cova da Iria to witness the Miracle of the Sun on October 13, 1917.

The crowd is transfixed and terrified by the Miracle of the Sun.

Father Joaquin Alonso, the official Fatima archivist for sixteen years until his death, who had unrestricted access to Sister Lucia. Father Alonso stated that the Third Secret, which follows the words "In Portugal, the dogma of the Faith will always be preserved etc.", probably foretells "the crisis of the Faith in the Church and the negligence of the pastors themselves."

DOSSIER

La Madonna come difesa della fede

«Perché occorre tornare a Maria»

...A una delle quattro sezioni della Congregazione spetta l'occuparsi di apparizioni mariane. «Cardinal Ratzinger, lei ha letto il cosiddetto "terzo segreto di Fatima", quello inviato da suor Lucia a papa Giovanni che non volle rivelarlo e ordinò di depositarlo negli archivi?». «Sì, l'ho letto». «Perché non viene rivelato?». «Perché, stando al giudizio dei pontefici, non aggiunge nulla di diverso a quanto un cristiano deve sapere dalla rivelazione: una chiamata radicale alla conversione, l'assoluta serietà della storia, i pericoli che incombono sulla fede e la vita del cristiano e dunque del mondo. E poi, l'importanza dei Novissimi. Se non lo si pubblica – almeno per ora – è per evitare di far scambiare la profezia religiosa con il sensazionalismo. Ma i contenuti di quel "terzo segreto" corrispondono all'annuncio della Scrittura e sono ribaditi da molte altre apparizioni mariane, a cominciare da quella stessa di Fatima, nei suoi contenuti noti. Conversione, penitenza, sono condizioni essenziali alla salvezza»...

The Italian text of the 1984 interview of Cardinal Joseph Ratzinger in *Jesus* magazine, wherein the Cardinal revealed that the Third Secret speaks of "dangers threatening the Faith and the life of the Christian and therefore of the world" and that it also contains "what has been said again and again in other Marian apparitions." The vision published by the Vatican in June 2000 does not correspond to these revelations of the Cardinal.

The decision of His Holiness Pope John Paul II to make public the third part of the "secret" of Fatima brings to an end a period of history marked by tragic human lust for power and evil, yet pervaded by the merciful love of God and the watchful care of the Mother of Jesus and of the Church.

Photographically reproduced text from *The Message of Fatima* in which Cardinal Bertone declares: "The decision of His Holiness Pope John Paul II to make public the third part of the 'secret' of Fatima brings to an end a period of history marked by tragic human lust for power and evil ..." This ludicrous assertion prompted Catholics to ask why the Vatican had not ended the period of tragic human lust for power and evil by revealing the vision of "the Bishop dressed in white" back in 1960, when Our Lady wished it to be revealed.

Sister Lucia in her coffin. Only after Lucia was dead did Cardinal Bertone introduce new purported statements by Lucia he had never mentioned before and for which there is no independent record.

In this photograph from *Life* magazine in 1949, Bishop José da Silva displays the outer envelope that he prepared containing a text of the Third Secret before its transmission to the Vatican in 1957.

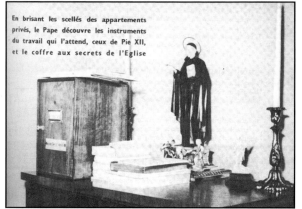

En brisant les scellés des appartements privés, le Pape découvre les instruments du travail qui l'attend, ceux de Pie XII, et le coffre aux secrets de l'Eglise

Photo from *Paris-Match* magazine in 1958, showing the wooden safe in the papal apartment of Pius XII in which a text of the Third Secret was safeguarded. The text in this safe was *not* the text in the Holy Office archives.

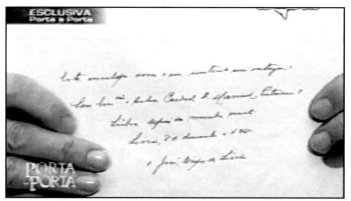

During his appearance on *Porta a Porta* on May 31, 2007, Cardinal Bertone displays on camera the outer envelope displayed by Bishop da Silva for *Life* magazine in 1949.

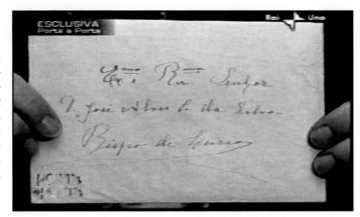

Bertone displays on camera an unsealed outer envelope for a text of the Secret, on which Lucia wrote the name of the Bishop of Leiria — the bishop in charge of Fatima.

Cardinal Bertone displaying the seal on the back of the outer envelope prepared by Bishop da Silva.

Cardinal Bertone's *Last Visionary of Fatima* purports to be an answer to Socci's book, but fails to address any of his points, while making new disclosures that are devastating to Bertone's claim that he has revealed the entire Third Secret.

The two Third Secret envelopes.

Top and middle: **The front and back (showing wax seals) of Third Secret envelope #1, bearing Sister Lucia's handwritten notation of the "express order of Our Lady" that this envelope can only be opened in 1960.**

Bottom: **Third Secret envelope #2, also bearing Sister Lucia's handwritten warning "by express order of Our Lady" that also this envelope can only be opened in 1960.**

Cardinal Bertone failed to mention the existence of these two envelopes, and the "express order of Our Lady" written on each, at any time from June 26, 2000 until the telecast of May 31, 2007. Bertone had always represented before May 31, 2007 that there was only one envelope and that Lucia had never received an order from the Blessed Virgin regarding 1960.

Bertone reveals on camera that the text of the vision of the Bishop in white was written on a *single folio* (sheet) of notebook paper, even though his own book, published weeks before, states that when he met with Lucia in April 2000 she authenticated *folios* (*sheets*) of paper. Thus, there is at least one missing sheet of paper pertaining to the Third Secret of Fatima.

A close-up of the single folio on which the text of the vision was written by Lucia showing that it is clearly not the "letter to the Bishop of Fatima" in which she had confided contents of the Secret. Bertone admitted on camera that the folio he displayed is *not* a letter. The missing letter would probably explain the meaning of the vision.

After appearing on television to display the text of the vision of "the Bishop dressed in white," Bertone attends an event headlined as "The whole truth and nothing but the truth"—an ironic commentary on the doubts surrounding his purported disclosure of the entire Third Secret.

L'OSSERVATORE ROMANO

EDITORIAL AND MANAGEMENT OFFICES VATICAN CITY
WEEKLY EDITION IN ENGLISH
FORTIETH YEAR
N. 35 (2068) - 29 August 2007
UNICUIQUE SUUM   NON PRAEVALEBUNT

Editorial Office: Via del Pellegrino, 00120 Vatican City, Europe - Telephone 39/06.698.99.390 - Telefax 39/06.698.83075 INTERNET: www.vatican.va/news_services/or/home_eng.html E-MAIL: ormet@ossrom.va

The whole truth and nothing but the truth

The 28th Meeting for Friendship Among Peoples recently concluded in Rimini, Italy. For the text of Secretary of State Cardinal Tarcisio Bertone's Opening Mass homily, see page 5.

Archbishop Loris F. Capovilla, the still-living secretary to Pope John XXIII. The Archbishop revealed to Solideo Paolini that there are two envelopes and two texts pertaining to the Third Secret of Fatima, and that one of the texts was kept in the papal apartment inside a larger envelope (the "Capovilla envelope") on which Capovilla had written the dictation of John XXIII ("I give no judgment") and the names of all those to whom Pope John had revealed its contents. Bertone has never produced this envelope, even though Capovilla confirmed its existence during a telecast in September 2007 arranged by Bertone himself.

Solideo Paolini, the young Italian intellectual to whom Archbishop Capovilla revealed the existence of two different texts and envelopes (the "Bertone envelope" and the "Capovilla envelope") comprising the entirety of the Third Secret.

Antonio Socci, the Italian intellectual, journalist and television host whose book *The Fourth Secret of Fatima* concludes: "[T]hat there is a part of the Secret not revealed and considered unspeakable *is certain*. And today—having decided to deny its existence—the Vatican runs the risk of exposing itself to very heavy pressure and black-mail."

The publication of *Fourth Secret* reignited the Third Secret controversy and forced the Vatican to attempt to answer Socci's overwhelming evidence demonstrating a cover-up of a text of the Third Secret.

such disturbing truths from the realm of possibility. Therefore, any text of the Fatima message in which the Mother of God warns of apostasy in the Church would not, according to this very mentality, be an "authentic" part of the Message—especially if the apostasy predicted in the conveniently "inauthentic" text is taking place on the watch of Bertone and his fellow Vatican prelates.

But now to the most explosive moment of the telecast: Bertone's own confirmation of the "two envelopes" theory.

The envelope, please!

A full 50 minutes into the 100-minute broadcast, host Vespa uttered the words the viewers had been waiting to hear: "Now, Eminence, the envelope." Over the next ten minutes Cardinal Bertone, while never appearing to miss a beat, would nullify the "official reconstruction" of the Third Secret, completely vindicate the claims of Socci and the "Fatimists," and confirm the well-founded suspicions of millions of Catholics around the world.

Our examination here must be meticulous, but the effort will be rewarding. First, we will examine the fatal problems for the official account posed by the envelopes Bertone produced during the telecast. Then we will consider how Bertone's revelations concerning the contents of the ultimate envelope, the text of the vision of the bishop in white, only provided further substantiation (if that were necessary) for the existence of a missing text of the words of the Virgin explaining the vision.

First, the envelopes. Recall that in June 1944 Bishop da Silva finally received from Sister Lucia a sealed envelope containing her handwritten text of the Secret, which she had written down six months earlier, and the Bishop placed Lucia's envelope in a larger envelope of his own, also sealed with wax, on which he wrote the following instruction:

> This envelope with its contents shall be entrusted to His Eminence Cardinal D. Manuel [Cerejeira], Patriarch of Lisbon, after my death.
>
> Leiria, December 8, 1945
> † Jose, Bishop of Leiria[243]

---

[243]Ibid: *Este envelope com o seu conteudo sera entregue a Sua Eminencia O Sr. D. Manuel, Patriarca de Lisboa, depois da minha morte.*
Leiria, 8 Dezembro de 1945
† Jose, Bispo de Leiria

Thus, the historical record shows that the "packaging" of the Secret involved an assemblage of two envelopes: the sealed envelope of Sister Lucia and the outer sealed envelope of the Bishop of Fatima. What Bertone produced during the telecast, however, was dramatically different; and the differences fatally contradicted the official account of the previous seven years, while revealing the long-hidden truth.

"First I will show you the orange envelope," Bertone began. This was not the envelope containing the purported Third Secret, but rather "the Italian translation of the Third Secret of Fatima, March, 6, 1967. We are in the times of Paul VI: this is the envelope that always accompanied the envelope, the older *authentic* envelope, that contains the original of the Third Secret..." (Notice the reference to an "authentic" envelope, as if some "inauthentic" envelope were in the picture.) Questions immediately abounded.

What was the point of showing an Italian translation of the purported Secret dated March 6, 1967? That translation did not even exist until two years after Paul VI had already read the Secret, according to the official account (on March 27, 1965), and nearly four years after Pope Paul read a text of the Secret (the one in the papal writing desk called "Barbarigo") on June 27, 1963, as confirmed by Archbishop Capovilla's testimony—which, of course, everyone on the show was in the process of ignoring. Further, this translation was dated nearly *eight* years after the date John XXIII had read a text of the Secret (August 17, 1959) with the aid of a translation by Monsignor Tavares.

Obviously, then, according to everyone's account, the 1967 translation was not prepared for the personal use of Paul VI or John XXIII in reading and understanding the Secret. Who, then, was it for? We can gather that Cardinal Ottaviani used it for the plenaria of Cardinals on the Third Secret, because the date of the translation is only days after his February 11, 1967 address to the Fifth Mariological Conference on the same subject, as we also saw in Chapter 3. It is reasonable to conclude, then, that the Third Secret plenaria, whose existence Bertone himself had just revealed during the telecast, must have been in March of 1967. Bertone himself appeared to confirm this on camera when he stated, in response to Vespa's question about whether there was a typewritten transcript of the Secret: "Yes, certainly, it was transcribed and then it was translated into Italian for the convenience of the cardinals of the plenaria." But Bertone neither opened the orange envelope nor discussed any further its contents. The transcript and translation have never been produced, although they would have been quite helpful to the Italian audience watching the show. This was another circumstance that could not fail to arouse suspicion.

Why, then, bother with the orange envelope at all? Perhaps this was a case of showing more envelopes than necessary to give the impression of "transparency." But the result was not favorable to the official account. Bertone held the orange envelope up to the camera long enough to allow one to see exactly what is written on it; and what one could see raised more questions.

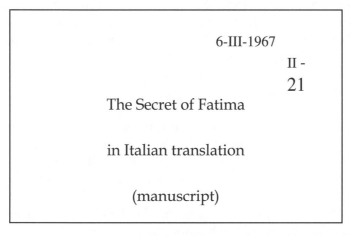

6-III-1967

II -
21

The Secret of Fatima

in Italian translation

(manuscript)

Figure 1

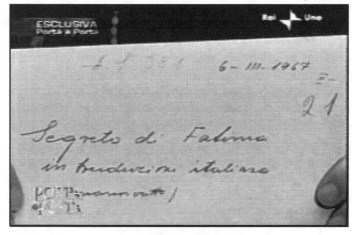

Figure 2

Why does the envelope state "manuscript" in parentheses? Is it not obvious that an Italian translation of "The Secret of Fatima" is a manuscript? Or is it not the case that inside is the Italian translation of the manuscript portion of the Third Secret, the four-page description of the vision of the bishop in white comprised of 62 lines? So that, in another envelope, one would find the Italian translation of the letter portion of the Secret: the "letter to the Bishop of Leiria," wherein Lucia said she had related the contents of the Secret; the one-page text of 25 lines testified to by Cardinal Ottaviani. Does not the Roman numeral "II" on the right-hand side of the envelope indicate that it is the second of two related documents? Admittedly, based on the evidence of the orange envelope alone, this is far from certain, but Bertone's following disclosures would only confirm the suspicion.

Not one envelope, but four!

"And we come to the white envelope," Bertone continued, as he put down the orange envelope and held up another. "This is the first envelope, very large, you can see, with the writing of Bishop Jose da Silva, Bishop of Leiria. An envelope written by the Bishop of Leiria that *contains the other envelopes* until [sic] the *authentic envelope* that contains the Third Secret." The other *envelopes*? Once again, the historical account of the "packaging" of the Third Secret in 1944 speaks of Sister Lucia's *lone envelope* inside the Bishop of Fatima's outer envelope—two envelopes in all. Now, suddenly, Bertone was introducing the notion of a series of nested envelopes—envelopes within envelopes. This alone caused fatal problems for the official account, as I will discuss presently. Notice also the second peculiar reference to "the *authentic* envelope," as if there were some inauthentic envelope floating around.

The envelope Bertone was now displaying—we shall call it Envelope #1—appeared to be the one in which Bishop da Silva had placed Lucia's own sealed envelope containing "the letter" to which Lucia, the Vatican itself (in the 1960 press release) and various witnesses already mentioned had referred; the letter in which Lucia confided to the Bishop contents of the Secret. Bishop da Silva allowed this envelope to be photographed for *Life* magazine, taking it out of his safe for that purpose.[244] The photographs

---

[244]*See The Whole Truth About Fatima (WTAF)*, Vol. III, p. 52 and photograph at photo insert section circa p. 426.

from the 1940s corresponded to the envelope Bertone was now showing on television, which contained the Bishop's handwritten instructions on how to handle the Secret in the event of his death. Envelope #1, as Bertone showed the camera, had been sealed with a large blob of wax, although its top edge had long since been slit open with a letter opener. So far, then, no apparent problem for the official account.

From this large outer envelope, however, Bertone withdrew a smaller, yellowed envelope "with the handwriting of Sister Lucia"—Envelope #2—on which was written the name and title of Bishop da Silva. Envelope #2, said Bertone, is "without seals because it was put inside the large sealed envelope" of Bishop da Silva (Envelope #1). Note well: Bertone had just admitted to millions of viewers that an envelope inside a larger, sealed envelope *does not require a seal of its own*. That admission would have a telling impact a few moments later.

> *Question:*
>
>> Why is it that neither *Message* nor *Last Visionary* nor any other statement by Bertone and his collaborators over the past seven years has mentioned the yellowed envelope with the Bishop of Fatima's name on it in Lucia's handwriting, which Bertone had just now produced?
>
> *Answer:*
>
>> It may well be the outer envelope for the text we have yet to see.

Next, Bertone withdrew from the unsealed yellowed envelope "a further envelope, *with seals*, and with the writing of Sister Lucia, the *authentic* writing of Sister Lucia, where she speaks of the year 1960..." This envelope—Envelope #3 in the series—had three wax seals on the back, but, like Envelope #1, its top edge had long ago been slit open. At this moment Bertone, for the first time ever, finally revealed that Sister Lucia had written on the outside of this envelope, which he displayed for the camera and read aloud, the following:

> "*By express order of Our Lady*, this envelope can only be opened in 1960 by the Cardinal Patriarch of Lisbon or the Bishop of Leiria."[245]

---

[245]"Por ordem expressa de Nossa Senhora este envelope só pode ser aberto em

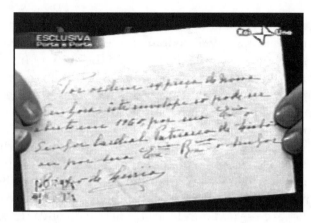

Figure 3

Not once in the years between June 26, 2000 and the telecast of May 31, 2007—not in his Introduction to *Message*, not in his entire book attempting to respond to Socci, not in his many interviews and other statements on the subject—had Bertone ever revealed that Sister Lucia had written on the envelope an *express order* of the Virgin that the Secret should be opened in 1960. All references to the precise wording of what can be called the "1960 order" from the Virgin had been carefully avoided on the occasions when Bertone was alleging (in *Message*, his book and elsewhere) that Sister Lucia "confessed" to him that she never had any communication with the Virgin concerning 1960. It was now apparent to millions, however, that all the while Bertone was telling the world Sister Lucia had never heard from the Virgin regarding 1960, he was in possession of an envelope stating *precisely the opposite* in Sister Lucia's own handwriting. Yet Bertone acted as if nothing were amiss, as if everyone had known all along that an "express order of Our Lady" concerning 1960 had been inscribed on Envelope #3. In a moment, however, Bertone would make an even more explosive disclosure.

The second Third Secret envelope appears!

After displaying Envelope #3, Bertone made the disclosure that, in and of itself, destroyed the credibility of the official account and confirmed once and for all the truth of the "two envelopes" theory (as if Capovilla's testimony were not enough). Bertone withdrew from Envelope #3, not the text of the vision which the official account claims is the whole of the Third Secret, but rather *Envelope*

1960, por Sua Ex.cia Rev.ma o Senhor Cardeal Patriarca de Lisboa ou por Sua Ex.cia Rev. ma o Senhor Bispo de Leiria."

#4—a second sealed envelope, on the outside of which was a *second, identically worded* "1960 order" in Sister Lucia's handwriting:

> "*By express order of Our Lady*, this envelope can only
> be opened in 1960 by the Cardinal Patriarch of Lisbon
> or the Bishop of Leiria."

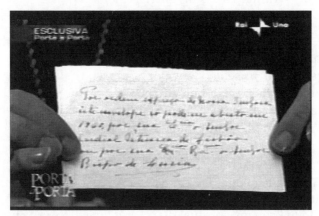

Figure 4

Figures 3 and 4 are the two Third Secret envelopes produced on camera by Cardinal Bertone during the telecast of May 31, 2007. Note the differing lineation of the Portuguese words "Nossa Senhora" (Our Lady) in the first two lines of each envelope.

Bertone had, incredibly, just blithely confirmed that there are indeed two envelopes pertaining to the Third Secret, each with three wax seals of its own and each with its own separate "1960 order"! An order Sister Lucia had twice recorded in her own handwriting, despite Bertone's now demonstrably false representation that Lucia "confessed" she had never received any such order from the Virgin. Yet neither *Message*, nor Bertone, nor anyone else at the Vatican had ever made reference to these identical twin envelopes before. On the contrary, in *Last Visionary*, published weeks before the telecast, Bertone told De Carli there was only *one* internal envelope referencing 1960, enclosed in an outer envelope that was *not Sister Lucia's*:

> De Carli: More than one envelope there were *two*.
> Bertone: Yes. An external with the note "Third part
> of the Secret" and an internal *of Sister Lucia* with the
> date '1960'.[246]

Moreover, Bertone's account in *Last Visionary* has Sister Lucia

---

[246]Bertone, *The Last Visionary of Fatima (Last Visionary)*, p. 49.

"authenticating" the text of the Secret by touching her sheets of paper and only one envelope during the purported April 27, 2000 meeting with him:

> Yes, these are my sheets of paper and the *envelope* is mine, they are the sheets of paper that I used and this is my writing. This is my *envelope*...[247]

Thus, during the alleged "authentication," only *one* "1960" envelope prepared by Sister Lucia was shown to her, not the two Bertone had just produced on camera. (This is not even to mention Lucia's yellowed, unsealed envelope, also not shown to her in 2000.) In fact, Sister Lucia herself reported that she had placed *a* text of the Secret into *a* sealed envelope, not *two* sealed envelopes. To recall Sister Lucia's earlier mentioned statements in 1943-44:

> *As reported by Father Alonso:*

> "They [Bishop da Silva and Canon Galamba] tell me either to write it in the notebooks in which I've been told to keep my spiritual diary, or if I wish, to write it on a sheet of paper, put it in *an envelope*, close it and seal it up."[248]

> *From Lucia's letter to Bishop da Silva of January 9, 1944:*

> "I have written what you [Bishop da Silva] asked me; God willed to try me a little, but finally, this was indeed His will: it [the Secret] is sealed in *an envelope* and it is in the notebooks..."[249]

Question: Why was the second sealed "1960" envelope not shown to Lucia during the "authentication" in 2000 if, as Bertone was now claiming, *the two belonged together, one inside the other*?

Answer: The two envelopes did not belong together, but were used for two different but related texts of the Third Secret.

Question: Why had Bertone never mentioned Sister Lucia's second "1960" envelope to the public between 2000 and the television appearance on May 31, 2007?

Answer: He did not want the public to know that there were two

---

[247]Ibid.

[248]Father Joaquin Alonso, *La verdad sobre el Secreto de Fátima*, p. 39; quoted in *WTAF*, Vol. III, p. 44.

[249]Father Alonso, *Fátima 50*, October 13, 1967, p. 11; quoted in *WTAF*, Vol. III, pp. 46-47.

such envelopes, because that would indicate that there were two parts to the Third Secret, each with its own "1960" envelope, one of which is (or was) lodged in the papal apartment and "officially" does not "exist."

Question: Where is the external envelope bearing the note "Third Part of the Secret?" that Bertone identifies in *Last Visionary* as the outer envelope that held only *one* sealed internal "1960" envelope from Sister Lucia?

Answer: Impossible to say. This is just another of the major inconsistencies that riddle Bertone's telling and retelling of the story. But it does indicate that Bertone withheld on camera an envelope he had earlier mentioned in print.

Here it must be noted that in his Introduction to *Message* back in 2000, Bertone provided a version of the facts that departs from what he says in both *Last Visionary* and the telecast in 2007: "Before giving the sealed *envelope* containing the third part of the 'secret' to the then Bishop of Leiria-Fatima, Sister Lucia wrote on the *outside envelope* that it could be opened only after 1960 [failing, as always, to mention the 'express order of Our Lady']..."

So, according to Bertone's 2000 version of the facts in *Message*, rather than the *three* envelopes Bertone had just showed during the 2007 telecast, Sister Lucia prepared only *two* envelopes for transmission of the Secret: *one* "outside" envelope bearing a "1960 order", apparently *not* sealed, and *one* internal sealed envelope, apparently *without* a "1960 order." Thus, according to *Message* in 2000, there was only *one*, not two, "1960" envelopes. And, as we have just seen, *Last Visionary* likewise refers to only *one* "1960" envelope. Yet on camera Bertone had just displayed *two* such envelopes for the first time in the seven-year-long controversy.

Follow the bouncing envelopes

Clearly, something is gravely amiss with Bertone's ever-changing account of the envelopes pertaining to the Third Secret. All told, Bertone has given three conflicting versions of the "packaging" of the Secret. Depending on which version one consults, according to Bertone: (a) Lucia prepared one, two or three envelopes for transmission of the Secret; (b) either one or two of the envelopes she prepared was sealed; and (c) the total number of envelopes involved in transmitting the Secret, including those not prepared by Lucia, is either three or four.

The only thing common to all three versions is that there is at least one outer envelope prepared by the Bishop of Fatima, bearing his handwritten instructions for disposition of the text inside upon his death. Otherwise, Bertone's three versions of the facts are irreconcilable. This can be seen from a study of Table 2.

TABLE 2
BERTONE'S THREE VERSIONS OF SISTER LUCIA'S
"PACKAGING" OF THE THIRD SECRET

June 26, 2000 (*Message*)[250]	May 10, 2007 (*Last Visionary*)[251]	May 31, 2007 (telecast)
Two envelopes from Sister Lucia:	*One* envelope from Sister Lucia, and another, not hers, of unknown origin:	*Three* envelopes from Sister Lucia:
(1) Lucia's *unsealed* outer envelope with "1960 order" (*never produced*); and	(1) An outer envelope, *not* Sister Lucia's, with the note "Third Part of the Secret" (*never produced*);	(1) Bishop da Silva's outer envelope;
		(2) Lucia's *first* inner envelope (the yellowed envelope), *unsealed*, bearing the Bishop's name in her writing, but no "1960 order" (not mentioned in *Message* or *Last Visionary*);
(2) Lucia's sealed inner envelope containing the Secret, but *no* "1960 order" (*never produced*).	(2) Lucia's sealed inner envelope, with "1960 order," containing the Secret.	(3) Lucia's *second* inner envelope, sealed, bearing a "1960 order" (not mentioned in *Message* or *Last Visionary*);
		(4) Lucia's *third* inner envelope, also sealed, bearing a "1960 order" (no mention in *Message* or *Last Visionary* of three inner envelopes, including two bearing a "1960 order").

---

[250]*The Message of Fatima*, p. 29.

[251]Bertone, *The Last Visionary of Fatima*, p. 49.

As the table makes clear, Bertone's differing accounts, when read together, point directly to the existence of one or more envelopes that have been withheld from the faithful. Despite the many inconsistencies in Bertone's story, however, there can be no doubt of what Bertone had just revealed on *Door to Door*: two sealed envelopes from Sister Lucia, each of which bear an express order from the Mother of God that its contents could only be revealed in 1960. The only logical explanation for the existence of these two envelopes is this: two texts, one for each envelope, just as Socci, the "Fatimists," millions of Catholics and, of course, Archbishop Capovilla maintain.

What all the envelopes mean

Seemingly oblivious to his own stupefying disclosure, Bertone was acting as if no one should think it the least bit strange that Sister Lucia would redundantly create two sealed envelopes inscribed with the identical "1960 order" for what he claimed was only *one* text, and then, just as redundantly, place one sealed envelope inside another sealed envelope. Of course, it would have been senseless for Lucia to prepare an envelope bearing an order that it could not be opened until 1960, only to place it inside *another* envelope bearing the same order. It would also have been rather strange for Lucia to place a sealed envelope *inside* another sealed envelope.

In fact, only moments before he revealed Lucia's two sealed inner envelopes—Envelopes #3 and #4—Bertone himself had been careful to note that Envelope #2—the yellowish outer envelope with Bishop da Silva's name on it in Lucia's handwriting—*had not been sealed* because *it was already inside sealed Envelope #1*, the outermost envelope inscribed with Bishop da Silva's instructions for disposition of the Secret upon his death. Following the very logic Bertone had indicated, if Lucia did not seal her yellowish envelope, Envelope #2, because it was placed inside the Bishop's sealed outer envelope, Envelope #1, then why would she have sealed Envelope #4, which allegedly was placed inside *sealed* Envelope #3?[252] On the other hand, if the yellowish envelope on which Lucia wrote the Bishop's name—again, Envelope #2—was intended to contain her

---

[252]While Bertone was careful to show that Envelope #1 *was* sealed, that Envelope #2 was *not* sealed, and that Envelope #3 *was* sealed, when it came to Envelope #4 he avoided pointing out the strangely redundant seal, which was revealed only inadvertently as Bertone handled the envelope on camera.

Envelopes #3 and #4, *then why was Envelope #2 not sealed* to protect the two inner envelopes on their way to the Bishop of Fatima?

From all of this one can only conclude that the four envelopes Bertone revealed on camera do not logically belong together in a single nested assemblage. Rather, it is obvious that the assemblage, logically arranged, would involve two outer envelopes each holding *one* of the two inner envelopes sealed with wax and bearing the "1960 order." *That, indeed, is precisely why Bertone's account in* Last Visionary *reflects only one inner envelope and one outer envelope.* Thus, in a possible arrangement of the envelopes produced on camera, Envelope #1, that of Bishop da Silva, would hold Envelope #3, the first sealed envelope bearing the "1960 order", while Envelope #2, Lucia's yellowish unsealed envelope, would hold Envelope #4, the second envelope bearing a "1960 order."

Still more inconsistencies

Add to these inconsistencies the facts revealed by the contemporaneous written account of Archbishop Capovilla, already discussed, that Pope John XXIII directed him to write on the "envelope" (*plico*) or "wrapping" (*involucro*) containing the Secret the phrase "I give no judgment," along with Capovilla's signature and the names of all those to whom Pope John deemed it necessary to disclose the Secret. Assuming this "wrapping" was some outer envelope and not the Third Secret envelope proper, Bertone failed to produce it during the telecast.

Question: Where is this outer envelope?

Question: Is it the same outer envelope Bertone mentioned in *Last Visionary* but has never produced, the envelope bearing the note "Third Part of the Secret"?

Question: Is this envelope not indeed the outer envelope for a text of the Secret that has not yet been produced?

In any event, there is a missing envelope whose existence Bertone himself revealed in *Last Visionary*. This is yet another disclosure that undermines the official account.

The official account demolished

The confusion concerning the envelopes is Bertone's to unravel, and the faithful have a right to hear his attempt at an explanation. But this much is certain: the official account has been demolished.

The never-before-mentioned "extra" sealed envelope with the "1960 order" could only have been prepared for a separate and distinct portion of the Secret that has not yet been produced. Once again, we know this because even according to Bertone's account before the May 31st telecast—in *Message* and in *Last Visionary*—there was *no second sealed envelope* from Sister Lucia containing a "1960 order," or indeed any other sealed envelope from her as part of the "packaging" of the text of the vision.

Therefore, the second sealed envelope produced during the telecast could only have been meant for another text—the very text that found its way to the papal apartment. No other explanation makes sense, especially in view of Bertone's and the Vatican's otherwise inexplicable failure to mention the "extra" envelope *at any time during the past seven years.*

Possible objections

In concluding our discussion of this point, it is necessary to consider certain objections that will present themselves to the thoughtful reader:

Objection: Why would Bertone display the second sealed envelope on camera and demolish his and the Vatican's entire position, if that envelope really were a "smoking gun" that proves the existence of a second and related text of the Secret? Why would Bertone not simply hide the envelope and never produce it?

Answer: Bearing in mind that Bertone had indeed *never mentioned the second envelope* in the seven years preceding the telecast of May 31, 2007, only to introduce it *after* its existence was revealed by Capovilla, the answer to the objection seems clear: The existence of the two envelopes had been confirmed by an unimpeachable living eyewitness, Archbishop Capovilla, who was no less than the personal secretary of Pope John XXIII. Other evidence, no matter how compelling, could safely be ignored as the product of feverish "Fatimists," but not Capovilla's testimony. Since the Vatican could not refute or even comment on Capovilla's testimony because it is true (the only reasonable explanation for the wall of silence concerning Capovilla), more and more members of the faithful, following Socci's lead, would become convinced that there *are* two envelopes, one of which the Vatican is hiding from the world. The "two envelopes" problem, then, would never go away so long as the Vatican continued to deny the existence of two envelopes while failing to answer Capovilla. There could be only one way out: *suddenly introduce the second envelope as if it had always been there,* but merely as one of two envelopes meant to shelter a single text—the text of the vision.

Only this would explain why, even a few weeks before the telecast, Bertone was still claiming in *Last Visionary* that (a) there was only *one* sealed inner envelope bearing a "1960 order;" (b) Sister Lucia had identified only *one* inner envelope as hers; and (c) the only outer envelope (aside from Bishop da Silva's, which is not in dispute) was not Sister Lucia's envelope, but one marked "Third Part of the Secret"—which, again, Bertone has never produced.

It is reasonable to conclude, therefore, that sometime between the publication of *Last Visionary* and the telecast it was decided to reveal the second "1960" envelope as a mere "extra" envelope for the text of the vision. Hence, only a few weeks after negating the existence of a second "1960" envelope in his own book, Bertone suddenly introduced it on television for the first time in the history of the controversy.

This would also explain why Bertone was at pains to describe Envelope #4, the innermost envelope, as "the *authentic* envelope that contains the Third Secret." Was there some *inauthentic* envelope in this regard? Were the other envelopes in the four-part assemblage he had just disclosed, including the never-before-mentioned "extra" envelope bearing the "1960 order," *not* "authentic"?

Objection: What of the fact that the "extra" envelope bearing the "1960 order" has not appeared in any account of the chain of custody of the Third Secret written over the past 60 years?

Answer: Since we know the "extra" envelope exists, as Bertone himself showed us, the failure of any historical account to record its existence *must be the result of it having taken a more hidden path to (and within) the Vatican than the one taken by the envelope holding the text of the vision*—a more hidden path that ended in the papal apartment with no record in the Holy Office archives.

In any case, Archbishop Capovilla, in testimony Bertone would not answer or even mention, has confirmed the existence of not only two different envelopes, but two different *texts* comprising the same Third Secret. So did Father Schweigl, almost as directly, with his revelation that the Third Secret "has *two parts*: One part concerns the Pope. The other part is the logical continuation... of the words: 'In Portugal, the dogma of the Faith will always be preserved etc.'"[253] And no one has disputed Father Schweigl's testimony either.

An explosive "folio"

We have examined sufficiently the fatal problems for the official account posed by the envelopes Bertone produced on the telecast. Let us now consider the contents of the last envelope in the series: Envelope #4, the so-called *"authentic* envelope that contains the Third Secret." Notice, again, the curious description of this last envelope as "authentic," as if there were some inauthentic envelope vying for our attention.

As was to be expected from the official account, Bertone withdrew from Envelope #4 the text of the vision of the bishop in white. But here too there was a stunning new revelation: the text of the vision was not written on four *separate* sheets of paper, as *Message* had made it appear in the photo-reproduction provided in 2000,[254] but rather on four *attached* pages which clearly appeared to be a folio *of ruled notebook paper.* Here it must be noted that in English usage "folio" means "a *sheet of paper* folded once to make two leaves, or four pages, of a book or manuscript."[255] Likewise, the Italian word "foglio" means a "leaf, sheet" or "clean, loose *sheet of paper."*[256] Hence the English "folio" and the Italian "foglio" are equivalent— both mean "sheet of paper." Bear this in mind as we continue.

Bertone identified the notebook folio on camera as follows: "the folio (sheet of paper)... the only *authentic* folio, the only folio in which is contained the Third Secret" ("il foglio... l'unico foglio *autentico,* l'unico foglio in cui è contenuto il terzo segreto").[257] Again we must ask: Is there an *inauthentic* folio somewhere of which Bertone has knowledge? A sheet of paper, perhaps, that did not "actually exist in the archives of the Holy Office," but which might exist (or have existed) in the papal apartment? Why else this

---

[253]*WTAF,* Vol. III, p. 710.

[254]*See The Message of Fatima,* pp. 17-20, showing what appear to be four separate sheets of ruled paper, without explaining that they were all part of one notebook folio.

[255]*Random House Unabridged Dictionary,* © Random House, Inc., 2006.

[256]*Oxford Paravia Concise English-Italian, Italian-English Dictionary* (Oxford, England: Oxford University Press, 2002).

[257]Again, the Italian "foglio" means a two-sided sheet of paper, not a page in a book or manuscript.

harping on the "only *authentic*" folio?[258]

As the camera revealed, then, the text of the vision had been written on a folio of four ruled notebook-style pages, front and back. And, curiously, the four-page folio had been folded in half yet again in order to make it small enough to fit into Envelope #4. Why would Sister Lucia have done that, as opposed to using a larger envelope that would have allowed her to send the document flat? Bertone himself had just demonstrated that Sister Lucia had access to larger envelopes, two of which were part of his assemblage!

Neither *Message*, nor Bertone, nor any other Vatican official had ever before revealed that the vision was written on four *contiguous* pages that clearly comprised a single folio of ruled notebook paper. On the contrary, in *Last Visionary*, published a few weeks before his television appearance, Bertone points the reader away from this fact. Let us recall once again what Sister Lucia said, according to *Last Visionary*, during the purported "authentication" meeting in April 2000:

> "Yes, these are my *sheets* of paper (fogli)... *they* are the *sheets of paper (fogli)* that I used...."[259]

Thus, according to Bertone's own prior account of the "authentication" of the Secret in *Last Visionary*, the Third Secret was written on *sheets* of paper—*not* what Bertone called "the only authentic *sheet* of paper" (*l'unico foglio autentico*) during the telecast weeks later. Two conclusions are suggested by this major inconsistency, both destructive of the official account:

First, Sister Lucia did indeed refer to "my sheets of paper" during the April 2000 "authentication" meeting with Bertone, in which case *there is at least one missing sheet of paper* pertaining to the Third Secret, given that Bertone represented on television in May 2007 that what he was showing the camera was "the only authentic *sheet* of paper (*l'unico foglio autentico*), the only *sheet* of paper in which is contained the Third Secret."[260] This would mean

---

[258]During the telecast Bertone revealed that Lucia had to use a *magnifying glass* to read her own handwriting in order to "authenticate" it: "Then, looking carefully with a magnifying glass, because she was a little myopic [a little?], first with her eyeglasses and then with the magnifying glass..."

[259]Bertone, *Last Visionary*, p. 49.

[260]Compare the Italian text of Sister Lucia's alleged statement in *Last Visionary* with Bertone's statement on the telecast:
> Lucia in *Last Visionary*: "sono i miei fogli... sono i fogli che ho usato" (p. 49).
> Bertone on TV: "il *foglio*... l'unico *foglio* autentico... l'unico *foglio* in cui è contenuto il terzo segreto."

that sometime after Lucia had "authenticated" *two or more sheets of paper* as those she had used to write down the Third Secret, it was decided to reveal only *one* of them—the text of the vision on the notebook-style folio—while withholding the other, which contains the missing words of the Virgin.

Second, in the alternative, Sister Lucia did *not* speak of "sheets of paper" (*fogli*) as reported in *Last Visionary,* but only one sheet (*foglio*). In that case Bertone's account in *Last Visionary* is unreliable—or his account is calculated to give the false impression that the vision was written on four separate sheets that did *not* comprise a folio of ruled notebook paper.

But why would Bertone want to give the impression that the vision was not written on four contiguous sides of one notebook folio, but rather on four separate sheets? What difference does it make? Here we must reexamine under a different aspect Sister Lucia's revealing statements in 1943-44, quoted above:

> *As reported by Father Alonso*:

> "They [Bishop da Silva and Canon Galamba] tell me either to write it in *the notebooks* in which I've been told to keep my spiritual diary, or if I wish, to write it *on a sheet of paper*, put it in an envelope, close it and seal it up."[261]

> *From Lucia's letter to Bishop da Silva of January 9, 1944*:

> "I have written what you [Bishop da Silva] asked me; God willed to try me a little, but finally, this was indeed His will: it [the Secret] is sealed in an envelope *and* it is in *the notebooks*..."[262]

That is, Sister Lucia herself revealed that she had written down the Secret *both* on a *sheet* of paper that she placed in a sealed envelope *and* in her diary, which was in *notebook* form. That is, she exercised *both* of the options given to her. What Bertone displayed on camera is what came from the *notebook,* whereas the sheet of paper in the sealed envelope—Lucia's letter to the Bishop of

---

[261]Father Joaquin Alonso, *La verdad sobre el Secreto de Fátima*, p. 39; quoted in *WTAF*, Vol. III, p. 44.

[262]Father Alonso, *Fátima 50*, October 13, 1967, p. 11; quoted in *WTAF*, Vol. III, pp. 46-47.

Fatima—has *not* been produced.

Thus, Bertone would have a good reason not to reveal that the text of the vision he displayed on camera is from a notebook: If he revealed that the text was from Lucia's *notebook*, this would call attention to the fact Lucia had also written a *letter* to the Bishop of Fatima, which was not being produced. After all, one does not write letters to bishops in a notebook! This might explain why Bertone's account in *Last Visionary* gives the impression that the vision was written, not in a notebook, but on four separate sheets of writing paper.

Objection: In January 1944 Sister Lucia referred to only one sealed envelope, and did not say that what was in her notebooks was in a second sealed envelope, so how can it be maintained that there are two sealed envelopes pertaining to the Third Secret?

Answer: Cardinal Bertone *showed* us two sealed envelopes! And, since Lucia's letter to Bishop da Silva on January 9, 1944 states that contents of the Secret were "sealed in *an* envelope"—not *two* envelopes, one inside the other, as Bertone was now claiming—it can only be the case that Sister Lucia later decided to place the folio from her diary into a *separate* sealed envelope bearing its own "1960 order." Since Lucia did not finally relinquish the Third Secret documents to Bishop Gurza for delivery to Bishop da Silva until six months after her January 9th letter to da Silva—again, Gurza received the documents from Lucia on June 17, 1944—her decision to use the second sealed envelope would not have been reflected in the January 9th letter and thus would be outside the historical record. Hence, what Bertone displayed during the telecast was the folio from Sister Lucia's diary, which had its own separate "1960" envelope. By process of elimination, whatever was in the sealed envelope referred to in the letter of January 9, 1944 has not been produced.

That Bertone had shown us a folio from Lucia's notebook/ diary was apparent to host Vespa. After a commercial break, Vespa stated that Bertone had just shown "an extraordinary document, a letter, a document, *a folio from a diary*" and then asked Bertone: "To whom is it addressed? Is it *a kind of diary*?" Bertone's revealing reply was: "It is a declaration. It is *not addressed to anybody...*" Hence, by Bertone's own admission, the text of the vision could not possibly be the "letter to Bishop da Silva" that she sent inside of *one* sealed envelope. But it could be, and very probably is, what Vespa perceived it to be and what it so plainly appears to be: "a folio from a diary" that Sister Lucia had kept in notebook form and which she ultimately transmitted in *another* sealed envelope—a sealed envelope that would otherwise be redundant.

On the other hand, if it is objected that the document Bertone displayed does not at all appear to be a folio from a diary and that the "Fatimists" are merely fitting the evidence to their preconceived conclusions, then one must answer the question why Vespa *twice* suggested that Bertone had shown a folio from a diary? Did Vespa have information from Bertone to which the viewers were not privy? Why did Vespa describe the document as *both* a letter *and* a folio from a diary and then ask Bertone if it was "a kind of diary"? Was he somehow aware that the Secret involved *both* a letter and a diary entry? Bertone, as he had with so many other issues, conceded this one by evading the question, stating that the document was "a declaration" addressed to no one, but failing to deny that it was from Lucia's diary. There is no reason to doubt that Vespa's perception was well founded, especially since Lucia herself wrote of committing the secret to "the *notebooks* in which I've been told to keep my spiritual *diary...*"

Another major disclosure

The disclosure of the notebook folio, which the official account had presented as four separate sheets of paper for the past seven years, only added to the mountain of discrepancies and conceded testimony demonstrating the existence of a missing text of the Secret. But the debacle did not end with Bertone's presentation of the envelopes and their contents. In another of his many revealing but inadvertent disclosures, Bertone—stressing yet again the new theme of the "authentic text" that "actually existed in the archives"—insisted that "there was only this folio *in the archive of the Holy Office* in 1957, when by order of Our Lady and the Bishop of Leiria, Sister Lucia accepted that the Secret be brought to Rome *from the archives of the Patriarch of Lisbon....*"

The archives of the Patriarch of Lisbon? But the document that concerns us *was never in the archives of the Patriarch of Lisbon*. It is an undeniable historical fact that in 1957 copies of all Lucia's writings and the envelope containing the Secret were personally delivered by auxiliary Bishop Venancio *directly from the chancery in Leiria* to the papal nuncio in Lisbon, Msgr. Cento, who took the documents directly to Rome.[263] It was just before departing to make that very delivery that Venancio held Bishop da Silva's sealed outer envelope under the light to see Sister Lucia's envelope and the one-page text inside.

So, it would appear that the "authentic text" in the archives of the Patriarch of Lisbon is the same "authentic text" that "actually existed in the Holy Office archives" in 2000. But it is not the text we are looking for, which evidently took a different path to Rome: a path that went from Bishop da Silva to Monsignor Cento, the papal nuncio, and by him to the papal apartment of Pius XII—as Bertone has tacitly admitted by his resounding silence concerning the dispositive testimony of Archbishop Capovilla (not to mention to all the other witnesses who place a text of the Secret in the papal apartment).

No answer to Ottaviani!

By this point in the broadcast Bertone himself had demolished the official account. But the debacle was not entirely finished. Once the four-page folio of 62 lines had been presented on camera, Bertone received the one mild challenge he encountered during the 100-minute telecast. It concerned Cardinal Ottaviani's testimony that the Secret is a one-page document comprising 25 lines of handwritten text. In response to the challenge, Bertone, despite his calm appearance, floundered badly.

Marco Politi, while assuring Bertone that "we are in agreement with Cardinal Bertone that there do not exist other documents" (what better proof that the fix was in?), did remark that

> However there are oddities, and also in the book by De Carli (*Last Visionary*). Cardinal Ottaviani said that, as far as the contents, it was 25 lines, while we have here a text of 62 lines. Papa Wojtyla, to a group of German intellectuals, hinted that the Secret of Fatima speaks of great trials that *await* Christianity... that it treats of huge catastrophes, of cataclysms, while instead, reading the text of the vision, it depicts persecutions of the Church that appear to have already passed [according to Bertone and the official account].

In response, Bertone ignored Politi's pointed reference to John

---

[263]*The Whole Truth About Fatima*, Vol. III, pp. 480-481.

Paul II's reported remarks at Fulda (in 1980) on the apocalyptic elements of the Secret, thus conceding the point (as he had so many others). Concerning Cardinal Ottaviani's testimony, Bertone not only failed to issue any firm denial, but instead offered an amazing affirmation which only substantiated Politi's objection: "To me it was a little amazing that Cardinal Ottaviani *had said categorically a sheet of 25 lines...*"

That is, Bertone himself had just acknowledged before millions of witnesses Cardinal Ottaviani's "categorical" testimony undermining the official account. Yet Bertone found this testimony only a *little* amazing? Why would it not be *hugely* amazing, even a cause for panic, requiring immediate public denials and corrections, given Bertone's "official" position that no such text has ever existed? Why would he not hasten to say, with all due respect to the late Cardinal, that Ottaviani could not possibly have been correct? Instead, Bertone offered another telltale affirmation about why he found the Cardinal's testimony "a little" amazing: "...because the Cardinal, then Pro-Prefect of the Congregation of the Holy Office, had in his hand physically and different times the Third Secret, also showing it himself to the plenaria of Cardinals..." But that is precisely why Ottaviani *knew what he was talking about* when he spoke "categorically" of a text of one sheet comprising 25 lines!

Bertone, on the other hand, was not an eyewitness to Ottaviani's handling of the Third Secret back in the 1960s. At that time, as a young priest, Bertone was at the Pontifical Salesian University of Rome, an association that he continued in various academic posts until 1991, when he was made Archbishop of Vercelli. Bertone could not, therefore, tell us of his own knowledge what document or documents Ottaviani had in his hands on various occasions, including the aforesaid "plenaria" (full assembly) of cardinals regarding the Secret—a newly revealed indication of its great importance and delicacy.[264] Nor did Bertone cite the testimony of any actual eyewitness to rebut Ottaviani. Quite the contrary, his next statement revealed that *he knew nothing and no one that could contradict Ottaviani's decisive evidence.* Examine carefully these

---

[264]Bertone was a faculty member, dean and then rector of the Salesian University in Rome until 1991, when Pope John Paul II appointed him Archbishop of Vercelli. In June 1995 "the same pope asked him to return to Rome to be Secretary of the Congregation for the Doctrine of the Faith, whose Prefect was Cardinal Ratzinger." See "Cardinal Bertone prefers activity to study," Zenit, at permalink: http://www.zenit. org/article-16979?1=english. Bertone was not involved in the meanderings of the Third Secret documents in the hands of Cardinal Ottaviani and others in the 1960s.

words from the broadcast:

> ... *it may be* that he had given a rather hasty summary
> [of the Secret], that he was mistaken.[265] I don't *believe*
> that this element is *so convincing* as to say that there
> exists a sheet of paper (*foglio*) of 25 lines respecting
> the other of around 60 lines.

Cardinal Bertone doesn't *believe* Cardinal Ottaviani's testimony
is an "element" that is "so convincing" as to say there is a missing
text of 25 lines respecting the published text of 62 lines? *Maybe*
Ottaviani gave a hasty summary of the Secret's contents? *Maybe*
he was mistaken? Are these the words of a man who is certain
Ottaviani's "categorical" statement had to be wrong? Or, rather, are
they the words of a man who has adopted the rhetorical posture of
appearing to be perplexed by something he knows or has reason
to suspect is true?

Consider that, as Vatican Secretary of State, Bertone had ready
access to witnesses or documentation that could have refuted
Ottaviani's statement conclusively, if such witnesses or documents
existed. For example, at any time between 2000 and 2007 Bertone
could have inquired of any of the still-living cardinals who
attended the Third Secret plenaria presided over by Ottaviani; or,
if not the cardinals, then any still-living members of their staffs. It
would have been a simple matter to ask these witnesses if they had
ever seen in Ottaviani's hands or heard him describe a one-page
document of 25 lines pertaining to the Secret, or if they had seen
such a document themselves. Bertone could also have consulted
the minutes of the plenaria and the personal papers of Ottaviani
himself. Or he could have made inquiry of any number of other
witnesses in the Vatican, from the Pope on down, as to whether
they or anyone had ever seen or heard of the text whose existence
Ottaviani had "categorically" affirmed.

Yet, Bertone had appeared on national television totally
unprepared to refute Ottaviani's "categorical" statement
undermining the official account. Why? Because *there is no
refutation*. Cardinal Ottaviani was telling the truth.

---

[265]In the Italian: "*può darsi che* abbia fatto un calcolo sommario, che sia sbagliata..."
The phrase "può darsi che" means "it may be," "perhaps" or "perchance." See *Oxford
Paravia Concise English-Italian, Italian-English Dictionary* (Oxford, England: Oxford
University Press, 2002).

Some fishy arithmetic

After a four-minute commercial break to think this problem over, however, Bertone offered an improvised "attempt at an explanation" which demonstrated that he was prepared to "fudge" the facts in order to save the official account from demolition. Bertone suggested that Cardinal Ottaviani had somehow counted the lines of text on only *two* pages of the four-page folio:

> An attempt at an explanation of the affirmation of Cardinal Ottaviani. Ottaviani, perhaps—one could find, if we calculate in the first page of the folio [*foglio* in Italian] first and last—maybe Cardinal Ottaviani held it in his hand like this [holding up one side of the folio on which the first and fourth pages appear], and one sees that there are, there would be in itself 16 lines [indicating the fourth page] plus 9 [indicating the first page]—remember that there are there 9 written lines on the first page. Therefore, 16 plus 9 are 25, without counting the following pages. This could be an explanation.

Could be? If this was the best the Cardinal could do to answer Ottaviani, then clearly he had no answer—not even this implausible one—because the total of the lines of text on the first and fourth pages of the folio is 32, not 25: 13 on the first page and 19 on the fourth; or 30 lines in total if one excludes the "J.M.J" on the first page and the dateline at the end of the fourth page.

Now, during the preceding four-minute break Bertone had ample time to count the lines on the two pages (I did this myself in less than 30 seconds), in which case he would have discovered immediately that his "explanation" was untenable. Thus, either the Cardinal counted the number of lines and deliberately misstated it on camera, or he never bothered to count them and simply ventured an imprecise guess as if it were a determined fact. In either case, the Cardinal showed himself to be a smooth operator willing to mislead millions of people if it served his purpose. Further, the idea that Cardinal Ottaviani could have overlooked two of the vision's four pages was so ridiculous as to indicate that Bertone knew quite well Ottaviani was telling the truth and that only some hasty contrivance on camera could obscure this fact.

In sum, Bertone addressed the crucial matter of Ottaviani's testimony—it was far more than the "oddity" Politi had called it—as if he were in no better position to know the truth than the members of the viewing audience, even though he had access to anything and everything that could have refuted Ottaviani's testimony. Yet all Bertone had provided was a patently misleading "attempt at an explanation."

Only four conclusions are possible concerning Bertone's affirmations, all of them unfavorable to the official account: (1) Bertone does not wish to look into the truth of Ottaviani's testimony because he does not wish to learn that it *is* true, so that he can continue to pretend it is some mysterious "element" that "amazes" him "a little," but is not "so convincing"; (2) Bertone knows very well that Cardinal Ottaviani spoke the truth and that the document he "categorically" identified does indeed exist, in which case Bertone is simply concealing the fact dishonestly; (3) under the posited "broad mental reservation," the document Ottaviani identified, being in Bertone's estimation "inauthentic" (since it speaks of apostasy in the Church, which Bertone excludes *a priori*) does not "exist"; or (4) under another mental reservation, the text at issue does not "exist" because it was not in the Holy Office archives, but only in the papal apartment, of which latter text Bertone will not admit to any knowledge until (as we will see in Chapter 10) September 2007.

March of the multiple versions

Having flubbed the rather meek challenge from Politi, Bertone used the closing minutes of the telecast to continue his attempt to debunk the "express order of Our Lady" that the Secret could only be revealed in 1960. After De Carli pointed out that the connection of the Third Secret to the year 1960 "can present some problems" for the "interpretation" that the Secret culminates with the 1981 attempt on John Paul II, Vespa added: "But you, Cardinal, said [when reading aloud on camera the '1960 order' on the two envelopes] that Our Lady said not before 1960." Ignoring the two envelopes he had just produced on camera, Bertone, holding up his hand defensively, replied with his ready explanation that Sister Lucia had invented the date:

> Yes, a prescription of the Virgin. *But I asked her*: "Is it *really* the Madonna who ordered that the envelope not be opened before 1960, or was it *you* who set that date?" And Sister Lucia answered me literally: "It was

I who set that date." The Madonna did not want that the Secret be known. This is a firm point, even if she [Lucia] decided to write it with the permission of the Madonna, but to deliver it as a secret that could not be published. "It was I who thought that 1960 would be a term sufficient to be able to open the envelope." And she said: "And I thought that perhaps I would be dead and not be involved in the Secret."

"But *I asked her*" said Bertone, as if Sister Lucia had only been waiting to abandon a lifetime of testimony upon a single question from the Cardinal. Here, complete with alleged "literal" quotations, Bertone gives his *third* different version of Sister Lucia's alleged confession that she had concocted the express order of Our Lady inscribed on the two envelopes. Bertone's alleged question and Sister Lucia's alleged answers had, yet again, been reworded completely. Let us put this third version alongside the two we have already compared.

TABLE 3

BERTONE'S THREE VERSIONS OF SISTER LUCIA'S ALLEGED
"CONFESSION" CONCERNING THE "EXPRESS ORDER OF OUR LADY"

June 26, 2000 (*Message*, p. 29)	May 10, 2007 (*Last Visionary*, p. 92)	May 31, 2007 (telecast)
Bertone: "Why only after 1960? Was it Our Lady who fixed that date?"	Bertone: "Was it the Madonna who suggested that date, to indicate a deadline so precise?"	Bertone: "Is it *really* the Madonna who ordered that the envelope not be opened before 1960, or was it *you* who set that date?"
Lucia: "It was not Our Lady. I fixed the date because I had the intuition that before 1960 it would not be understood, but that only later would it be understood."	Lucia: "It was a decision of mine because I felt that 1960 would be a date very far from the writing of the 'Secret' in 1944 and because I had thought that I would be dead in that year, therefore the last obstacle to the interpretation and to the disclosure of the secret would have been taken away. The Madonna did not communicate anything to me in that regard."	Lucia: "It was I who set that date. It was I who thought that 1960 would be *a term sufficient to be able to open the envelope*. And I thought that perhaps I would be dead and not be involved in the Secret."

Notice that the alleged wording of the questions, the wording of "Sister Lucia's" alleged answers and the concepts she allegedly expressed in those answers are different in each version. Aside from the continuing problem of the shocking "liquidity" of the quotations Bertone attributes to Lucia, we see that in the third version Bertone has Lucia uttering the words: "It was I who thought that 1960 would be *a term sufficient to be able to open the envelope.*" This newly worded rationale of "Sister Lucia" for inventing heavenly orders and writing them on envelopes seems to savor of Bertone's own claim, expressed in *Last Visionary*, that Lucia arbitrarily selected 1960 because it provided "a sufficiently wide temporal arc for the comprehension of the sense of the vision."[266] It appears that between early May and late May of 2007, Bertone's *"sufficiently wide temporal arc"* had blended conceptually with "Sister Lucia's" revised rationale of "a *term sufficient* to be able to open the envelope."

But, to repeat the question I posed earlier in discussing *Last Visionary*, why would exactly 16 years from 1944 be a "term sufficient to be able to open the envelope"? Why not 10 years, 15 years, or 20 years? Why would a date 16 years hence leap into Sister Lucia's head from out of nowhere? And why would Sister Lucia even think in the first place that the revelation of the Secret had anything to do with completion of a "temporal arc" or "sufficient term"? How would she know the Secret was "time sensitive" unless the Virgin had told her so? And if the Virgin *had* told her so, why would the Virgin not also have told her *when* the envelope could be opened? Bertone's claim was unbelievable on its face. Once again, if Sister Lucia had said such a thing to him, it could only have been a product of coercion or undue influence. Otherwise, the words attributed to Sister Lucia by Bertone were not hers but rather Bertone's fabrication.

As had so often happened before, however, Bertone's own statement undermined his position. Notice that in the above-quoted statement from the telecast Bertone says: "The Madonna *did not want that the Secret be known.* This is *a firm point*, even if she [Lucia] decided to write it with *the permission of the Madonna*, but to deliver it as a secret that could not be published." So, according to Bertone, Our Lady did not want the Secret known or published, and would not even allow it to be written down without her

---

[266]Ibid.

permission, yet Sister Lucia, knowing this, decided on her own to have it published in 1960 and to forge on two envelopes a non-existent express order to that effect from the Virgin!

One must reject as nonsensical Bertone's suggestion that Our Lady merely gave some sort of grudging "permission" to write down a Secret that "could not be published." What would be the point of writing down a text that no one was allowed to see? Rather, the Virgin *directed* Lucia to write down a text that *was* to be published—in 1960. Yet the viewers were asked to believe that while the Blessed Virgin was giving Lucia an "express order" to write down the Secret,[267] she had nothing to say concerning *when* the Secret was to be published. Even more implausibly, the viewers were expected to believe that Our Lady *never* said anything to Lucia about when the Secret was to be revealed to the world. It was all left up to Lucia's imagination, including her *ad hoc* calculation of "temporal arcs" and "sufficient terms."

Further undermining himself, Bertone gave this answer to Vespa's question why Sister Lucia had waited so long (from 1917 to 1944) to write down the Secret:

> Because she had the prohibition: the Third Secret she had to preserve within herself and not reveal it to anyone. This was *the order of Our Lady.*

So, Bertone was quite ready to accept that Lucia had received "the order of Our Lady" for some purposes but not for others. As for the *express* order of Our Lady, written on two different envelopes and communicated to Lucia's bishop, the Cardinal Patriarch of Portugal, the whole Catholic Church and the entire world, well, that order was made up. A very convenient conclusion indeed, considering that a heavenly order linking the Third Secret to 1960 would not only destroy Sodano's/Bertone's "preventative interpretation" linking the vision of "the Bishop dressed in white" to a failed assassination attempt in 1981, but would also point directly at Vatican II and its aftermath as the focus of the Secret. The thoughtful viewer could only laugh at the sheer audacity of it all—and then become angry at this cavalier treatment of the deceased seer and her incomparably intimate relationship with the Mother of God.

The "march of the multiple versions" continued with Bertone's

---

[267]To recall, the order was given during the Virgin's apparition at Tuy on January 2, 1944. *See WTAF*, Vol. III, pp. 47-48.

latest assertion that Sister Lucia had "accepted" Sodano's/Bertone's "interpretation" of the vision: "When she heard the news of the attempt of May 13—all the convent had prayed all night—she thought that *this was the moment of the realization of that terrible prophecy, and that he was the Pope of the Third Secret*. She said: 'Yes, I thought of that'—a further proof of the interpretation..." Compare this with the *four* prior versions of Bertone's account set forth in Table 4, on the following page.

As we can see from a study of this table: (1) In the 2000 version of Bertone's account, Lucia merely agrees that Mary's maternal hand deflected the bullet that would have killed John Paul II, but she does not actually accept the "interpretation," although Bertone is suggesting that she does. (2) Yet in the same 2000 version, Bertone cites a fragment from a letter purportedly sent by Lucia to the Pope in 1982 in which the seer makes no reference to the assassination attempt and warns that we have *not yet seen* the complete fulfillment of the Secret. (3) By December of 2001, however, Lucia "fully confirms" the interpretation that the Pope in the vision is John Paul II. (4) Yet, by early May 2007 Bertone admitted "not in these terms"—meaning, no—when asked directly whether Lucia accepted the interpretation. (5) Finally, during the telecast in late May 2007, only a few weeks later, Bertone suddenly has the deceased seer declaring positively that the assassination attempt was "the moment of the realization of that terrible prophecy, and that he [John Paul II] was the Pope of the Third Secret." Notice, however, that in this fifth version the only words actually attributed to Sister Lucia are: "Yes, I thought of that." Lucia's alleged unequivocal statement in November 2001—"I fully confirm the interpretation..."—has long since been forgotten. Also forgotten is Bertone's own citation in 2000 to the purported 1982 letter from Lucia to John Paul II, flatly contradicting the notion that the 1981 assassination attempt is the "realization" of the Third Secret.

Although the subject of the Consecration of Russia is not the focus of this book, Bertone's comment on this subject during the telecast does provide another example of Bertone's inability to quote Sister Lucia the same way twice on any subject on which he claims she spoke to him during his "meetings" with the seer. After Bertone observed that Sister Lucia "probably had other apparitions, so long was her life," Vespa asked if she had ever spoken of these other apparitions with him. Bertone replied: "*She did not speak of that to me*, but indirectly—I asked for verifications, or I tried to verify.

BERTONE'S FIVE VERSIONS OF SISTER LUCIA'S ALLEGED ACCEPTANCE OF SODANO's/BERTONE's "INTERPRETATION" OF THE THIRD SECRET

June 26, 2000 (*Message*, p. 29 - reporting on the April 27, 2000 interview of Lucia by Bertone)	June 26, 2000 (*Message*, p. 9 - reproducing purported letter from Lucia to Pope John Paul II on May 12, 1982)	December 21, 2001 (communiqué re: the November 17, 2001 interview of Sister Lucia by Bertone, published in *L'Osservatore Romano*, p. 4)	May 10, 2007 (*Last Visionary*, p. 65 - unspecified interview of Lucia by Bertone)	May 31, 2007 (telecast - reporting unspecified interview of Lucia by Bertone)
"As regards the passage about the Bishop dressed in white, that is, the Holy Father… who is struck dead and falls to the ground, Sister Lucia was in full agreement with the Pope's claim that 'it was a mother's hand that guided the bullet's path and in his throes the Pope halted at the threshold of death.'"	Lucia purportedly declares, in fragment of letter allegedly addressed to Pope John Paul II in 1982, *a year after the attempt:* "*if we have not yet seen the complete fulfillment of the final part of this prophecy, we are going towards it little by little …*"	Lucia allegedly states to Bertone: "…I fully confirm the interpretation made in the Jubilee Year."	De Carli: "All of this you explained to Sister Lucia and she accepted the interpretation?" Bertone: "Certainly, *even if not in these terms*. She insisted on the force of prayer and on the conviction, like granite, that the Hearts of Jesus and Mary cannot be deaf to our supplications."	Bertone: "When she heard the news of the attempt of May 13… she thought that this was the moment of the realization of that terrible prophecy, and that he was the Pope of the Third Secret. She said: 'Yes, I thought of that'—a further proof of the interpretation…"
Note: Lucia merely agrees God deflected the assassin's bullet; she does *not* actually agree with the interpretation.	**Note:** The letter Bertone cites in *Message* contradicts his own suggestion in *Message* that the vision depicts the 1981 assassination attempt. The letter *makes no mention of the attempt* even though it was purportedly written a year later.	**Note:** "Lucia" allegedly "fully confirms" that the vision culminates in the 1981 assassination attempt. But her purported letter to the Pope in 1982, cited by Bertone himself in *Message*, states the opposite: "*if we have not yet seen the complete fulfillment of the final part of this prophecy, we are going towards it little by little…*"	**Note:** Lucia no longer "fully confirms" the interpretation.	**Note:** "Lucia" now allegedly "thinks" that John Paul was the Pope in the vision and that the vision was "realized" with the assassination attempt. But, again, her purported letter to the Pope in 1982 says the opposite: "*if we have not yet seen the complete fulfillment of the final part of this prophecy…*"

For example, after the famous act of consecration of John Paul II to the Immaculate Heart, she told me that the Madonna told her that that was the consecration she was awaiting and that she was content, and we are in 1984." That statement varied dramatically from Bertone's statement in *La Repubblica* two years earlier in which he said: "Lucia *had a vision* in 1984, the last 'public' one, of which it has never been spoken, during which the Madonna thanked her for the consecration in his [God's!] name..."[268]

Bertone's latest version of Sister's Lucia's alleged about-face on the inadequacy of a consecration of the world departed from the account of his purported interview with the seer on November 17, 2001, during which Lucia is alleged to have stated: "I have already said that the consecration desired by Our Lady was made in 1984, and has been accepted in Heaven." There was no claim back in 2001, as Bertone was now claiming on television in 2007, that the Madonna personally "told her that that was the consecration she was awaiting and she was content." So, the 2007 television version of what Lucia allegedly told Bertone departed from the versions Bertone had given in 2000 (in *Message*), 2001 (the alleged interview of Lucia) and 2005 (the statement in *La Repubblica*), all of which departed from each other. Let us compare Bertone's four different versions of Lucia's alleged testimony on this point. (See Table 5 on the following page.)

An absurd finale

In the closing minutes of the telecast, Politi, at least, served the truth by rejecting the "preventative interpretation," flatly declaring that the vision of the bishop in white "certainly is not connected to the attempt on the Pope." Sitting in a gilded chair, but without any real authority in the matter, Bertone could offer nothing more than his contrary opinion:

> I don't think one can affirm, as Politi categorically affirms, that the Third Secret does not have any reference to the [assassination] attempt. But how can he say this? It refers exactly to the attempt, the bishop dressed in white, 'we had the impression it was the Holy Father.' I interviewed Sister Lucia. Now we must dwell also on what Sister Lucia said, then we can discuss as much as we wish....

---

[268]*La Repubblica*, February 17, 2005; quoted in *Fourth Secret*, p. 123.

TABLE 5

BERTONE'S FOUR VERSIONS OF SISTER LUCIA'S ALLEGED

"APPROVAL" OF THE 1984 CONSECRATION OF THE WORLD

June 26, 2000 (Message, p. 8)	December 21, 2001 (communiqué re: November 17, 2001 "meeting" with Sister Lucia)[270]	February 17, 2005 (La Repubblica)[271]	May 31, 2007 (telecast - Door to Door)
Sister Lucia allegedly personally "confirmed" that the 1984 ceremony sufficed.	Lucia allegedly says: "I have already said that the consecration desired by Our Lady was made in 1984, and has been *accepted in Heaven*."	Bertone claims "Lucia had a vision in 1984, the last 'public' one, of which it has never been spoken, during which the Madonna thanked her for the consecration in his [God's!] name…"	Bertone claims that while Lucia *did not tell him* directly "[S]he told me that the Madonna told her that that was the consecration she was awaiting and [that] she was content…"
Note: *No* statement by Our Lady to Lucia "approving" the 1984 ceremony, and no statement by Lucia to Bertone, but only a debunked letter to an unknown addressee, created by a computer Lucia never used.[269]	**Note:** First alleged reference by Lucia to a communication from "Heaven," but still no statement or apparition of Our Lady. ("If I had had new revelations, *I would not have spoken of them to anyone*, but would have told them directly to the Holy Father!")	**Note:** Heaven's alleged "acceptance" is now a full-blown apparition of the Virgin Mary in 1984, "of which it has never been spoken," during which the Virgin allegedly expresses thanks for the 1984 ceremony in God's name.	**Note:** Bertone drops his claim in 2005 that Our Lady appeared to Lucia in 1984 to convey a divine "thank you" in God's name.

As we have already seen, by the date of the telecast Bertone had given five different versions of what "Sister Lucia said" regarding his "interpretation" of the vision, in the fourth of which Bertone admits "not in these terms," when asked outright if Lucia accepted the interpretation. Lucia, it seems, was no more

---

[269] As already noted, Bertone admitted in *Last Visionary* that Lucia "never worked with the computer." *See* footnote 158.

[270] See "Incontro di S.E. Mons. Tarcisio Bertone con Suor Maria Lucia de Jesus e do Coração Imaculado," *L'Osservatore Romano* (Italian edition), December 21, 2001, p. 4; and "Archbishop Bertone met Sr. Lucia: Convent of Coimbra, Portugal, 17 November 2001", *L'Osservatore Romano* (English edition), January 9, 2002, p. 7.

[271] *La Repubblica*, February 17, 2005; quoted in *Fourth Secret*, p. 123.

persuaded than Politi. What strikes one in watching—again and again, as I have—this televised debate over the meaning of the vision of the bishop in white is the utter absurdity of the situation: a Vatican cardinal bantering with a journalist on a talk show about the meaning of what the Mother of God conveyed ninety years ago for the good of all humanity. We are asked to believe that the only One who had nothing to say about what the vision means is the very One who confided it to Lucia with instructions to reveal it in 1960! As Socci rightly asks: "Is it possible that the Madonna appeared so sensationally at Fatima to give a message-warning so important that nevertheless remains incomprehensible, confused or susceptible of various and opposing interpretations?"[272] Could anyone possessed of his faculties still believe, especially after the Cardinal's performance on *Door to Door*, that there is *no* text containing words of the Virgin explaining the vision?

A final objection

One final objection must be addressed, an objection encompassing this entire discussion: If Bertone and his collaborators were really engaged in a plan to conceal a text of the Third Secret containing such terrible prophetic words of the Virgin, would they have executed that plan as clumsily and with as many blunders as these pages have presented? Are we not confronted here with a kind of bumbling honesty as opposed to cunning?

The answer is that, on the contrary, Bertone and his collaborators are not bumblers but highly intelligent men with advanced academic degrees. Yet in this controversy they were faced with a classic Hobson's choice: Say nothing and run the risk of Socci and the "Fatimists" persuading too many of the faithful that there has been a cover-up, with a consequent loss of credibility on the part of the Vatican apparatus. Or, respond to Socci and "the Fatimists" and thereby incur the even graver risks of being evasive, of making public statements demonstrably at variance with known facts, of self-contradiction and further unintended revelations, thereby suffering an even greater loss of credibility. Bertone and company chose the latter course, and the outcome was inevitable. As Scripture says: "He that diggeth a pit, shall fall into it..."[273]

---

[272]Socci, *Fourth Secret*, p. 73.

[273]Ecclesiastes, 10:8.

Embarrassing beyond the Tiber

The Cardinal's performance had been smooth, charming, pleasing to the eye. He was, after all, an "ottimo telecronista"—a great television commentator—as De Carli had called him during the telecast. But to anyone able to think critically, the performance was, as Socci put it, "embarrassing beyond the Tiber." Embarrassing, that is, throughout the world. For Bertone had refuted nothing, avoided every major issue, and yet had revealed much—first and foremost, the sensational disclosure of the two envelopes and the diary folio—that only confirmed what Socci and "the Fatimists" had suspected and had already proven independently.

As Socci concluded in his reply to the telecast from which he had so suspiciously been excluded, despite the absence of any real challenge to Bertone's version of the facts the Cardinal had only succeeded in demonstrating that the doubt Pope John professed to have concerning the supernatural origin of the Third Secret

> could not refer to the text of the vision revealed in 2000, that does not contain anything "delicate." But only to that "fourth secret" that—as Cardinals Ottaviani and Ciappi revealed—spoke of apostasy and the betrayal by the upper ecclesiastical hierarchy. That "fourth secret" of which John Paul II, in 1982, said that it "had not been published because it could be badly interpreted." That "fourth secret" of which Cardinal Ratzinger, in 1996, said that at the moment certain "details" could be harmful to the faith....[274]

And that "fourth secret," one must add, that Cardinal Ratzinger, in 1984, described as a warning of "dangers threatening the faith and the life of the Christian and therefore of the world," which contains "things" that "correspond to what has been *announced* in Scripture and has been *said* again and again in many other Marian apparitions...", but "is not published, at least for now... to avoid confusing religious *prophecy* with *sensationalism*." And, finally, that "fourth secret" which prompted the future Pius XII to declare, in 1931, in words very similar to Ratzinger's in 1984: "I am worried by the Blessed Virgin's messages to little Lucia of Fatima. This persistence of Mary about the dangers which menace the Church

---

[274]"Bertone nel 'Vespaio' delle Polemiche" ("Bertone in the 'Wasp's Nest' of the Polemics"), loc. cit.

is a divine warning against the suicide of altering the faith, in her liturgy, her theology and her soul..."

Thus far, Bertone's every effort to answer Socci had only dug a deeper pit for him and the other defenders of the official account. Just as Socci had said in defense of himself, Bertone had "offered the proof that I am right"—that there is indeed a missing text of the Secret. And that text, as Socci puts it, remains "well hidden." With the dramatic collapse of the cover-up on live television, Bertone and his collaborators found themselves in a desperate position. Soon they would launch further attempts to rescue the official account from the damage they themselves had inflicted upon it. In keeping with the pattern that has developed throughout this controversy, however, those attempts would only further confirm that something is being hidden.

Chapter 9

Desperate Measures

Cardinal Tarcisio Bertone is nothing if not an intelligent man. A man of Bertone's intelligence could not fail to see that the official account has been thoroughly discredited by his own attempts to defend it. That result, as I have shown, is not due to any incompetence on Bertone's part, but rather the impossibility of denying convincingly that which, as Socci puts it, "is certain." What is certain is that there is a text of the Third Secret containing the precious words of the Virgin Mary that must explain the meaning of what the former Cardinal Ratzinger himself called the "difficult to decipher" vision of "the Bishop dressed in white."

If the claims that such a text exists were "pure ravings," as Bertone would have it, then the Cardinal would be content to allow that fact to speak for itself, to let the ravers rave on. Yet the Cardinal will not let the matter drop, precisely because he is an intelligent man. He knows too well that there is now a mountain of evidence, to which he himself has contributed mightily, that the posited missing text, to quote Socci again, "exists yet is well hidden"—well hidden by those who have persuaded themselves that the text is "not authentic" and declare that they have revealed what they call the "authentic" Secret.

Thus, Bertone has felt compelled to continue attempting to manage the Third Secret controversy since his disastrous appearance on *Door to Door*. He is still trying—privately and unofficially—to bring closure to a matter that will not be closed. Bertone's efforts have taken on the aspect of a personal crusade in defense of his own reputation and credibility. Meanwhile, the Vatican, especially the Pope, continues to maintain a wall of silence, without a single official reply to Socci's contentions or the testimony of Archbishop Capovilla.

A revealing radio appearance

On June 6, 2007, only a few days after his appearance on *Door to*

Door, Cardinal Bertone made a brief appearance on Vatican Radio to continue lobbying for an end to the controversy. The online transcript of the interview is tendentiously entitled: "There do not exist unrevealed parts of the Secret of Fatima: to our microphones, Cardinal Bertone recalls his meetings with Sister Lucia, described in the book 'The Last Visionary of Fatima'."[275] In answer to questions by the interviewer, one Giovanni Peduto, Bertone only inflicted major new damage to the official account.

To begin with, Bertone described Sister Lucia as "a sister who had *memorized with a meticulous perfection* everything that 'Our Lady', as she called the Madonna, had communicated to the three shepherds and in a particular way to her, because she—compared to Francisco and Jacinta—was the most mature and would thus have had the mission of communicating the famous three secrets of Fatima." Bertone failed to explain why Sister Lucia's meticulous memorization of what the Virgin communicated to her had failed completely when it came to the "express order of Our Lady," which Lucia had inscribed on two separate envelopes, that the Third Secret could only be revealed in 1960.

Next, in reply to Peduto's question: "What was Sister Lucia's impression of the attempt on John Paul II of 1981, that Pope Wojtyla always connected to the vision of the Secret of Fatima?", Bertone gave this answer, in pertinent part:

> .... I explicitly questioned Sister Lucia on her first reaction to the attempt precisely in connection with the third part of the Secret, and she replied: "I thought immediately of the bishop dressed in white," in that wording of the Third Secret which had already stated: "We had the impression that it was the Pope." And therefore she herself connected the thing, from the beginning—even before Pope John Paul II, because John Paul II connected the attempt to the mystery of the Secret of Fatima after he had brought to himself the text of the third part of the Secret. I would say that she from the beginning connected this terrible event to the prophecy of Fatima....

With this remark Bertone provided no less than his *sixth* different version of Lucia's alleged "acceptance" of Sodano's/

---

[275]Radio Vatican broadcast, June 6, 2007; transcript available at http://www. radiovaticana.org/it1/Articolo.asp?c=137631. All translations are based on this transcript.

Bertone's "interpretation" of the vision. Recall that in the fifth of the five versions set forth in the comparative table in Chapter 8 (see Table 4), that being the version Bertone presented during the telecast of May 31, 2007, the Cardinal claimed: "When she heard the news of the attempt of May 13... she thought that this was the moment of the realization of that terrible prophecy, and that he was the Pope of the Third Secret. She said: 'Yes, I thought of that'—a further proof of the interpretation..." On Vatican Radio only days later, however, Bertone has suddenly retreated to the claim that "I would say" Lucia merely "connected" the assassination attempt to the Secret. He has abandoned his claim, days earlier, that Sister Lucia "thought that this was the moment of the realization of that terrible prophecy, and that he [John Paul II] was the Pope of the Third Secret." Bertone revealed yet again that his accounts of "my meetings with Sister Lucia" are extremely "fluid" and wholly unreliable.

Bertone's self-inflicted wounds were further aggravated by his answer to this curiously worded question: "Notwithstanding publication of the third part of the Secret, there are still numerous criticisms and objections on the part of those who maintain that in reality not everything was revealed: what is your *opinion* on this point?" Opinion? Has the existence of a hidden text of the Third Secret suddenly become debatable even for the Cardinal? Incredibly, the Cardinal suggested precisely that in his answer:

> I have also presented in a television broadcast the *authentic* text, the four little pages, that is the only *folio* compiled by Sister Lucia. The words of the Third Secret are contained in that *folio* and there are not other words written by Sister Lucia regarding the Third Secret. The other words have been invented, formulated by other persons, but do not correspond to the writings of Sister Lucia. Therefore, *I am firmly convinced* by the documentation that was *in the Secret Archive of the Holy Office*, which was brought—as is known—in 1957 to Rome; and by the explicit declarations of Sister Lucia in the presence of the Bishop of Fatima, that there is nothing else: the Third Secret is this, from the first to the last word.

He is *"firmly convinced"* that there is no other text of the Third Secret? Why is this suddenly a matter of the Cardinal's personal *conviction* as opposed to a matter of cold, hard *fact* he could have verified simply by *asking Sister Lucia* the questions he had steadfastly refused to ask over years of controversy: Is there a text containing the words of the Virgin indicated by your "etc" following the phrase "In Portugal, the dogma of the faith will always be preserved etc."? Is there a text in which the Virgin *explains* the "difficult to decipher" vision of the bishop in white?

It seems that at this point in the controversy Bertone is feeling the enormous pressure of the weight of evidence in favor of the existence of a missing text—a text of which he cannot or will not speak—and that he has responded to the pressure by retreating into the safe harbor of a personal "conviction" on the matter, as if in the apprehension that sooner or later the whole truth will come out. And notice that here again Bertone placed conspicuous verbal emphasis on an "authentic" text of the Secret located in the Holy Office archive, while ignoring once again the burning issue of the text located in the papal apartment.

Notice also Bertone's curious reliance, not on anything Sister Lucia said directly to him in answer to a direct question, but rather an allusion to "explicit declarations of Sister Lucia in the presence of the Bishop of Fatima." *What* declarations? These newly revealed "explicit declarations" of Sister Lucia—still another posthumous "surprise"—have never been reported in any part of the official account over the past seven years, nor did Bertone provide any details during the radio broadcast.

Recall that in Chapter 5 we saw that since 2000 the *only* specific "declaration" on this point ever attributed to Sister Lucia consists of the following nine words, presented in Bertone's patently incredible December 2001 communiqué concerning his alleged interview of the seer at Coimbra on November 17, 2001: "Everything has been published; there are no more secrets." But as we have already seen, these alleged nine words were *not uttered in the presence of the Bishop of Fatima.*[276] As Bertone himself states in the communiqué, the interview was conducted "in the presence of Rev. Luis Kondor, SVD, Vice-Postulator of the cause of Bl. Francisco and Bl. Jacinta, and of the Prioress of the Carmelite

---

[276]Furthermore, when appearing on Cardinal Bertone's television show on September 21, 2007, the retired Bishop of Fatima, Serafim de Sousa Ferreira e Silva, would conspicuously fail to attest to *any* declaration by Sister Lucia to the effect that the vision of the bishop in white is all there is to the Third Secret and nothing remains to be published. Rather, he would make it a point to affirm before the camera that he was testifying to *"only one fact"*: that Lucia had authenticated the text of the vision, which is not even in dispute. *See* Chapter 10.

Convent of St. Teresa, to obtain explanations and information directly from the only surviving visionary." I note once again that *neither Father Kondor nor the Prioress has ever come forward to authenticate Bertone's purported quotation*—an omission made all the more telling by the fact that Bertone's alleged quotations of the seer have a demonstrated tendency to change dramatically over time.[277]

Where, then, can we find the alleged "explicit declarations of Sister Lucia in the presence of the Bishop of Fatima" concerning whether there is a yet-to-be-revealed text of the Third Secret of Fatima? What exactly did the Bishop ask her, and what exactly did she answer, if anything? Add this to the list of inadvertent disclosures and glaring omissions that undermine the credibility of the official account.

During the radio broadcast Bertone continued to bungle his attempt to explain the testimony of Cardinal Ottaviani that there is a one-page text of the Secret, comprising 25 lines. In Chapter 8 we saw how during his appearance on *Door to Door* Bertone flubbed Marco Politi's polite challenge concerning this testimony. On the radio Bertone did no better. He simply repeated his blatantly contrived "attempt at an explanation" on television days before:

> There are 62 lines [in the text of the vision]. Here, if you like, 25 lines from one side of the folio—as is cited by Cardinal Ottaviani, *who spoke of a folio of 25 lines*, I have also attempted perhaps to interpret, to explain, to justify *this affirmation of Cardinal Ottaviani*; and then the other lines—16 plus 16—from the other part of the folio and therefore there is nothing else! Now, *I cannot accept* that there are other secrets, that there is a fourth secret.

So, once again Bertone argued that 25 lines of text on two pages is the same thing as 25 lines on one page, and that Cardinal Ottaviani somehow failed to realize the document he was referring to consisted of four pages (on one folio) rather than a single page. But, of course, *none* of the four pages of the folio on which the vision is written contains 25 lines, nor is there any combination of

---

[277]We must recall that even the isolated statement of nine words allegedly uttered before Kondor and the Prioress is not supported by any transcript of the interview, and that we have no way of knowing the precise question alleged to have elicited the cropped quotation, or its crucially important context within the purported two-hour interview.

two pages yielding 25 lines, as Bertone had now falsely suggested twice. Bertone's arithmetic here was just as fishy as it was during the telecast.

Even if Bertone could offer the excuse that he seized upon this flimsy explanation under the pressure of the moment on TV—and he could not, as he had more than enough time during the four-minute commercial break to make an accurate count of the lines on each page of the folio—he could hardly offer that excuse a week later during the radio broadcast. Why, then, would Bertone persist in what he had to know was a patently false "explanation" of Cardinal Ottaviani's decisive testimony? Why would he once again fail to suggest politely that Cardinal Ottaviani must have been mistaken, that there is no one-page text and never has been? Again, the only reasonable answer is that Bertone knows that Ottaviani was *not* mistaken, because there is indeed a one-page text of 25 lines pertaining to the Secret—a text now conveniently deemed "inauthentic" and thus not part of the Third Secret; a text that was not "in the archives" but rather in the papal apartment.

Most telling of all were Bertone's remarks concerning the "etc" issue, with which he concluded his answer to Peduto's request for his "opinion" about the claim of a missing text:

> ...That famous phrase "In Portugal the faith will always be kept intact" [*serberà intatta la fede*] is contained in *another writing* of Sister Lucia and *closes with ellipses* [*puntini*], as we know, a part of the memoirs of Sister Lucia. Enough: there is nothing else!

Aside from misquoting the key phrase—"In Portugal the *dogma of the faith* will always be *preserved*"—the Cardinal has evidently decided to *eliminate the telltale "etc" altogether* by replacing it with ellipses, representing to his audience that "we know" the phrase ends in an ellipsis. Of course, what "we know" is that Bertone was deliberately misleading his listeners. There can be no other reasonable conclusion, as it is quite impossible to believe that after seven years of controversy precisely over the "etc", the Cardinal has suddenly forgotten the "etc" exists and now believes there is only an ellipsis, which would mean that the words of the Virgin to the seers simply trailed off in mid-sentence or that Lucia's "meticulous memorization"—the Cardinal's own words!—of what the Virgin told her suddenly became sketchy toward the end of the Virgin's momentous opening reference to the preservation of dogma in Portugal.

Attention must be paid to Bertone's attempt to demote what are plainly the opening words of the Third Secret to the status of "another writing of Sister Lucia... a part of the memoirs of Sister Lucia," as if to say the words in question are mere scribblings of Lucia in her "memoirs," rather than a direct quotation of the Virgin. Bertone conveniently failed to mention that what he dismissed on the radio as "another writing" and mere "memoirs" of Lucia are *the very source of the text of the Message of Fatima*, and that *he himself* had relied on Lucia's "memoirs"—the Third Memoir, to be exact—for the text of the first two parts of the Great Secret published by the Vatican in *Message*. Nor did Bertone mention that he (and his collaborators) knowingly avoided the more complete Fourth Memoir for the very reason that it contains what they so earnestly seek to avoid: the "etc" that is the gateway to the missing text. It will be helpful here to set forth again the pertinent portion of the Fourth Memoir:

> ...In the end, my Immaculate Heart will triumph. The Holy Father will consecrate Russia to me, and she will be converted, and a period of peace will be granted to the world. *In Portugal the dogma of the Faith will always be preserved etc. Tell this to no one. Yes you may tell it to Francisco.*

Cardinal Bertone knows full well that the words represented by the "etc" are situated within the integral message conveyed by the Virgin, which Sister Lucia *meticulously memorized*, but that the seer could not commit these particular words to paper because she did not yet have the Virgin's permission to reveal them. Why, then, would the Cardinal take the risk of going on the air to make the demonstrably false claim that the "etc" is an ellipsis and that the phrase at issue is merely some unimportant "other writing" of Lucia's? The answer is clear: he took the risk because he feels that he must, at any cost, remove the "etc" from everyone's memory, as the "etc" points directly to the text he and his collaborators have hidden from the Church and the world.

Finally, what of the dispositive testimony of Archbishop Capovilla that there are indeed two separate envelopes and two separate texts pertaining to the Secret? As he had over the previous eight months since Socci published that testimony, Bertone acted as if that testimony had never been given. He had not one word to say about Capovilla during the radio broadcast. This continued silence in the face of Capovilla's explosive revelations could not have been more revealing.

In sum, therefore, the radio interview, like Bertone's other private interventions, had only made it more apparent that the official account is not worthy of belief. Yet again an attempt at damage control had inflicted more damage. But *still* Bertone would not let the matter drop.

Capovilla under pressure

Knowledgeable observers of this controversy knew that it was only a matter of time before Archbishop Capovilla came under immense pressure to "retract" his testimony to Solideo Paolini, just as Sister Lucia came under pressure to "retract" her testimony about the "express order of Our Lady" concerning 1960 and the necessity of an explicit consecration of Russia by name.

As of September 2007 Capovilla had voiced no objection to the account of his testimony in Socci's *Fourth Secret*, published nearly a year before (November 2006). Moreover, Capovilla had voiced no objection to the even wider publicity his testimony received in a front-page story in November 2006 in the Italian newspaper *Libero*, which published the testimony as part of a preview of *Fourth Secret*. Nor did Capovilla raise any doubts about his testimony in two meetings with Paolini after the Archbishop was aware that his testimony was to be published: a meeting in November of 2006, and another on June 21, 2007, which Paolini tape-recorded in anticipation of pressure on Capovilla to "retract."[278] There were, in fact, a total of four face-to-face meetings between Paolini and Capovilla: early April 2003; July 5, 2006; November 2006 and June 21, 2007. There was also a telephone conversation on July 18, 2006, and, beyond any possibility of "retraction," Capovilla's "confidential note" of May 17, 1967, a copy of which he provided to Paolini, as already discussed.[279] That note confirms every detail of the location of the never-produced "Capovilla envelope" in the

---

[278]Solideo Paolini, "Report from Italy: My Meetings with Archbishop Capovilla and the Socci-Cardinal Bertone Struggle," address at Fatima conference in Botucatu, Brazil, August 2007. *See* transcript at http://www.fatimapeaceconferences.com/ solideo_paolini_2007_en.asp.

[279]Ibid. See also Appendix I.

papal apartment of John XXIII and Paul VI.

In the meeting with Paolini on June 21, the Archbishop seemed "quite annoyed by the turmoil caused by his declarations," and he revealed that he was under pressure from the Vatican as a result.[280] During the meeting Capovilla was in the process of "preparing a written report consisting of documents, photocopies, papers" and he told Paolini "'there were things that I have to reply to…' It seemed like the Vatican had asked him to give them his statements; it is as if they said to him: 'What exactly did you say to him [Paolini]? And why?'"[281] Capovilla protested to Paolini that when he made his revelation of the existence of two texts and two envelopes he "was speaking in a free-wheeling manner (*parlando a ruota libera*), which in Italian does not mean that what he said was not true, but that he had said too much."[282]

Yet, during the same meeting Capovilla *amplified* his prior testimony by "hint[ing] at the existence of an attachment of some sort to the four pages published in the year 2000 [the vision of the 'Bishop dressed in white']," which attachment contains what Vatican authorities had characterized as "the thoughts of Sister Lucia" that she "might have thought—at least at the beginning— came from Our Lady!"[283] Was this Capovilla's way of revealing that certain Vatican officials had decided to demote the words of Our Lady following the "etc" to "some annotations" of Sister Lucia, just as Bertone had suggested in *Message*? Would this not indicate a mental reservation, as suggested throughout this book, according to which Bertone and his collaborators could state that they had revealed the entirety of the Third Secret without having to mention Sister Lucia's mere "annotations," which she only "thought" were from the Virgin?

By September of 2007, however, the undoubtedly heavy pressure on Capovilla had apparently begun to have its effect. On September 11, *Telegraph.co.uk* reported on an interview of Capovilla by none other than Bertone's ally, Giuseppe De Carli, co-author of Bertone's *Last Visionary*. According to the *Telegraph*, during this interview "Msgr. Capovilla, who witnessed Pope John XXIII opening the envelope of the third secret, said: 'There are not

[280]Ibid.

[281]Ibid.

[282]"Declaration of Dr. Solideo Paolini", ¶ 3(b), reproduced at http://www.cfnews.org/Paolini-Sept18.htm.

[283]Paolini, "Report from Italy," loc. cit.

two truths from Fatima and nor is there any fourth secret. The text which I read in 1959 is the same that was distributed by the Vatican. I have had enough of these conspiracy theories. It just isn't true. I read it, I presented it to the Pope and we resealed the envelope.'"[284]

A close reading of the statement attributed to Capovilla shows that it actually denies nothing of his prior testimony. First of all, in saying that the text he read in 1959 is "the same that was *distributed* by the Vatican," Capovilla is *not* saying that the text he read in that year is the text of the vision published by the Vatican in June 2000. Quite the contrary, as we will see in Chapter 10, weeks later, in another failed attempt to defend his account, Bertone himself will reveal during his own television broadcast Capovilla's further statement that he does not consider the Third Secret to have been hidden because *certain select Vatican prelates* were allowed to read it in 1959—*not* because the text of the *vision* was published to the world in 2000. Thus, by the phrase "distributed by the Vatican" Capovilla could be signifying nothing more than that he and certain prelates in the Vatican read a text *distributed* to them in 1959.

Granted, there is a major ambiguity here. But the ambiguity arises because Capovilla—no doubt quite deliberately—has *not* been asked specifically to deny that there are two different texts and two different envelopes pertaining to the Secret; the "Capovilla envelope" and the "Bertone envelope," as he had called them when he informed Paolini of their existence. Capovilla does not even mention his revelations to Paolini in the *Telegraph* article. Instead, Capovilla denies what no one has claimed in the first place: that there are "two truths from Fatima" and literally a "fourth secret" of Fatima, which is merely the ironic title of Socci's book. The real question, of course, concerns the existence of two *parts* of the one Third Secret: the text of the vision and a text in which the Virgin explains its meaning. In the statement reported in the *Telegraph*, Capovilla does not deny that there are indeed two texts. His prior testimony remains completely intact.

As for Capovilla's purported remark: "I have had enough of these conspiracy theories," here too the Archbishop conspicuously fails to deny the precise information he provided to Paolini: that a text of the Secret was contained in an envelope kept in the right-hand drawer of Pope John's writing desk, called "Barbarigo". That

---

[284]"Catholic Church isn't hiding apocalypse secret," Telegraph.co.uk, September 11, 2007. *See* also "Declaration of Dr. Solideo Paolini," loc. cit.

revelation was no "theory." In fact, as we will also see in Chapter 10, weeks later Capovilla will confirm on Bertone's own television show that this envelope exists, and Bertone *to this day has failed to explain why he has never produced it.*

In sum, the statement in the *Telegraph* seems to be a carefully worded attempt to give the *appearance* of a denial where none is actually stated. And, in a rather comical development, it turns out that the *Telegraph* article was derived from—of all places—a story in a *women's lifestyle and fashion magazine* called *Diva e Donna,* which features breathless stories on the latest details of the lives of female Italian celebrities, along with pictures of scantily clad movie stars, songstresses and models. Strange business indeed: a non-denial from Capovilla in an interview published by a women's magazine—*ten months* after the publication of *Fourth Secret,* which had presented Capovilla's testimony to the world without the least objection from the witness. The choice of this bizarre forum to publish Capovilla's non-denial was a classic public relations "trial balloon." The Vatican, meanwhile, was continuing to observe a thunderous official silence regarding a witness whose testimony had extinguished the official account. Bertone had been left to fend for himself.

But Bertone had yet another stratagem to deploy in his private and unofficial campaign to put a damper on the controversy his own statements had helped fan into worldwide flames. Since his appearance on *Door to Door* had been a disaster, Bertone would produce his own television show!

Chapter 10

The Cardinal Bertone Show

On September 21, 2007 Cardinal Bertone staged a special televised event in an auditorium at the Pontifical Urbaniana University in Rome near the Vatican. Scores of VIPs were in attendance, including a number of Vatican clerics, former Prime Minister of Italy, Giulio Andreotti, the former Mayor of Rome, the Vice Minister of Government, assorted other politicians, prominent bankers and businessmen, and the recently retired Bishop of Fatima, Serafim de Sousa Ferreira e Silva. The 400-seat auditorium was nearly filled to capacity with these invitees.

Brought to you by...

The emcee for what could be called "The Cardinal Bertone Show" was Father Federico Lombardi, director of the Vatican Press Office, who was not appearing on behalf of the Vatican and had no message from the Pope. Lombardi began by thanking the various sponsors of the event, none of which was a Vatican department. The sponsors included a banking concern, a tourism center, and a prominent artist, Giuseppe de Lucia.

Why had an audience of the rich, the famous and the powerful assembled in an auditorium to attend a privately sponsored event at Bertone's invitation? The American idiom for such an event is "dog and pony show," meaning an elaborate public relations presentation that is long on style but short on content. The ostensible purpose of the event, broadcast live on the private religious television channel *Telepace*, was a "presentation" of *Last Visionary* by Cardinal Bertone. But *Last Visionary*, published in May 2007, had already been presented to the public a number of times at other venues, including a summer book fair at Piazza Maggiore De Palma in Scalea, Italy, where a capacity crowd came to hear co-author De Carli discuss the book and answer questions from three journalists (Michele Cervo, Michela Gargiulo and Giorgio

Santelli).[285]

Lombardi himself evidently felt obliged to offer an excuse for another "presentation" of a book that had long since been presented: "The book has already been published for a while," he admitted, but "it is right to return to speak of it" in view of the 90th anniversary of the Fatima apparitions, which "will culminate next October with the trip of Cardinal Bertone to Fatima…" (where the Cardinal would dedicate the hideous new "basilica" constructed at the site of the apparitions). But why should the Cardinal's trip to Fatima in October require a televised "presentation" of his book in September, when that book had already been presented to the public back in May? In that Roman manner, Lombardi was merely stating the polite pretext that concealed the real purpose of this dog and pony show: another attack on Socci's book and the claims of the "Fatimists," which Bertone had thus far not only failed to refute but had actually helped to substantiate. Bertone could hardly admit that he had taken to the airwaves *again* in an effort to salvage his position, for that would make him look like a worried man. And yet that is exactly what he had done.

Socci and Paolini are shown the door

As with the appearance on *Door to Door*, Bertone had arranged things so that there would be no opportunity to confront him. No questions would be permitted from any member of the audience, including the representatives of the press. Nevertheless, both Antonio Socci and Solideo Paolini are in attendance in the hope that Socci will be able to pose to Bertone the question the Cardinal had been ducking for more than seven years:

> Your Eminence, are you ready to swear on the Gospel that the famous phrase of the Madonna contained in the Third Secret of Fatima noted by the Vatican in 2000 — "In Portugal, the dogma of the Faith will always be preserved etc", said the Madonna — is not followed by anything else?[286]

Socci and Paolini, along with other journalists, had positioned

---

[285]"Plaza full for De Carli and *The Last Visionary of Fatima*," http://www. unlibroperlestate.org/notizia.php?id=15.

[286]Paolo Rodari, "On the Road to Fatima, Socci is Stopped by the Swiss Guards," *Il Riformista*, September 22, 2007.

themselves outside the auditorium before the start of the event, expecting to encounter Bertone as he entered. *Corriere della Sera* later carried Socci's account of what happened next:

> It was a shameful thing. I had only wanted to ask one question for one minute and to receive a terse response: yes or no. But Cardinal Bertone, alerted to my presence, entered directly into the auditorium through a service door. A stratagem that made everyone present laugh. Afterwards, three Vatican gendarmes pushed me outside the place, saying that I could not give interviews. A ridiculous scene that astounded my colleagues who were present and put me in a difficult position, seeing that I am a strenuous defender of the Vatican.[287]

The Cardinal had literally run away from Socci's question! And the keepers of the hidden text of the Third Secret of Fatima had descended to the use of brute force in order to silence the questioner, who happens to be one of Italy's most prominent and respected Catholic journalists and intellectuals, a vice-director of *Rai Due*, one of the primary Italian television channels, and the host of his own television show. As Socci is forcibly removed from the premises (together with Paolini), he is heard to remark: "The Church of dialogue has become a Church of monologue."[288]

The Bishop of Fatima plays it close to the vest

Once the pretext for the gathering—the "presentation" of an already presented book—has been stated, the real agenda begins immediately with some brief comments by the retired bishop of Fatima, Bishop Serafim de Sousa Ferreira e Silva. Serafim, however, provides no real assistance to Bertone. Rather, reading from a prepared text, the Bishop begins his remarks by noting pointedly that he had come to say "*Nothing, almost nothing*" and that "I wish to testify *only to one fact* and it is the following," whereupon the Bishop said that he was present with Bertone during the meeting of April 27, 2000 at which Sister Lucia authenticated "the original *envelope* which contained the secret" (failing to mention the *two* sealed envelopes Bertone had displayed on television) and "the

---

[287]"'Fourth Secret' of Fatima: Socci challenges Cardinal Bertone, thrown out by gendarmes," Bartolini Bruno, *Corriere della Sera*, September 22, 2007.

[288]Ibid.

four little pages written by hand." That is, the Bishop affirms what is not in dispute: that the text of the vision is authentic.

Tellingly, the Bishop does *not* corroborate Bertone's claim during the radio broadcast in June 2007 (see Chapter 9) that Sister Lucia had made "explicit declarations... in the presence of the Bishop of Fatima" that the vision of the bishop in white is all there is to the Third Secret. Serafim has nothing to say on this point, even though Bertone had staked his entire position on the Bishop's alleged witness of these never-quoted "explicit declarations," which Bertone had never mentioned until after Lucia's death. Serafim's silence on this crucial issue could not have been a mere oversight of the moment, given that the Bishop was speaking from a prepared text.

Nor does Serafim offer any corroboration of Bertone's claim in *Message, Last Visionary* and during his appearance on *Door to Door*, that during the same meeting of April 27, 2000 Lucia had "confessed" with "disarming candor" that she had never received any "express order of Our Lady" that the envelope(s) containing the Secret "can only be opened in 1960," but rather 1960 was "a fictitious date."

The Bishop's evident unwillingness to corroborate Bertone's account on such major points could not be more conspicuous to those familiar with the facts. Instead of backing Bertone to the hilt, as one would expect Serafim to do if Bertone's account were completely truthful and the Cardinal had been unjustly accused of prevarication, Serafim plays it very close to the vest, making it clear that he would testify only to *one* fact. But surely he knows *many* facts about the April 2000 meeting, including whether Lucia really did declare that the vision is the entire Secret and that the Virgin had never spoken to her concerning revelation of the Secret in 1960. Already "The Cardinal Bertone Show" was following the pattern of the Cardinal's other interventions: telling silence on matters concerning the credibility of his entire account.

Bishop Serafim does state, however, that "the Secret of Fatima has now been revealed in *an authentic* and integral *way*." Here again we encounter the curious locution adopted by Bertone in response to Socci's overwhelming presentation of the evidence of a cover-up: that the "authentic" Secret has been revealed; the "authentic" Secret in the Holy Office archives as opposed to some "inauthentic" Secret somewhere else, perhaps in the papal apartment.

Question: Why does Serafim not simply declare—why has *no one* in Bertone's camp simply declared—that the entire Third Secret has been revealed? Why use such equivocal language as "revealed in an authentic and integral way"?

Answer: Serafim will not state simply that "the entire Third Secret has been revealed" because he is not comfortable with such an unequivocal affirmation. He is not comfortable with it because he knows there is something else that has not been revealed, something that might have been deemed "inauthentic" by certain parties acting in secrecy.

One can appreciate the inescapability of this conclusion by considering how it would appear if this sort of equivocal language were used in any other context where absolute candor is required, such as testimony in a courtroom, where a witness must tell the truth, the whole truth, and nothing but the truth:

> Prosecutor: Have you revealed the entire contents of the message you received from Mr. Jones?
>
> Witness: I have revealed the message in an authentic and integral way.

Now, if a jury heard that question and that answer, how could it fail to conclude that the witness was hiding something? That is what juries rightly find when a question that calls for a "yes" or a "no" is answered equivocally. And that is what the jury of public opinion ought to find here. Enough is enough. With the Church and the world in peril, the faithful are entitled to a simple answer to a simple question, rather than clever "Roman" nuances that obviously indicate some sort of mental reservation.

Messori plays the authority card

Bertone's next witness is the renowned Vaticanist and author, Vittorio Messori, who worked with John Paul II on his best-selling book, *Crossing the Threshold of Hope*. Like Bishop Serafim, Messori offers nothing of substance, but his appearance does serve a purpose: Messori calls for nothing less than mindless trust in Cardinal Bertone, simply because the Cardinal is a high-ranking Vatican official.

As Messori puts it: "[I]f we can no longer place our trust in the pastors of the Church, at the top of the Church, in a matter such as this, if we have really been misled, led down the garden path in things like this, where the protagonist is Mary herself... and where these truths, from the perspective of Faith, come directly from Heaven, and these truths have been twisted, cropped and manipulated, well, as a Catholic it is difficult if not impossible for me to accept this perspective." Messori added that while he himself had lent credence to the claim that the Third Secret must involve a prediction of apostasy in the Church as found in the words indicated by the famous "etc", he was now "repentant" because "I am a little old fashioned, I am with *Roma locuta est, causa finita est* (Rome has spoken, the case closed) in the sense that it is absolutely not possible for me to follow those who are also friends, who I esteem and respect, because... it is not possible for me to accept the hypothesis that the very heights of the Church would mislead and manipulate us."

Messori is a subtle and intelligent man, and so it is disappointing to see him abandon all subtlety and intelligence in favor of a public plea for unthinking acceptance of the affirmations of a prelate who, in the first place, *has never really denied* that there is a hidden text of the Third Secret, and who, moreover, has given an account so patently unbelievable that Messori's own esteemed and respected colleagues, no less faithful Catholics than he, cannot accept it.

Now, of course, Cardinal Bertone is not a "pastor of the Church," but rather a Vatican functionary with no pastoral authority whatsoever over the faithful. But even if Bertone had pastoral authority over individual Catholics such as Messori, one cannot say *Roma locuta est, causa finita est* concerning Bertone's representations, for that ancient maxim is reserved only to definitive papal pronouncements, not the affirmations of a lone cardinal, as Messori well knows. The Pope has said nothing about this controversy that in any way binds the faithful to accept Bertone's account. And, as Messori surely also understands, the promises of Christ regarding the indefectibility of His Church most certainly did not include a promise that any given cardinal will always be candid and above the temptation to withhold or manipulate the truth. On the contrary, as Saint Paul warned his own fellow bishops concerning the future of the Church:

> Take heed to yourselves, and to the whole flock,
> wherein the Holy Ghost hath placed you bishops,
> to rule the church of God, which he hath purchased
> with his own blood. I know that, after my departure,
> ravening wolves will enter in among you, not sparing

the flock. *And of your own selves shall arise men speaking perverse things, to draw away disciples after them.*[289]

Thus Scripture itself warns us that certain members of the hierarchy can *and will* mislead the faithful, and high-ranking prelates have done so more than once in Church history. And, as we saw in Chapter 3, Sister Lucia repeatedly warned of "diabolical disorientation" in the Church in connection with the Third Secret, which she herself linked to the Book of the Apocalypse. Yet Messori, like Bertone, appears to have adopted the position that it is simply inconceivable that there could be betrayal and deviation from the truth by members of the Vatican apparatus, a position that finds no warrant in Sacred Scripture, Church teaching, Church history or indeed the Message of Fatima itself.

But surely Messori would agree that not even the Pope could make demonstrably unbelievable statements and expect them to be believed. It is a defined doctrine of our religion that the Faith can never contradict reason;[290] and, as Saint Thomas says, against a fact there is no argument. Sad to say, Messori's remarks can only be seen as an appeal to abandon reason in this affair, to ignore the facts, to place blind faith in a particular prelate who is no less a fallible human being than Messori is. One had the right to expect more from Messori, especially given his earlier recognition that Socci and the "Fatimists" have raised objectively valid points. Messori's "repentance" is all the more disappointing given that Bertone has not actually denied those points, but has only given the appearance of a denial—something a man as astute as Messori should be able to discern.

Bertone's surprise witness

The next segment of "The Cardinal Bertone Show" is a surprise the Cardinal evidently thinks will be an unanswerable rejoinder to the critics of the official account: a videotaped interview of Archbishop Capovilla touted as a "denial" that there is any "Fourth Secret" of Fatima. That Capovilla had finally been enlisted in Bertone's campaign was not particularly surprising, given the pressure that had been applied to the Archbishop over the previous year. Also not surprising, however, is that, just as

---

[289]Acts 20:28-30.

[290]*See, e.g.* VATICAN COUNCIL I, Faith and Reason, Chapter 4, Canons 5 and 10.

with Capovilla's statements floated earlier in the ridiculous venue of *Diva e Donna* magazine, the videotaped interview contains no denial at all. Rather, the interview backfires as badly as *Last Visionary* and Bertone's own television appearance on *Door to Door*. In fact, during the four-minute segment of the interview broadcast on *Telapace*, Capovilla actually *confirms* key facts that undermine the official account, while leaving untouched his testimony to Paolini. Before discussing what Capovilla actually says on the videotape, I must make a few preliminary observations.

First observation: This interview of Capovilla was not conducted by any Vatican representative on an official mission of the Church, but rather by Bertone's lay co-author of *Last Visionary*, Giuseppe De Carli. In his written introduction to the transcript of the interview distributed to the press, De Carli states that on August 22, 2007 "this writer found himself at Sotto Il Monte [Capovilla's home town] to gather in person an invaluable version, the only one, of the events that happened almost a half century ago."[291] He "found himself" in Sotto Il Monte? Had he just happened to be in the neighborhood with a video crew and thought he would drop in on the Archbishop? He and the video crew had perhaps arrived at Sotto Il Monte in a collective hypnotic trance, to be awakened by a snap of the Archbishop's fingers?

To be serious, De Carli's choice of words was designed to eliminate any need to explain *who* had sent him to see Capovilla—obviously, Cardinal Bertone—and why Bertone was using a lay journalist as his agent instead of the Vatican dispatching an official representative to clear up this vexing matter. Clearly, the Vatican wanted absolutely no official connection with any attempt to have Capovilla suddenly "retract" statements he had made a year earlier and which had been published to the world without the least objection by him. This, then, was yet another of those strange private and unofficial moves by which Bertone was seeking to shore up the official account while the Vatican looked on silently.

Second observation: It had been more than a year since Capovilla's testimony to Paolini admitting that there are two envelopes and two texts pertaining to the Third Secret, and Capovilla had expressed no objection to Paolini's account of that testimony as published by Socci ten months earlier. But now, so De Carli's introduction claims,

---

[291]Transcript provided to the press on September 21, 2007, p. 1. Questions by Giuseppe De Carli; answers by Archbishop Loris Capovilla. All further quotations are translated from this transcript.

"Monsignor Capovilla has decided to break his silence after having read Cardinal Tarcisio Bertone's book *Last Visionary of Fatima...* and, in a particular way, the reiterated criticisms addressed to the thesis sustained by the Secretary of State in his account." Notice that Capovilla has *not* "broken his silence" because Paolini or Socci had misrepresented his testimony. We are asked to believe it was Cardinal Bertone's book that inspired Capovilla to come forward. To say what? To say nothing, as we shall see, except disclosures that inflict more damage on Bertone's "thesis."

Third observation: De Carli does not do Bertone any favors by noting in his introduction that during the interview at which De Carli had "found himself," Capovilla

> consulted his personal diary of that period, but *the precision of his recollection is absolute*. Capovilla, notwithstanding his advanced age, is *a miracle of lucidity* and oratorical verve. He is a man one could listen to for hours. The reconstruction of events was *minute, rich with particulars*, filled with suggestions, even pastoral and spiritual.

So much for any possible claim that Capovilla's memory had been inaccurate when he spoke with Paolini a year earlier.

Fourth observation: Just how cleverly contrived the videotaped interview would be is shown by De Carli's disclosure in the introduction that "In July of this year Monsignor Capovilla sent a dossier to Cardinal Bertone"—evidently the same dossier Paolini saw Capovilla preparing during their meeting of June 21, 2007. De Carli offers the following quotation from the dossier: "The assertion which has come to be attributed to me, according to which I would have explicitly declared that there is a part of the Third Secret not revealed, is not borne out by any *document*." But who ever claimed there is a *document* in which Capovilla states that a part of the Secret has not been revealed? His testimony to Paolini on this point was *oral*. The introduction makes it clear that hairsplitting and carefully worded evasions would be the order of the day when De Carli "found himself" at Sotto Il Monte.

Fifth and final observation: It is necessary to recall briefly the main points of Paolini's account of what Capovilla told him, an account whose devastating details confronted De Carli when he "found himself" in Capovilla's presence with a video crew:

- Paul VI first read the Third Secret on June 27, 1963, almost two years before the date given (March 27, 1965) in the official account of June 2000, showing that Paul VI earlier read a text whose existence the official account has not disclosed.

- This huge discrepancy in dates is accounted for by the fact that, as Capovilla stated: "perhaps the Bertone envelope [*plico*] is not the same as the Capovilla envelope [*plico*]."

- Both John XXIII and Paul VI read a text of the Third Secret that was kept in the papal apartment in an antique desk called "Barbarigo" — *not* in the Archives of the Holy Office, where the text referred to in the official account was located — and it was from this antique desk that Paul VI had retrieved the text he read two years before the date given in the official account.

- In answer to Paolini's precise question: "Therefore, both dates are true, because there are two texts of the Third Secret?", Capovilla gave this absolutely decisive answer: "Exactly so! (*Per l'appunto!*)."[292]

All these affirmations had been in print for nearly a year without objection from the Archbishop, as had his signed and sealed document of May 17, 1967, a copy of which he had provided to Paolini.[293] Any "retraction" of those affirmations and that document now would be patently unworthy of belief. But, in any event, no "retraction" that failed *explicitly to negate each of the affirmations* would even constitute a denial in the first place. That De Carli understands this is shown by his introduction to the transcript, wherein *he*, but *not* Archbishop Capovilla, makes the following declaration:

> For decades there have been attributed to Monsignor Capovilla phrases which have fed the legend of a "Fourth Secret." The "Capovilla envelope", evoked by Fatimists as something dark and threatening (in "The Fourth Secret" it is spoken of a planetary apostasy of the Catholic Church and of a Rome without faith destined to become the seat of the Antichrist), coincides with the "Bertone envelope." The Vatican has not hidden the truth, has not had attitudes of a

---

[292]Socci, *Fourth Secret*, p. 142.

[293]*See* Appendix I.

code of silence ["*omertá*"], has not omitted to publish acts and documents, has not responded to the need for clarity with silence. Therefore, all that there is has been brought into the light of the sun.

So, according to *De Carli*—*not* the Vatican itself in an official statement!—the "Bertone envelope" and the "Capovilla envelope" "coincide" (whatever that means) and the Vatican has not hidden the truth. But De Carli's indignant pronouncement is manifestly false. In the first place, as De Carli's own evidence would show in a few moments (and as I showed in Chapter 6) it is quite impossible for the "Capovilla envelope" to "coincide" with the "Bertone envelope," for Capovilla's envelope bears notations in his handwriting, including the dictation of Pope John XXIII, and Bertone *has never produced* this envelope. De Carli's introduction simply ignores the known facts, evidently in the hope that no one will notice.

But what does *Archbishop Capovilla* have to say about the two envelopes in the actual transcript of the interview that follows De Carli's laughably biased "journalistic" introduction? Not surprisingly, given the history of this controversy, on the videotape Capovilla does not deny *a single one* of the affirmations he made to Paolini. Incredibly, Paolini and the four meetings he had with Capovilla *are not even mentioned*. There is an ironic parallel here: Just as Bertone appeared on *Door to Door* without mentioning Capovilla, so does Capovilla appear on "The Cardinal Bertone Show" without mentioning Paolini!

And bear in mind that Capovilla does not actually appear in person during the show. Nor does he appear by a remote live video link, as no less than Bertone, the Vatican Secretary of State, had done on *Door to Door*. That Capovilla had been kept away from live television cameras could not fail to engender suspicion, given that the Archbishop is "*a miracle of lucidity* and oratorical verve" and a "man one could listen to for hours." The last thing Bertone wanted was that his star witness actually *be* a witness, for that would mean the Archbishop could not be confined to carefully edited utterances, frozen on tape and delivered to the audience without any possibility of contradiction.

Another disastrous interview

Now let us examine the actual statements of Archbishop

Capovilla during the four-minute taped interview screened in the auditorium during "The Cardinal Bertone Show."

In yet another of the irregularities and contradictions that plague Bertone's presentations, the printed transcript of the interview is substantially longer than the soundtrack of the video segment broadcast from the auditorium. Moreover, while the video segment is some four minutes in length, the total interview, according to De Carli, was thirty minutes long. The soundtrack, therefore, was clearly subjected to heavy editing, much of it concealed by "covering shots" of graphics or stock film footage that filled the screen while Capovilla was speaking in the background, so that the viewer would not see Capovilla's image jump at each edit. I shall rely on the more complete printed transcript.

De Carli's introduction to the transcript states that the videotape and audiotape of the interview are "irrefutable proof," but fails to say *what* they prove. In fact, they prove that the "official" account is not believable. Let us examine the pertinent portions of the printed transcript:

> **Excellency, Pope John knew immediately of the "Third Secret of Fatima"?**
>
> ...Pope John ascended to the Papal throne on October 28, 1958. In December, Cento [the papal nuncio to Portugal], who became a cardinal in the meantime, told him of this envelope and hinted to him that the secret of Fatima had been sent to Pius XII.

Here Capovilla already suggests, contrary to the official account, that an envelope containing the Third Secret was in the personal custody of Pius XII—that is, in the papal apartment, not in the Archives of the Holy Office, as the official account claims. In a few moments, Capovilla will confirm precisely that.

> **How did Pope John react?**
>
> *He was not in a hurry to read it. He had other priorities.* He had to commence the Petrine service and *call the Second Vatican Council.* In August of 1959 he was found at Castelgandolfo. It was a moment of calm, of tranquility. At the summer residence arrived the Dominican Father Pierre Paul Phillipe, with the text of the "Third Secret." And anxious to know its contents. Not so the Pope. "I will look at it Wednesday with

my confessor."

So far, not one word about Capovilla's explosive revelations to Paolini, but the Archbishop has confirmed precisely Socci's thesis, noted earlier, that Pope John deliberately deferred reading the Secret because "he wanted to announce the convocation of Vatican Council II, almost as if to put before Heaven a *fait accompli*."[294] Notice also the level of detail in Capovilla's recollections, including dates, times, places and even the day of the week nearly fifty years ago. The Cardinal clearly has both an excellent memory and detailed written memoirs of his time as secretary to Pope John XXIII.

> **The first Pope who came to a knowledge of the "mystery of the century" chose an almost sacramental context. Who was his confessor?[295]**

> It was Alfredo Cavagna, eighty years old, theologian and jurist. Together they opened the envelope. The Pope rang me up. He said: "We are taking a look at the text of Sister Lucia but cannot figure it out. Can you give us a hand?" At that moment I felt myself privileged, and I agreed with much humility. I, however, did not know the Portuguese language. *I must add that, at times, I have said and written that in the text there were dialect expressions. In reality there were not.* The fact is that I did not know the language, I misinterpreted. There came to be called a recordist [taker of minutes] from the Secretariat of State, the Portuguese Paolo Tavares, a very good and holy priest. They called him after one or two days. He made a translation. The Pope saw, read, considered, prayed.

Still not a word about the revelations to Paolini. But here Capovilla, obviously under off-screen prompting, suddenly claims he was mistaken in his repeated oral and written testimony over the decades (discussed in Chapter 2) that the text of the Secret that Pope John read in August 1959 contained difficult expressions peculiar to the Portuguese language, requiring that an Italian

---

[294]Socci, *Quarto Segreto*, p. 205.

[295]This question is not posed during the video segment, but it appears on the written transcript, whereas the answer on the written transcript differs in content from Capovilla's answer on the video, which is in response to an entirely different question. This indicates that Capovilla's answers on the tape segment have been spliced from the 30 minutes of footage De Carli claims to have taken, and to some extent rearranged.

translation be prepared by Father Tavares before the Pope could comprehend it. As Capovilla here confirms, that translation was not ready until a day or two after Pope John opened the sealed envelope and tried to read the text on his own.

Why would Capovilla go out of his way to claim now, fifty years later, that he was mistaken about the linguistic peculiarities of the text Pope John read in 1959? Recall that in Chapter 2 I also noted Cardinal Ottaviani's testimony that in 1960 Pope John read a text of the Secret in *another* sealed envelope, and that the Pope had no trouble reading this text: "*Still sealed*, it was taken later, *in 1960*, to Pope John XXIII. The Pope *broke the seal*, and opened the envelope. Although it was in Portuguese, he told me afterwards that he understood the text in its entirety."[296] Capovilla does not dispute this testimony. Recall also that in *Fourth Secret*, Socci provides as an appendix the analysis of a Portuguese linguist who concludes that the vision of "the Bishop dressed in white" published in 2000 is *devoid* of any difficult Portuguese dialect expressions.

These facts point clearly to the existence of two different texts: the one the Vatican published in 2000, which contains "regular" Portuguese, and the one not yet published, which contains more difficult, idiomatic Portuguese expressions. It seems apparent, then, that in an effort to rebut Socci's presentation, Capovilla has been induced suddenly to suggest that his consistent oral and written testimony, which stood for a lifetime, was a "mistake" (but not a lie).

But Capovilla's excuse for his "mistake" makes no sense: "I did not know the language, I misinterpreted." If Capovilla did not know Portuguese, it would never have occurred to him in the first place to state that the text contained particularly difficult Portuguese expressions, since *all* Portuguese expressions would be difficult (indeed incomprehensible) to him. Therefore, he could not have known that the text contained particularly difficult Portuguese *unless someone told him so*—either the Pope or Father Tavares. Since Capovilla's testimony could only have been based on the advice of others, his sudden declaration that *he* was mistaken, that *he* misinterpreted, uttered nearly fifty years after the fact, has the earmarks of an improvisation designed to explain away statements which seriously undermine the official account, but without Capovilla having to call himself a liar. Nevertheless,

---

[296]*WTAF*, Vol. III, p. 557.

Capovilla confirms the accuracy of reports by Frère Michel and other Fatima scholars concerning the Archbishop's prior testimony on this point.

De Carli's next question concerns the Italian translation of the Secret prepared by Father Tavares, and here Capovilla drops a bombshell—one of the many inadvertent disclosures that have wrecked Bertone's attempt to defend the official account:

> **He [Pope John] also read the translation from Portuguese to Italian?**

Yes, *certainly*.[297]

Capovilla reveals for the first time that a *written* Italian translation of the Third Secret was prepared for Pope John XXIII in 1959. Well, where is it? According to the official account, the only written translation was prepared on or about March 6, 1967, four years after Pope John died. This is the same translation whose dated envelope Bertone displayed on *Door to Door*, but without showing the translation itself.

Now, what was the point of the 1967 translation of the Secret if a translation had already been prepared for Pope John in 1959 under the auspices of the Secretariat of State and at the Pope's specific request? Obviously, there would have been no point— *unless the 1959 translation was of a different document*. A document we have yet to see. A document that contains particularly difficult Portuguese expressions, which Capovilla mentioned repeatedly in oral and written testimony that he now suddenly declares was all a mistake. This would explain why neither the 1959 translation *nor* the 1967 translation has ever been published. It would also explain why there is no mention of the 1959 translation anywhere in the official account, even though there would have been no reason *not* to mention it *if* the translation were really of the same document the Vatican published in 2000.

So, Capovilla has revealed that just as there are two different but related texts of the Third Secret, precisely as he told Paolini, so are there two different but related translations. Thus far we have seen only one of the texts of the Secret and an envelope purportedly containing the 1967 translation.

---

[297]This question and answer are neither seen nor heard on the videotape, but appear only in the written transcript—yet another indication that Capovilla had much more to say than Bertone was willing to broadcast on television.

There is, however, a possible alternative conclusion: that *both* the 1959 and the 1967 translations are of the same text of the Third Secret, the one containing difficult idioms that we have yet to see. Perhaps the 1967 translation of this text was considered an "improvement" over the 1959 translation. In any case, since we have not been shown *either* the 1959 or the 1967 translation—another suspicious circumstance in a mountain of suspicion—we can only speculate on this point.

De Carli's next question demonstrates that Capovilla's carefully controlled video appearance would be another exercise in evasion from beginning to end:

> **Monsignor Capovilla, this is an extremely important point. The text that you read corresponds to that which was presented to the world in June 2000 by Cardinal Joseph Ratzinger and by Monsignor Tarcisio Bertone?**
>
> But of course! I have said it, and I repeat it gladly now: that is the text. *I don't recall it word for word, but the central nucleus is the same.*

Of course, no one, including Socci, has ever suggested that the vision of "the Bishop dressed in white" is not an authentic *part* of the Third Secret, or that it is not *one* of the texts Pope John read. The question, as both De Carli and Capovilla know quite well, is whether Pope John read *a second* text in which the Blessed Virgin explains the vision, so that there would be two related texts comprising the entire Third Secret. Capovilla admitted to Paolini precisely that there are two texts: "Exactly so!" he said. During the De Carli interview, Capovilla has not denied what he said to Paolini. Indeed, he has not even *mentioned* Paolini.

Here we encounter a damning omission: *De Carli does not show Capovilla the published text of the vision to refresh his recollection.* Instead, Capovilla is allowed to offer the vague observation: "I don't recall it word for word, but the central nucleus is the same." The central *nucleus*? What is that supposed to mean? Why does De Carli not simply *show* the text to Capovilla, rather than having him rely on his memory about a "nucleus"?

De Carli's failure to exhibit the very text at issue to the witness who is being asked to authenticate that text appears at first blush to be inexplicable. But there is an explanation. Capovilla is *not* relying on his memory about the text of the vision because he knows down to the last detail what the text contains. He knows this, if for no other reason, because he, like countless other people, has a copy of *The Message of Fatima*, which reproduces the text in its entirety. In fact, as we saw in Chapter 6, Capovilla recommended to Paolini that he obtain a copy of *Message* for himself in order to understand what Capovilla was about to tell him concerning the Secret. Now, since Capovilla has ready access to a copy of the published text of the vision as reproduced in *Message*, he would have no difficulty remembering on camera exactly what is in the document. He would not say something as strangely evasive as "the central nucleus is the same." Moreover, Bertone himself had displayed the text on television, less than three months before De Carli's interview of Capovilla. Are we to believe that Capovilla has not seen this telecast or at least a tape of it? Capovilla could also have been given access to the original text at the Vatican if Bertone were really interested in having it authenticated.

Therefore, one can only conclude that Capovilla's vagueness of recollection is a rhetorical pose. Since he does not have the document in front of him at the moment he is being questioned about it, he can plead a lack of precise memory concerning its contents and thus avoid making any definite affirmations about whether the text of the vision is *the* text—the one and only text—that Pope John read. The Archbishop is unwilling to commit himself to that proposition because he knows there is *another* text, just as he told Paolini. Hence the vague remarks about the "nucleus" of a document he no doubt has near at hand and had read before the videotaped interview.

Consider the absurdity of what we are being asked to believe: that Capovilla cannot answer precisely questions that *anyone in the world could answer precisely* simply by examining the reproduction of the text of the vision in *Message*, a copy of which *Capovilla himself possesses*. We are undoubtedly witnessing one of those typically "Roman" evasions by which one dissembles without actually lying outright.

This would also explain why De Carli will not ask Capovilla to deny outright that he told Paolini there are two texts pertaining to the Secret. No "Roman" evasion would be possible in answer to such a direct question. The Archbishop cannot deny that he told Paolini there are two texts, because he knows that there are. That is why the Archbishop cannot even *mention* Paolini. And neither can De Carli.

> **In the text read by you in 1959 it speaks of a "bishop dressed in white" who is killed at the foot of a large cross?**
>
> Yes, it speaks of this; this appeared to us to be *the nucleus* of that private revelation received by the children of Fatima.

Again, the Archbishop makes a curious reference to the "nucleus" of a text that is literally at his fingertips, but which, quite tellingly, he is not shown on camera. And Capovilla has still not even mentioned Solideo Paolini, much less denied the statements he made to him. Notice that Capovilla has twice been asked to affirm that which no one is denying in the first place: that John XXIII read a text pertaining to the "bishop dressed in white." Not once, however, has De Carli asked Capovilla to deny that there is *another* text, containing the words of the Virgin, which explains the vision.

The next question and answer will demonstrate even more clearly the skillful evasiveness with which the entire interview was conducted:

> **And why, according to you, does it continue to be written that John XXIII would have read not this text, but another text, the so-called "Fourth Secret" that the Church would have thus far kept hidden?**
>
> How can it be said that it was hidden? The Third Secret was read by John XXIII; his confessor read it; I, his little secretary, have seen it; Cardinal Tardini has seen it; the two most important personages of the Secretariat of State, Monsignor Antonio Samore and Monsignor Angelo Dell'Acqua; all the heads of the dicasteries beginning with Cardinal Ottaviani. While on holiday, at the College of Propaganda Fide, there is Cardinal Agagianian. The Secretary of the Congregation, Sigismondi, saw it.

The question is misleading, but the answer is astounding. For the *third* time De Carli falsely suggests by his question that the "Fatimists" claim Pope John did not read the text of the vision, but rather some other text, when he knows full well that what they actually claim is that the Pope read *both* the text of the vision *and* another text which explains the vision's meaning. De Carli continues to feign ignorance of the real issue—the existence of a second text—and the Archbishop continues to fail to address it.

But look at Capovilla's answer: He *does not deny that there is another text*. Rather, he denies only that the text at issue has not been hidden *because* a select group of prelates he identifies has read it. And notice that *Capovilla does not declare that the whole world knows the Secret because the Secret is contained entirely in the vision published in 2000*. Why would the Archbishop—"a miracle of lucidity"—forget to make such an obvious point if the vision already published were really the Secret in its entirety? There can be only one reasonable answer: the Archbishop knows there is more to the Secret than the vision. That is why he will not simply declare, when given the perfect opportunity to do so, that the world has known the entire Third Secret since 2000.

Consider also that whatever that select group of prelates read must have been very grave indeed for so many of them to be summoned by the Pope to the task of reading it. Surely the ambiguous vision of a "bishop dressed in white," standing alone, could not have had such urgent importance that the Secretary of State and the head of every Vatican department would be called upon to scrutinize it under a vow of absolute secrecy that has been maintained for almost five decades.

More than halfway through the interview segment, Capovilla still has made no effort to retract his testimony to Paolini, while De Carli continues to avoid the subject of Paolini entirely. In answer to De Carli's next question, however, Capovilla drops another bomb on the already demolished edifice of the official account:

> **And the conclusion of this collective reading?**
>
> That none of those who had read the text asked the Pope to publish it, to speak of it. The Pope hesitated, then decided: "I have seen it, I have read it, we will reseal it." He dictated to me a text to write on the envelope: I give no judgment. He deferred to others: to a commission, to a congregation, or to his successor.

Capovilla reveals, just as he revealed to Paolini, that there is an envelope containing the Third Secret on which Capovilla wrote at the Pope's dictation: "I give no judgment." We also know, as mentioned in Chapter 6, that Capovilla wrote on the same envelope "a note concerning the manner of arrival of the envelope in his [Pope John's] hands and the names of all those to whom he considered it necessary to make it known."[298]

As I have already noted, *this envelope has never been produced by the Vatican and has never even been mentioned in the official account.* Why? What reason could there be to withhold the missing envelope besides a desire to hide its contents? If there were nothing to hide, the envelope surely would have been produced or at least mentioned in the official account. Given all the evidence presented, there can be only one conclusion: the missing envelope contains the very text at issue, the still-hidden portion of the Third Secret of Fatima.

Nor can one avoid this conclusion by supposing that the envelope bearing Pope John's dictation and the further note and list of witnesses by Capovilla was merely an outer envelope containing Sister Lucia's inner envelope, and that the outer envelope has since been discarded. It is inconceivable that an envelope bearing papal dictation and other key information, a document therefore of major historical importance, would be tossed in the garbage— unless, again, there is something to hide. But even if the envelope had, by some terrible mistake, been discarded, why would Bertone not simply explain the mishap and thus avoid creating still more grounds for suspicion?

Capovilla's revelation had only further corroborated his testimony to Paolini, testimony Capovilla is *still* not being asked to deny even as the interview draws toward its conclusion.

> **Excellency, of how many lines is composed the third part of the message that you read with Pope John XXIII?**
>
> I do not know with exactitude.
>
> **Were there four pages?**
>
> To me it seemed a long enough message, in small writing. *Probably* four small pages. *I don't know if it was pages or sheets.* But this is a particular on which I did not linger.

Once again—quite incredibly—Capovilla is not asked to examine the text published by the Vatican in 2000 and displayed by Bertone on television in 2007 in order to confirm that it was

---

[298]Socci, *Fourth Secret*, p. 142.

the same text he read with Pope John in 1959. The Archbishop is asked to recall from "memory" the number of lines and pages in a text he read some fifty years ago rather than simply taking a look at the document *he has available at that very moment*. The Archbishop declares with a poker face that a document at hand, a document he has no doubt read many times since 2000, "seemed a long enough message" and is "probably" four pages long, when he has to know *exactly* how long it is. And Capovilla suggests he cannot recall whether the document consists of contiguous pages (on a folio) or separate sheets of paper, when Bertone had shown the whole world only weeks before that the text of the vision is written on the four contiguous pages of one folio. There is no question a game is being played. And, yet again, no effort is made to address the Archbishop's testimony to Paolini.

> **I would not want to force your hand or reach hasty conclusions, nor arouse further polemics. Can we affirm, after what you have said, that the secret read by John XXIII is not the "Fourth Secret," but is, simply, the Secret published and discussed by the Congregation for the Doctrine of the Faith?**
>
> I will tell you more. When I heard talk of "Fourth Secret" I was amazed. It had never passed through my head that there exists a fourth secret. No one has said that to me, neither have I affirmed anything of that kind. I have always held that this will not be the last time that the Lord is revealed through the Mother of Jesus or the saints. As far as Fatima is concerned, I read with much joy that which has been defined precisely by then Cardinal Ratzinger and that which has been excellently collected in a volume by Cardinal Bertone. I have from the Magisterium of the Church everything I need. That which has been said truly represents a spiritual food for all of us.

By now it ought to be clear to any discerning reader that the interview is a sham designed to mislead the gullible and the uninformed. Here Capovilla denies yet another proposition not at issue: that there is a "Fourth Secret" of Fatima. Capovilla knows very well that "Fourth Secret" is merely the ironic title of Socci's book. The real issue, once again, is whether there is a missing part of the *Third* Secret, as Capovilla admitted to Paolini.

Instead of addressing the real issue, Capovilla answers De Carli's carefully framed question—carefully framed to *avoid* the real issue—about whether the text that Pope John read is the text published by the Vatican. Of course it is! But what about the *other* text, the one *not* published by the Vatican, whose existence Capovilla disclosed to Paolini? What does Capovilla have to say about that? *Not one word.*

As for Capovilla's declaration: "I have from the Magisterium of the Church everything I need," what does the Magisterium, the official teaching office of the Church, have to do with anything Bertone and the former Cardinal Ratzinger have said concerning Fatima? As we have already seen, Cardinal Ratzinger himself made it clear that *The Message of Fatima* commentary of June 2000, including its "attempt" to "interpret" the vision of the bishop in white, was and is in no way imposed on the faithful. And it is nothing short of insulting to suggest that the Magisterium has spoken through Bertone's *Last Visionary*, a secular book co-written with a lay journalist. Capovilla resorts to a fallacious argument from authority, when this sophisticated prelate certainly knows the difference between the Magisterium and the opinions of cardinals expressed in a commentary or a book.

De Carli "testifies" for Capovilla

At this point the video segment broadcast in the auditorium ends, although the written transcript continues for another page, embracing three more questions and answers. As soon as the segment ends, the camera returns to De Carli, who has the audacity to declare to the audience:

> I conclude, therefore, there is not a Capovilla envelope
> to contrast to a Bertone envelope. The two envelopes
> are the same document.

De Carli concludes? But what did *Capovilla* conclude, given that *De Carli has never asked him* whether there are two envelopes, the "Capovilla envelope" and the "Bertone envelope"? Even more audaciously, De Carli adds:

> I asked Msgr. Capovilla why he had never said
> these things in so many years. "I said them, I said
> them," he replied to me, "but no one ever came to
> ask me explicitly." As we can see, complex questions

sometimes have simple solutions.

One can only shake his head in wonderment at the clumsiness of the deception involved here:

First, it is De Carli, *not the witness*, who supplies the conclusion that there is only one envelope, not two envelopes, pertaining to the Third Secret. That De Carli was forced to resort to this ruse makes it virtually certain that he is complicit in a cover-up, for it is obvious that he could not extract this conclusion from Capovilla. Of course, Capovilla would not say this himself, because he had already told Solideo Paolini—and in fact he had just told De Carli!— that there is another envelope, bearing his handwritten notations at the direction of John XXIII, which Bertone has never produced. Moreover, Capovilla's contemporaneous "confidential note" (see Appendix I) confirms the existence of this other envelope, placing its existence beyond any possible manipulated "retraction" today.

Second, De Carli, seemingly alluding to a portion of the interview that does not appear in either the written transcript or the video segment (another indication of heavy editing of the 30-minute interview), suggests that Capovilla had only been waiting for someone to come and ask him explicitly about these matters, and that this is the "simple" answer to a seemingly complex question. *But Solideo Paolini had done precisely that on multiple occasions, and Capovilla told him of the existence of the other envelope.* Yet De Carli pretends Paolini has never questioned Capovilla on the very matters at issue. At the same time, De Carli suggests— without providing any transcript or video—that *he* has questioned Capovilla on these matters, when he presents no questions and no answers! Given that the videotaped interview went on for thirty minutes, of which only four minutes were shown to the audience, it is reasonable to assume that even if De Carli did ask Capovilla the right questions, he did not like the answers and does not wish to reveal them. Do De Carli and Bertone really think no one will notice the game they are playing?

Third, in the continuing written transcript, not reflected in the shorter video segment, *Capovilla himself again confirms the existence of a never-produced envelope containing a text of the Secret*, thus dropping a final bombshell on what is left of the official account:

> **Excellency, you have also followed the first years of the pontificate of Paul VI. Paul VI read the same message two times. Is that so?**

Yes, it is so.

The first time was a few days after his election, June 27, 1963; the second, March 27, 1965.

I have also demonstrated this. On June 27, 1963 I was, that evening, with the Sisters of the Poor in Via Casilina. A worried Monsignor Dell'Acqua telephoned me. The Fatima envelope could not be found. *I replied that probably it could be found in the writing desk called "Barbarigo,"* because it belonged to Saint Gregory Barbarigo and was gifted to Pope John by Count della Torre. *Pope John held it dear, in his bedroom, like a relic.* There were on the right and on the left five or six drawers. Later, Dell'Acqua telephoned me and communicated that *the envelope had been found.* On June 28 Pope Paul called me and asked *who had dictated the lines on the envelope.* I explained that it was the Pope himself who wanted to indicate the persons who had knowledge of the text. "Pope John did not say anything else to you?," Pope Paul asked me. "No, Holy Father, he left it to others to decide." "I will also do as much", responded Pope Montini. The envelope was resealed and *I don't know if it was spoken of further.*

Note well: Amazingly enough, the man who has become *Bertone's own witness* specifically confirms what he said to Solideo Paolini: that a text of the Secret was kept in the papal bedchamber in a writing desk called "Barbarigo," as opposed to the Holy Office archives, and that this text was enclosed in the envelope *Bertone has never produced,* bearing notations dictated by John XXIII.

But attention: Having finally admitted to the existence of the "Capovilla envelope," Bertone is now attempting (through leading questions posed to Capovilla by De Carli) to suggest that the text in the "Capovilla envelope" in the papal apartment is the same as the one in the Holy Office archives, even though this was never mentioned before. Let us examine the huge problems this crude "patch job" on the official account creates for Bertone.

A desperate about-face

Recall how in *Last Visionary* Bertone mocked the very idea of a text in the papal apartment: "And on what stands the apodictic certainty that the 'envelope' always remained in the 'apartment', even in a drawer of the bedside table of the Pope?"[299] Ha, ha, ha. Now, however, the very claim Bertone mocked is openly admitted in the very transcript De Carli created at Bertone's request. But why would Bertone include such damaging information in the transcript (while excluding it from the broadcast video segment) if he really is concealing a text of the Third Secret? Why the sudden about-face?

Quite simply, Bertone had no choice, as the existence of a text of the Secret in the papal apartment (never before mentioned by him or the Vatican) could no longer be denied. So, Bertone has adopted a tried-and-true tactic of the trial lawyer: When confronted by irrefutable evidence adverse to your position, try to make it *your* evidence; *embrace* it, even *repeat* it, as if to show the jury that you are not the least disturbed by it and that they too should pay it no mind. Thus Bertone, finally forced to admit there was a text in the papal apartment all along, now readily does so.

Bertone's new problems

Having been forced to admit the existence of the text in the papal apartment, Bertone has suddenly altered his version of the facts to assert that this text is the same as the text in the Holy Office Archive. He attempts to "prove" this by having De Carli pose the above-noted laughably leading questions, designed practically to force Capovilla to agree that Paul VI read the same text in 1963 and 1965: "...Paul VI read the same message two times.... Is that so? The first time was a few days after his election, June 27, 1963; the second, March 27, 1965?"

With questions like these, it is the questioner, not the witness, who is testifying. That is why leading questions are not permissible during the direct examination of a witness in legal proceedings. Leading questions defeat the search for truth by dishonestly suggesting to the witness the answer the *questioner* would like him to give, as opposed to the answer the *witness* would give if not prompted by the wording of the question.

At any rate, De Carli's phrase "Paul VI read the same *message* two times" is ambiguous enough to allow Capovilla to agree

---

[299]*Last Visionary*, p. 78.

without lying, as "the same *message*" could involve two different *texts* of the same Third Secret, or both parts (the vision and the Virgin's explanation) read together in 1963 and 1965. Notice, however, that Capovilla does not actually *say* that Paul VI read the contents of the "Capovilla envelope" as such for a second time in 1965. In fact, as De Carli's own transcript reveals, Capovilla *would not know* whether Paul VI did so, even if it were true. As Capovilla states: "The envelope was resealed [in 1963] and *I don't know if it was spoken of further*." Thus, De Carli has simply put words in Capovilla's mouth by means of his leading questions.

De Carli's clumsy leading questions aside, Bertone cannot succeed with this contrivance. First of all, if it were really the case that Paul VI read the same text twice—in 1963 and 1965—Bertone would have said so long ago, thus clearing up the apparent mystery. He would have mentioned this in *Message* back in 2000, or in *Last Visionary* or during his appearance on *Door to Door*. That Bertone says it now, only after the emergence of undeniable evidence of a text in the papal apartment, clearly suggests what the law calls a "recent fabrication"—a change of story designed to accommodate facts a witness did not think would come out: "You found a gun in my basement, detective? Oh yes, *that* gun. Of course, it was always there. The previous owner left it behind. Did I not mention this before?"

That tactic will not work here, however, because the evidence Bertone belatedly embraces and attempts to spin his way cannot fail to annihilate his "thesis." As Capovilla reveals to Bertone's own handpicked audience in the transcript quoted above, in 1963 Pope Paul's subordinate, Monsignor Dell'Acqua, asked Capovilla where the "Fatima envelope" was, and Capovilla told him where in the papal apartment it could be found. That is, Dell'Acqua (who was at the time no less than the Substitute of the Secretary of State) *did not make inquiry of the Holy Office because the text Paul VI wished to read was not there*. Yet we know that, as the official account reveals, Pope John did return *a* text of the Secret to the Holy Office before his death in 1963, and that it was *this* text that Paul VI read in 1965, as opposed to 1963:

> In fact Pope John XXIII decided to return the sealed envelope *to the Holy Office* and not to reveal the third part of the "secret."

> Paul VI read the contents with the Substitute,

> Archbishop Angelo Dell'Acqua, on 27 March 1965,
> and *returned the envelope to the Archives of the Holy
> Office*, deciding not to publish the text.[300]

Nowhere does the official account state that in 1963 Paul VI retrieved from the Holy Office the text that John XXIII had returned there, and not even Bertone is claiming that now. Therefore, the text that Capovilla helped Dell'Acqua locate in Pope Paul's apartment in June of 1963—the text kept in the late Pope John's prized writing desk called "Barbarigo"—could not possibly have been the one Pope John returned to the Holy Office before he died. Bertone's tactic has backfired, and there is no way out of the problem. His own witness has confirmed the existence of two separate but related texts of the Third Secret of Fatima: one in the Holy Office archives, the other in "Barbarigo"; one read by Paul VI in 1963—the text Pope John kept in "Barbarigo"; the other read by Paul VI in 1965—the text Pope John returned to the Holy Office.[301]

In sum, Bertone's belated admission of the presence of the "Capovilla envelope" in the papal apartment, and his failure to produce it or to explain its non-production, are the final blow to his position. He himself has demonstrated conclusively that he is hiding something. Bertone's contrivance—that Paul VI read the same text, contained in the same envelope, in 1963 and 1965—is riddled with gaping holes he cannot possibly explain:

- If Paul VI read in 1963 the same text he read again in 1965, and there is nothing to hide, then Bertone would have produced on television the envelope Paul VI resealed in 1963—the "Capovilla envelope" on which, as Bertone's own evidence proves, Capovilla wrote the words dictated by John XXIII, a list of names of those who had read the contents, and "a note concerning the manner of arrival of the envelope in his [Pope John's] hands..."

- The official account never mentioned that Paul VI read a text of the Secret in 1963, even though that reading was a momentous historical event.

- There would have been no reason for the official account

---

[300]*The Message of Fatima*, p. 4.

[301]The Italian original and English translation of the stamped "confidential note" by Archbishop Capovilla, dated May 17, 1967, in which he recorded the precise circumstances of the reading of the Third Secret by Pope Paul VI in 1963 are reproduced in Appendix I.

not to mention this momentous historical event *unless* the text Pope Paul read and placed back in the resealed "Capovilla envelope" in 1963 was (and is) being hidden.

- If Paul VI read in 1965 the same text he read in 1963, the official account of the 1965 reading would have mentioned this — unless, again, there is something to hide.

- As Bertone now reveals through Capovilla, Paul VI resealed the envelope containing the text he read in 1963, stating that he would "do as much as" Pope John had, meaning leave it to others to judge the text. Why, then, would Paul VI reopen the envelope he had resealed in 1963 in order to read the *same* text again in 1965? He wouldn't.

- If Paul VI decided to reopen the envelope he had resealed in 1963 in order to give it a second reading in 1965, how is it that neither his diaries, nor the records of the members of his staff, nor any Vatican document whatsoever, reflect that the Pope decided to revisit the same text he had previously decided to leave to others to judge?

But even if Bertone's leaky contrivance could hold water, he has still failed to explain away John Paul II's reading of a text of the Secret in 1978—three years before the date given in the official account—and Pope John's reading of a text of the Secret in 1960—the year following the date given in the official account. All told, the evidence, including Bertone's *own* evidence, shows that three different Popes have read texts of the Third Secret on two different occasions during their respective pontificates: John XXIII in August of 1959 and 1960; Paul VI in 1963 and 1965; John Paul II in 1978 and 1981. Apparently we are expected to believe that all three Popes read the same text twice, but by some incredible coincidence the Vatican's official records failed to note an historic second reading of the Third Secret by each Pope. Apparently we are expected to believe that although there are—

- *two* different Third Secret envelopes bearing the identical "1960 order" written on each of the two envelopes by Sister Lucia,

- *two* different locations of Third Secret texts,

- *two* different Third Secret translations in Italian, neither of which has been made public by the Vatican, and

- *two* different Third Secret readings in *two* different years by *three* consecutive Popes,

—there is only *one* text of the Third Secret of Fatima. But if anyone still believes that now, he has not given this matter the attention it deserves.

From beginning to end, and no denial

The final question and answer in De Carli's interview of Capovilla are of little consequence, except that Capovilla does confirm the "Fatimist" contention that when Paul VI went to Fatima in 1967 he declined to speak with Sister Lucia: "Sister Lucia requested a private conversation. But the Pope did not speak Portuguese, nor Sister Lucia Italian. 'Sister Lucia, tell everything to your bishop; it will be as if you told it to me.'" The claim that the Pope, accompanied on all his foreign trips by first-rate translators, could not speak to Lucia because of the language barrier must have been as insulting to Lucia's dignity as it is to our intelligence.

The interview concludes with Capovilla declaring: "And today I am happy to have read Cardinal Bertone's book, which in my opinion corresponds perfectly to that which the simplicity of this Sister had wanted to reveal through her life and through Mary. The Madonna says: 'Do what Jesus tells you.' Today He would say to us: 'Do what the Vicar of Christ tells you and you will all be more tranquil and in peace.'" And what has the Vicar of Christ told us to do regarding the Third Secret? Absolutely nothing.

So, Archbishop Capovilla will end the interview without denying a single word he said to Solideo Paolini, while nevertheless confirming that there is an envelope containing a text of the Third Secret that Bertone has never produced. The Archbishop will provide a series of irrelevant answers to a series of irrelevant questions designed to navigate around the crux of the matter: what Capovilla told Paolini. The Archbishop will conclude by telling us very cryptically that Bertone's book "corresponds"—that word again!—to the "simplicity" of what Lucia wanted to reveal in her life and through Mary. This is very conspicuously *not* the same as saying that what Lucia and the Virgin wanted to reveal in the *texts* of the Third Secret has all been published. He will recommend that everyone take the "papal tranquilizer"—just listen to the Pope and you will all be calm and peaceful. But the Pope has said nothing about this controversy that would require us to accept Bertone's representations, but rather has written privately to Socci thanking him for his book. Not even the Vatican apparatus has dared to launch an official defense of Bertone against the indictment Socci has published to the world—especially Capovilla's testimony to Paolini, which remains completely intact at the end of "The Cardinal Bertone Show."

Not with a bang, but a whimper

The final speaker on "The Cardinal Bertone Show" is Bertone himself. This is the Cardinal's moment to answer the many concerns raised by Socci and Catholics the world over concerning his version of events. But, as he has done for the past seven years, Bertone continues to duck every issue. After a brief discourse concerning the Church's approach to Marian apparitions, he says only this: "On the famous Third Secret, on the truth of the Third Secret, I will not return. Certainly, if there had been some further element, of commentary, of integration, it would have appeared in her [Lucia's] letters, in her thousands of letters—something that isn't there."

It seems that even as he avoids the issues, the Cardinal cannot help but raise further doubts about his account. Why would the Cardinal say that *if* there were a missing part of the Third Secret it would have appeared in Sister Lucia's correspondence with various people around the world, rather than in a text she wrote specifically at the direction of the Virgin? Why would Lucia reveal an element of the Third Secret in her *personal correspondence* when, as we know, the Secret was transmitted in two envelopes which state they "can only be opened in 1960 by the Cardinal Patriarch of Lisbon or the Bishop of Leiria"? Does the Cardinal mean to direct our attention away from those two envelopes, or the never-produced "Capovilla envelope" bearing the dictation of John XXIII? And on what basis does he assert that there is nothing pertaining to the Secret in Lucia's thousands of letters? Has he read and studied them all?

Although he had staged this entire television spectacle to defend his position, Cardinal Bertone has nothing further to say about the very controversy that had prompted him to stage it. Evidently, the Cardinal believes that the sheer spectacle of the event will create the impression that he has prevailed, even though the substance of what he has just presented only confirms that he cannot possibly be telling the whole truth.

Still more problems for Bertone

"The Cardinal Bertone Show" is, if that were possible, an even bigger disaster for him than *Last Visionary* and the appearance on *Door to Door*. For the Cardinal's own witness—the witness he tried to make his own in order to blunt the impact of the witness' testimony—has completed the destruction of the official account. Despite Bertone's elaborate attempt to suggest otherwise, Capovilla not only fails to deny even one word of his testimony to Paolini, he confirms key facts which demonstrate that there is a text, a translation, and an envelope pertaining to the Third Secret, none of which the Vatican has produced or even mentioned over the past seven years.

But that is not the end of the problems for Cardinal Bertone on this particular evening. Before the guards throw Socci out on the street, he is able to play for the assembled journalists an audiotape of Capovilla's statements to Paolini during their aforementioned meeting on June 21, 2007. As the major Italian daily *Il Giornale* reports, on the tape Capovilla is heard to state: "Besides the four pages [of the vision of the bishop in white] there was also something else, an attachment, yes." As the reporter from *Il Giornale* concluded, Capovilla's statement "would confirm the thesis of the existence of a second sheet with the interpretation of the Secret. The mystery, and above all the polemics, will continue."[302]

The mystery and the polemics will indeed continue. Meanwhile, however, not only the Church, but the whole world, is moving inexorably toward the ultimate consequences the missing text of the Third Secret no doubt foretells *and* gives us the means to avoid.

---

[302]"The Fourth Secret of Fatima does not exist," *Il Giornale*, September 22, 2007.

Chapter 11

Bertone's Method

In the preceding pages we have reviewed the evidence that led Antonio Socci (like millions of other Catholics) to conclude that it "is certain" there is a separate but related text of the Third Secret of Fatima, not yet revealed, containing "the words of the Madonna [which] preannounce an apocalyptic crisis of the faith in the Church starting from the top" and "an explanation of the vision (revealed on June 26, 2000) where there appear the Pope, the bishops and martyred faithful, after having traversed a city in ruins."[303] The hidden words of the Madonna would predict, as Socci writes, the "assassination of a Pope in the context of an immense martyrdom of Christians and of a devastation of the world."[304]

On these pages we have also examined how Cardinal Tarcisio Bertone has conducted an elaborate public relations campaign designed to give the appearance, but not the substance, of an explicit "official" denial that such a text exists, and how over the course of this campaign the Cardinal has only dug for himself a pit of inconsistencies, self-contradictions and new disclosures which have undermined his position. I stress that it is *his* position, not that of the Holy Catholic Church, that Bertone has undermined. For in his privately published book, *Last Visionary*, his radio broadcast, and his two television appearances, Bertone has in no way spoken with the authority of the Church's Magisterium, which is not his to exercise in any event. Nor, we must remind ourselves, is *The Message of Fatima* commentary of June 2000 in any way a binding teaching of the Church. Once again, as Cardinal Ratzinger himself made clear, the commentary presents nothing more than an "attempt" to interpret the vision of the bishop in white, and the Church has not limited the freedom of the faithful to reach their own conclusions about what it means. In the end, therefore, all of

---

[303]Socci, *Fourth Secret*, p. 82.

[304]Ibid., pp. 63-64.

Bertone's affirmations concerning this controversy are merely his own statements, not the Church's. And, when all is said and done, so is the "official" account as a whole.

The big picture

If one examines carefully the parade of presentations Bertone has conducted since Socci's *Fourth Secret* was published in November of 2006, as indeed we have done on these pages, one will discern the following elements of the "big picture":

First, Bertone has assiduously avoided making any unequivocal statement—much less a simple yes or no—about whether there is a text that contains the words of the Virgin following the famous "etc" and explaining the vision of the bishop in white. Instead, he harps on the idea of an "authentic text" in the archives of the Holy Office, and fails and refuses *either to ask or to answer* precise questions concerning a text involving the "etc" and the Virgin's explanation of the vision.

Second, Bertone will not disclose the existence of such a text, but neither will he deny it explicitly, since that would require an outright lie. However, his repeated references to an "authentic" text in the archives—as opposed to the text (and envelope) his own witness now admits was located in the papal apartment—evince a mental reservation concerning another text, not yet published and privately deemed "not authentic" by himself and others.

Third, Bertone and his collaborators have conducted a series of elaborate presentations which give the appearance of responding to the need for transparency, but which are really exercises in obfuscation—

- the commentary (*Message*) and press conference of June 26, 2000, which ducks the "etc" issue by using the Third instead of the Fourth Memoir;

- ten hours of purported interviews of Lucia in Coimbra, for which Bertone provides no videotape, audiotape, transcript or any other independent record, and from which he purports to extract only a few words of the seer in "quotations" which constantly change, seemingly as the need arises;

- a book co-written with De Carli (*Last Visionary*), published in May 2007, only a few pages of which even purport to address Socci's conclusions, but in fact evade them all;

- a television appearance on *Door to Door* on May 31, 2007, during which Bertone likewise fails to answer any of Socci's conclusions;

- a radio appearance on Vatican Radio on June 6, 2007, suffering from the same deficiency;

- a further television appearance on *Telepace* on September 21, 2007, a show filled with celebrities and speeches, but likewise failing to rebut Socci or the evidence he presented—including the testimony of Archbishop Capovilla to Solideo Paolini, which is not the least affected by the videotaped interview Bertone's agent, Giuseppe De Carli, conducted in a failed attempt to obtain a "retraction" that only further demonstrated Bertone must be hiding something.

Not one of these presentations addresses the very heart of the matter: whether Lucia wrote a text containing the Virgin's words following the "etc" and explaining the vision of the bishop in white. On the contrary, all of these presentations are designed precisely to avoid and obscure that question by focusing on matters not in dispute: that the text of the vision is authentic, and that John XXIII read the text of the vision.

Fourth, despite all these presentations, the testimony of Capovilla to Paolini that there are two texts and two envelopes comprising the Third Secret is not only not denied *but further confirmed* by the presentations themselves. The same is true as to the testimony of Cardinal Ottaviani that there is a one-page, 25-line text of the Secret.

Fifth, having done absolutely nothing with these presentations to disprove the accusations of Socci and the "Fatimists," but rather having actually *confirmed* the accusations, Bertone nonetheless projects a suave assurance that his position has been vindicated.

Sixth, Bertone has used the trappings of authority—his title, his ornate Vatican offices, his associates in the hierarchy, the dog and pony show featuring powerful and influential friends—to endow with a patina of officialdom what is really nothing more than a failed personal and private initiative to vindicate himself against Socci and all the other members of the faithful who are not persuaded by his representations.

Seventh, neither the Pope nor the Holy See has officially joined Bertone's campaign against Socci and the position he represents so ably. Quite the contrary, the Pope has made it a point to thank Socci for having written a book that resoundingly rejects Bertone's version of the facts and openly declares that Bertone and his collaborators have engaged in a cover-up!

One must pause to consider the wholly extraordinary nature of what the Cardinal has attempted here. In an effort to silence his critics, the Cardinal has written a book and appeared on television and radio like any other guest in the "crossfire" of a public controversy. When these public relations maneuvers backfired, the Cardinal even went so far as to arrange private sponsorship from bankers and other supporters for a television special of his own, assembling an audience of the elite and a panel of luminaries who had nothing important to say. These initiatives, all undertaken in less than a year following the publication of Socci's book, do not suggest a man confident he has nothing to hide and content to let the truth speak for itself. Rather, they suggest a man working furiously to create a distraction from the growing perception that he is, in fact, hiding something.

Consider also the audacity of the Cardinal's method. While resorting to the mass media to argue his case, the Cardinal refuses to answer questions from any member of the media except the one journalist he has handpicked to assist him in his media campaign: Giuseppe De Carli, his co-author. And when even De Carli attempts to pursue certain questions, the Cardinal ignores the questions or provides evasive answers, as we saw in Chapter 7. Yet the Cardinal expects the faithful to accept uncritically his claim that he has laid to rest all doubts about the completeness of the Vatican's disclosure of the Third Secret when (a) he will not answer questions, (b) neither his book, nor his radio or TV appearances, nor anything else he has said over the past seven years denies or refutes a single point Socci and the "Fatimists" have raised, and (c) his shifting statements and new disclosures have only heightened the certainty that there exists a hidden text of the Secret, just as Socci has observed.

Bertone says, in essence, "Trust me!" even as he refuses to address the many facts that cast doubt on the veracity of his account—facts that Socci, a devout and loyal Catholic, has so effectively marshaled. As these pages have shown, there are, quite literally, at least 101 grounds for doubt. (*See* Appendix II.) Relying on a publicity blitz that is all show and no substance, as opposed to providing forthright answers to simple questions, Bertone evidently believes the faithful will simply overlook the facts merely because the Cardinal Secretary of State has made appearances in various private forums, surrounded by prestigious and powerful friends, and we should "trust" and "obey" the pastors of the Church. But once again, contrary to what Messori has suggested, Cardinal Bertone has no pastoral authority over the faithful, nor has the Pope declared by his own authority that Bertone's version of the facts is to be accepted. If anything, the Pope has indicated (by his letter to Socci) that the faithful are entirely free to accept *Socci's* position as opposed to Bertone's. Much less does Bertone have any authority to compel assent to his statements where, as here, he acts in a private capacity as an author and a guest on a TV or radio show.

Therefore, regardless of the imposing manifestations Bertone's method has produced, the faithful have no obligation to believe a word he has said over the course of this controversy, unless what he has said is objectively worthy of belief. That Bertone's account is objectively *not* worthy of belief ought to be obvious from all the evidence presented here, much of it revealed by Bertone himself. Bertone's method—the simulation of authority, the semblance of a denial, the dog and pony show, the high-handed refusal to answer or even acknowledge serious questions, the appearance of imperturbability in the face of damning evidence—cannot trump the demands of truth. As Bertone himself has recently observed in another context: "The truth is the destiny for which we were made. For every human being, thirst for the truth has always been a deep desire and demanding challenge. Indeed, man is by nature 'curious': he is prompted to find answers to the many 'whys' of life and to seek the truth."[305] Irony of ironies, in the very midst of this controversy Bertone himself publicly proclaims the reason the faithful cannot accept his account.

Failing, yet still in charge

And yet the Third Secret of Fatima remains firmly under

---

[305]HOMILY OF CARDINAL TARCISIO BERTONE, Auditorium in the Trade Fair district, Rimini, Sunday, 19 August 2007, at http://www.vatican.va/roman_curia/secretariat_state/card-bertone/2007/documents/rc_seg-st_20070819_meeting-rimini_en.html.

the control of the Vatican Secretary of State, despite Bertone's increasingly embarrassing failure to persuade the faithful that everything has been revealed, that the Mother of God had nothing to say to her children about a vision Bertone, following Sodano, has taken it upon himself to "interpret" on the Virgin's behalf. It seems that Bertone, no less than his predecessor, is exercising a kind of shadow government in the Church that holds itself accountable to no one and believes it can say or do anything without fear of contradiction, even by the Pope.

In a column written two days after he was ejected from the Urbaniana during "The Cardinal Bertone Show," Socci makes this dramatic appeal to the Pope:

> Holiness, govern the Church which is falling into ruin! For charity, *do not leave the sheep of Christ, already lost and suffering great trial, in other hands. The cardinals to whom you have improvidently consigned the government of the Church are not one with you...* Let Padre Pio— of whom today is the feast—and the Madonna of Fatima illuminate you. We implore you, let yourself be guided by Heaven, taking the hand of the Mother of God who at Fatima came to rescue us... Have no fear. Do not flee. Be courageous. Thus will Benedict and his pontificate truly be a blessing for the Church. To the glory of God.[306]

In the accompanying article Socci notes that Pope Benedict finds himself surrounded by those who are tempted to govern the Church in his stead, including opponents of the Pope's historic *motu proprio, Summorum Pontificum*, which "liberated" the Latin Mass from its captivity under a non-existent "prohibition" for the past forty years. "But who commands the Vatican?" Socci asks. "The fact is," he writes, "that Benedict XVI is practically alone in the apostolic palace and the barque of Peter is tossed this way and that by clerical bureaucrats..." In an unmistakable reference to the alliance between De Carli and Bertone, Socci notes that "opportunism, servility and clericalism dominate the Catholic world. The intellectuals, generally, are dominated by hostile ideologies or are interested only in kissing the slipper of the powerful prelate of the moment."[307]

---

[306] "Appeal to the Pope!," *Libero*, September 23, 2007.

[307] Antonio Socci, "There is a caste, even in the Church," ibid.

Socci recalls Pope Benedict's "dramatic perception of conditions in the Church. This is shown by the cry he uttered during the historic Way of the Cross on March 25, 2005: 'How much filth there is in the Church, even precisely among those who, in the priesthood, should belong completely to Him. How much pride, how much self-complacency!'"[308] Certainly the Pope recognizes the situation that confronts him, the situation surely foretold in the missing words of the Virgin that belong together with what he himself (writing as Cardinal Ratzinger) called the "difficult to decipher" vision of the bishop in white. But, as Socci asks: "when, where and how is the cleansing to be done after such a resounding denunciation? The Pope alone cannot do it, but even he will sooner or later have to make courageous choices."

One of the "courageous choices" the Pope will have to make is finally to put an end to the charade that Bertone and his predecessor have been conducting. As Socci recognizes, giving voice to Catholics around the world, the text that explains the enigmatic vision of the Third Secret must be revealed for the good of all humanity, no matter what private opinions have been expressed as to its "authenticity." But if the Pope will not act, what can the faithful do to liberate that heavenly text from its captivity in human hands? How will they learn the whole truth the Blessed Virgin conveyed to her children for their earthly protection and eternal salvation? What is the remedy for an injustice that threatens the welfare of the Church and every living soul?

---

[308]Ibid.; quoting Homily of Benedict XVI during the Stations of the Cross on Good Friday 2005.

Chapter 12

What Can We Do?

As this discussion should make clear to anyone who has followed it attentively, Antonio Socci's conclusion is correct: "[T]hat there is a part of the Secret not revealed and considered unspeakable is certain. And today—having decided to deny its existence—the Vatican runs the risk of exposing itself to very heavy pressure and blackmail."[309] But what can *we* do about it? Even if we know that the Vatican is in possession of a hidden text of the Third Secret of Fatima which it refuses to divulge, and which certain members of the Vatican apparatus may have deemed "inauthentic," are we not powerless to do anything but lament the situation and await the dire consequences doubtless described in this hidden text? What remedy do we have to compel its disclosure?

In the first place, we must remind ourselves that the Catholic Church is not a merely human institution. The Holy Ghost guides the Church toward the ends that God Himself has established from all eternity. One of those ends is the final fulfillment of the Message of Fatima. As Our Lady of Fatima herself promises: "In the end, my Immaculate Heart *will* triumph. The Holy Father *will* consecrate Russia to me, and she *shall* be converted, and a period of peace *will* be granted to the world." These are the words of the very Mother of God, precisely as they are quoted in the Vatican's own commentary on Fatima.[310] The words of the Blessed Virgin Mary mean what they say; and, given their source, they are an infallible prediction of what will happen, regardless of the contrary designs of certain men.

We return, finally, to the subject of the Consecration of Russia. The Message of Fatima, including the part that is still hidden, will be fulfilled. It will be fulfilled when Russia is consecrated to the Immaculate Heart of Mary. Meanwhile, however, we must already be living through at least the beginning of what Our Lady prophesies in the words that undoubtedly explain the vision of

---

[309]*Fourth Secret*, p. 173.

[310]*Message*, p. 16.

"the Bishop dressed in white." The question is how much more suffering the Church and the world will have to endure before the Pope does what the Virgin requested. Will we first have to witness the annihilation of nations—of which Our Lady warns even in the Second Secret—before the promises of Fatima are realized? Is the vision of the Third Secret, then, the depiction of a blasted, post-apocalyptic world in which a wounded, limping Pope is hunted down and killed outside the ruins of Rome? Was Pope Saint Pius X speaking of this very scene when he revealed that he had been given a vision of a future Pope fleeing the eternal city amidst the bodies of his brethren?[311]

Rejecting the claim of Bertone and his collaborators that the Fatima prophecies belong entirely to the past, Socci draws a hopeful parallel between the Third Secret and the famous "dream of the two pillars" of Saint John Bosco. In this vision, the saint-prophet saw that a successor to a Pope killed during a great battle is able to steer the Church to a safe anchorage between the twin pillars of the Eucharist and the Immaculate Heart. So will it be, says Socci—along with every "Fatimist"—when Russia is finally consecrated and the Immaculate Heart triumphs. When the consecration takes place it will be a testament to the power of the papacy as a divine instrument of the grace mediated to the world through Mary, producing a victory even greater than the one against Islam at Lepanto. Socci calls this coming victory—and any Catholic who has hope must agree with him—"an extraordinary change of the world, an overthrow of the mentality dominating modernity, probably following dramatic events for humanity." The Triumph of the Immaculate Heart will mean also an end to the current ecclesial crisis, lamented so dramatically by Pope Paul VI with his reference to "the smoke of Satan" in the Church after Vatican II. As Socci writes, the triumph of Mary's Immaculate Heart will bring about

> a clear 'conversion' to doctrinal orthodoxy after the frightening deviations following the Council [and] a return also to adoration, therefore also a return to the bi-millennial liturgy of the Church... [A] different face from the Church of today: more adoring than

---

[311]To repeat what was earlier quoted: "I saw one of my successors taking to flight over the bodies of his brethren. He will take refuge in disguise somewhere; and after a short retirement he will die a cruel death. The present wickedness of the world is only the beginning of sorrows which must take place before the end of the world." Yves Dupont, *Catholic Prophecy, The Coming Chastisement* (Rockford, Illinois: Tan Books, 1970), p. 22.

worldly, more mendicant of the grace of salvation from God, than occupied by its own plans and projects… A Church that expects everything from Christ, not from political ability, from activism and from the mania of *aggiornamento*…[312]

Of course, this glorious fulfillment, although inevitable, cannot happen without the participation of the faithful. God deigns to use human instruments to achieve the ends of His Church, and He will not impose His graces without the cooperation of the freely acting human subject. As Frère Michel explained in 1985, it is probable that the Consecration of Russia will not take place until reparation is made for the insult to Christ and His Blessed Mother committed by those who have buried the prophecy of the Third Secret—and worse, have done so in direct disobedience to the "express order of Our Lady" that it be revealed in 1960.[313]

As Saint Paul warns the members of the Church: "Extinguish not the spirit. Despise not prophecies, but prove all things; hold fast that which is good."[314] In his *Summa Theologicae* Saint Thomas Aquinas, the greatest of all the Doctors of the Catholic Church, observes that God sends His prophets in every age of salvation history "not indeed for the declaration of any new doctrine, *but for the direction of human acts*"—that is, to tell men what they must do to save their souls.[315] To despise the prophets that God sends us for our correction is to invite divine retribution. As early as 1957 Sister Lucia warned that to ignore the Virgin of Fatima's prophetic message means "we can no longer hope for any type of pardon from Heaven, because we have stained ourselves with that which the Gospel calls a sin against the Holy Spirit. We cannot forget that Jesus Christ is a very good Son and that He will not allow His Holy Mother to be offended and despised."[316] And, as Socci rightly contends, it was an act of "superbia"—supreme pride—to censor part of the Third Secret for reasons of human prudence:

If the Madonna appeared at Fatima, with an event so

---

[312]Socci, *Fourth Secret*, p. 127.

[313]Address at the Vatican, in the Augustinium, Sunday, November 24, 1985. This Extraordinary Synod opened on the Feast of St. John of the Cross.

[314]I Thess. 5:19-21.

[315]*Summa Theologicae*, II-II, Q. 174, Art. 6.

[316]Cited in Socci, *Fourth Secret*, p. 109. *See* also Francis Alban and Christopher A. Ferrara, *Fatima Priest* (Pound Ridge, New York: Good Counsel Publications, 1997, Second Edition), p. 298 (also at http://www.fatimapriest.com/Appendix3.htm).

sensational, precisely to give a message "so delicate" and urgent for humanity and the Church, how can we Catholics "silence" her and censor her, holding that her message "is not destined to be made public"? Is it not an act of superbia to pretend ourselves more prudent than she who is venerated as "Virgin Most Prudent," and more wise than she who is defined as "Seat of Wisdom"? *How is it possible that political considerations, or human fear, have prevailed over the obedience due to Heaven?*[317]

How indeed? It would seem, then, that the only reparation possible is for the Pope to reveal entirely what those who think themselves more prudent than *Virgo Prudentissima* have concealed. For what they have concealed is that which God Himself has provided for the temporal and eternal welfare of every soul: a warning of the consequences of sin and human folly, and with that warning the way to safety.

But what role can ordinary Catholics play in bringing an end to this scandalous concealment of the Virgin's saving message? Their role is threefold: prayer, penance and petition.

Prayer

Before anything else, Catholics must pray to God, through Mary, the Mediatrix of All Graces, for the intention of full disclosure of the Third Secret of Fatima, and with this, the conversion of Russia and the triumph of the Immaculate Heart of Mary. How should we pray? The Virgin of Fatima prescribed, above all, the prayer of the Holy Rosary. Again and again the Virgin exhorted the Catholic faithful to daily recitation of the Rosary, which she mentioned in every one of her apparitions at the Cova da Iria:

> May 13, 1917: "Recite the Rosary every day in order to obtain peace for the world and the end of the war."

> June 13, 1917: "pray the Rosary every day..."

> July 13, 1917: "...continue reciting the Rosary every day in honor of Our Lady of the Rosary, in order to obtain peace in the world and the end of the war, because only She can help you."

---

[317]Ibid., p. 37.

August 13, 1917: "…continue praying the Rosary every day."

September 13, 1917: "Continue to pray the Rosary in order to obtain the end of the war."

Finally, on October 13, 1917, the day of the Miracle of the Sun, the Lady identified herself as none other than Our Lady of the Rosary: "I am the Lady of the Rosary. May you continue always to pray the Rosary every day." Sister Lucia would spend the coming decades telling everyone who would listen, in conversations, letters and other writings, that the Rosary is an indispensable spiritual armament in the midst of the chaos and "diabolical disorientation" that was already overcoming the world, even as the apparitions at Fatima were coming to a close.

Penance

Together with their prayers, the faithful must offer what Our Lady of Fatima also repeatedly prescribed: penance. That is, the faithful must be willing to make sacrifices, to endure sufferings offered to God for the intention they seek. And what is the Passion of Our Lord Himself if not a penitential sacrifice of infinite value, made by One who had committed no sin? If He who committed no sin offered up the penance of His very life for the redemption of sinners, how can the faithful, sinners all, fail to offer their own meager penances for the intention that the entire Third Secret be revealed and the Fatima message fulfilled, so that souls (including their own) will be saved and the world spared the chastisement it so richly deserves?

Nor should the faithful wait for any command by Church authorities to do penance, for Our Lord has already given the command through His Blessed Mother. As Sister Lucia declared to the Church: "[W]e should not wait for an appeal to the world to come from Rome on the part of the Holy Father, to do penance. Nor should we wait for the call to penance to come from our bishops in our dioceses, nor from the religious congregations. No! Our Lord has already very often used these means and the world has not paid attention. That is why now, it is necessary for each one of us to begin to reform himself spiritually. Each person must not only save his own soul but also help all the souls that God has placed on our path."[318]

---

[318]Quoted in *Fatima Priest*, p. 297 (also at http://www.fatimapriest.com/

Petition

Finally, the faithful must petition the authorities of the Church, beginning with the bishops of their dioceses and the priests of their parishes. They should also petition the other members of the hierarchy, and, to the extent they are able, communicate their concerns to fellow Catholics by the various means of social communication. The Church's canon law abundantly recognizes and secures the right of the faithful, by virtue of their baptism as Catholics, to petition the hierarchy and to communicate with each other regarding matters of concern in the Church, of which there can be none greater today than the Third Secret and the Message of Fatima as a whole.[319]

But above all, the faithful should petition the Pope in accordance with the God-given right of every member of the Church to have direct recourse to the Supreme Pontiff.[320] The petition can take many forms. Today it is possible to send the Pope a letter, a facsimile transmission or even an email at the papal email address the Vatican has established (benedictxvi@vatican.ca). Can petitions to the Pope actually produce the relief requested? Of course they can. The impact of perhaps millions of petitions delivered to the Pope cannot be doubted. For example, it is an historical fact that the worldwide petitions of the faithful were instrumental in moving Pope Pius XII to issue his infallible dogmatic definition of the Assumption of the Blessed Virgin Mary. Likewise, in issuing his *motu proprio* "liberating" the Latin Mass and declaring that it was "never abrogated [forbidden]" by Paul VI, Pope Benedict made explicit reference to "the insistent *petitions* of these faithful..."[321]

It is, in fact, precisely such forms of petition and communication, including Socci's book and the publications of Father Gruner's Fatima apostolate, that have prompted the Vatican apparatus to reveal as much of the truth as it has. Where would we be today if Catholics such as Socci and Father Gruner, out of timidity or human respect, had failed to exercise their right to speak out in defense of truth and had remained silent in the face of an "official"

Appendix3.htm).

[319]*See* Canons 212-228, 278, and 299, CIC 1983.

[320]This right is dogmatically defined by the Second Council of Lyons (1274) and the First Vatican Council (1870), and further codified in Can. 221 of the 1983 Code of Canon Law promulgated by Pope John Paul II.

[321]*Summorum Pontificum* (2007), Preamble.

account that is simply not credible? Recall the words of Pope Saint Gregory the Great, quoted at the beginning of this book: "It is better that scandals arise than that the truth be suppressed." Recall also the dramatic words of Socci himself: "The Church is not some kind of sect or Mafia gang that demands from us a code of silence. But it is the house of the sons of God, the house of liberty and of truth."[322] As members of the house of the sons of God, Catholics would fail in their duty and even sin by remaining silent under these circumstances. As Pope Saint Leo I declared: "He that sees another in error, and endeavors not to correct it, testifies himself to be in error." Pope Felix III taught likewise: "Not to oppose error is to approve of it, and not to defend truth is to suppress it..."

For what, precisely, should the faithful petition? First of all, they should petition the Pope (and the other members of the hierarchy) for disclosure of the hidden text now held hostage by the Vatican Secretary of State. The members of the hierarchy, including those of the highest rank in the Vatican—including even the Pope himself—can have no valid grounds for denying such petitions. As for the idea that by a mental reservation those who have control of the hidden text can continue to deny its existence in good faith based on their private judgment that it is "not authentic," let us recognize this for what it is: a vain attempt to justify the illicit suppression of what the faithful have a right to know for their own temporal and eternal safety.

The pastors of the Church have a duty before God to tell us *everything* the Mother of God revealed at Fatima. For Sacred Scripture teaches that God has appointed every pastor of the Church, especially the bishops and the Pope, a *watchman* over those in his charge. One of the duties of the Church's watchmen is precisely to warn the faithful about what the former Cardinal Ratzinger himself revealed to be the subject of the Third Secret: "dangers threatening the faith and the life of the Christian and therefore of the world." In the Book of Ezechiel we are reminded that before God visits a chastisement on his people He appoints a watchman whose duty is to sound the alarm, so that those who heed the watchman's warning may avoid the chastisement. The watchman who remains silent, however, will have the blood of those who are lost upon his hands:

---

[322] "Bertone nel 'Vespaio' delle Polemiche" ("Bertone in the 'Wasp's Nest' of the Polemics"), *Libero*, June 2, 2007.

> When I bring the sword upon a land, if the people of
> the land take a man, one of their meanest, and make
> him a watchman over them… And if the watchman
> see the sword coming, and sound not the trumpet:
> and the people look not to themselves, and the sword
> come, and cut off a soul from among them: he indeed
> is taken away in his iniquity, but I will require his
> blood *at the hand of the watchman*."[323]

And, what is worse than the watchman who remains silent, here we are dealing with watchmen *who have positively represented that there is no approaching danger!* Can anyone seriously contend that God approves of this conduct?

Thus, the moral obligation of our ecclesial watchmen to disclose the Third Secret in its entirety cannot be avoided by any mental reservation. The Church and the world have a right to know what has been hidden, and the watchmen have a divinely imposed duty to reveal it. Nor will it do to argue that since we have already been able to deduce the probable contents of the Secret there is no longer any need for a warning from the watchmen of the Church. On the contrary, the Church and the world *need to hear the words of the Virgin herself, precisely as she stated them.* For those words impart infallible divine wisdom and, no doubt, specific advice from Heaven that by its very nature is absolutely indispensable in its every detail. Further, absent a full disclosure of the Secret by Church authorities, many of the faithful will be led to believe that there is nothing to disclose.

Prayer, penance and petition. To obtain what God promises, we must *do* what He requires. In the end, the Message of Fatima, like every divine ordinance, involves the impenetrable mystery of the relation between grace and free will. It is a frightening truth, yet a testament to the love of the God who made us free, that whether the angel we see in the vision of "the Bishop dressed in white" destroys the world with the fire that is being repelled by the Virgin depends in large measure upon the prayers, penances and petitions of the simple faithful. The glorious fulfillment the Queen of Heaven has promised us, therefore, requires obedience not only by the Pope and the bishops, but also by the multitude of Christ's subjects, whose acts of faith, joined together in the vast economy of salvation, will help obtain for the Roman Pontiff the

---

[323]Ezechiel 33:2, 6.

grace to do what must be done.

Will a Pope come to be executed by soldiers atop a hill outside a ruined city in a world that has suffered divine retribution? Or will Benedict or his successor, avoiding this fate, reveal the hidden words of the Virgin, perform the Consecration of Russia, and bring on the triumph of the Immaculate Heart? That some Pope will do these things is certain. Therein lies our hope. But will it be this Pope or another; will it be now, or after the world has already borne a terrible witness as the consequence of its own rebellion against God? We ponder this question in fear and in hope as we expect, by the promise of Our Lady of Fatima, the light that is coming to deliver us from the darkness.

Appendix I

Some Certified Notes of Archbishop Capovilla Regarding the Third Secret

What follows are translations and true copies of the contemporaneous documentation of Archbishop Loris F. Capovilla, personal secretary to Pope John XXIII, confirming the existence of the "Capovilla envelope" pertaining to the Third Secret of Fatima, which was kept in the papal apartment. *Cardinal Bertone has never produced this envelope*, even though Capovilla's evidence has finally forced him to admit its existence.

———

LORIS FRANCESCO CAPOVILLA
ARCIVESCOVO DI MESEMBRIA

F A T I M A

A Reserved Note of L.F. Capovilla

17 May 1967

Thursday the 27th of June 1963, I was on duty in the Anticamera in the Vatican [the outer office where the Pope meets various persons]. Paul VI in the early morning received among others, Cardinal Fernando Cento (who had been Papal Nuncio to Portugal) and shortly afterwards the Bishop of Leiria Monsignor Joao [John] Pereira Venancio. Upon leaving, the Bishop asked for "a special blessing for Sister Lucia".

It is evident that during the audience, they spoke about Fatima. In fact in the afternoon the Sostituto [the Substitute Secretary of State] Monsignor Angelo Dell'Acqua telephoned me on Via Casilina (I was a temporary guest of the Sisters of the "Poverelle"):

"I am looking for the package [plico] of Fatima. Do you know where it is kept?"

"It was in the drawer on the right hand side of the desk, named 'Barbarigo'[1], in the [Papal] bedroom."

One hour later Dell'Acqua called me back: "Everything is okay. The envelope [plico] has been found."

Friday morning (28 June) between one meeting and another Paul VI asked me:
"How come on the envelope there is your (Capovilla's) name?"
"John XXIII asked me to write a note regarding how the envelope arrived in his hands with the names of all those to whom he felt he should make it known."
"Did he make any comment?"
"No, nothing except what I wrote on the outer file [involucro]: 'I leave it to others to comment or decide.'"[2]
"Did he later ever return to the subject?"
"No, never. However the devotion of Fatima remained alive in him."

1. It is called thus because it belonged to St. Gregory Barbarigo. The Pope received it as a gift from Co. Gius. Dalla Torre (1960).

2. See the attatched note of agenda of John XXIII, 10 November 1959.

From the Agenda of 1959
of John XXIII, 10 November, Feast of St. Andrew Avellino

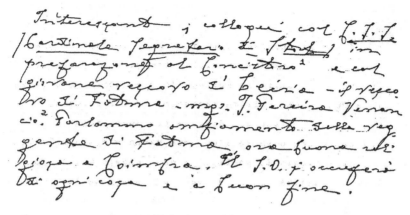

[handwritten note of John XXIII]

1. Consistory 14-17 December with the creation of eight Cardinals.

2. Joao Pereira Venancio, born 1904, titular Bishop of Eurea di Epireo 1954 | Bishop of Leiria 1958.

[The text below is a translation of Capovilla's typewritten copy of John XXIII's handwritten original document shown above.]

Interesting conversations with C.S.S. (Cardinal Secretary of State) in preparation for the consistory and with young Bishop of Leiria – the Bishop of Fatima – Monsignor J. Pereira Venancio. We have spoken at length of the seer of Fatima, who is now a good religious at Coimbra. The Holy Office will take care of everything to a good end.

L.F.C.

F A T I M A
Note riservate di L.F.Capovilla
17.v.1967

LORIS FRANCESCO CAPOVILLA
ARCIVESCOVO DI MESEMBRIA

Giovedì 27 giugno 1963 sono in servizio d'Anticamera in Vaticano.   Paolo VI in mattinata riceve, tra gli altri, il card. Fernan=
do Cento (che fu nunzio in Portogallo) e subito dopo il Vescovo
di Leiria mons. João Pereira Venancio.   Nel congedarsi , il Vesco=
vo chiede "una speciale benedizione per Suor Lucia".

E' evidente che durante l'udienza hanno parlato di Fatima . Di=
fatti nel pomeriggio il Sostituto mons. Angelo Dell'Acqua mi   tele-
fona in Via Casilina (sono ospite provvisorio delle Suore delle Po=
verelle) :

" Cercano il plico di Fatima. Lei sa dov'è custodito ?
" Sta nel cassetto di destra della scrivania detta "Barbarigo",[1]
in stanza da letto .

Un'ora dopo, Dell' Acqua mi ritelefona : " Tutto a posto. Il
plico è stato rinvenuto ".

Venerdì mattina (28.VI) tra un'udienza e l'altra, Paolo VI   mi
chiede :
" Come mai sul plico c'è il suo (di Capovilla) nome ?
" Giovanni XXIII mi chiese di stilare una nota circa le modalità
di arrivo del plico nelle sue mani con i nomi di tutti coloro ai
quali ritenne doveroso farlo conoscere .
E Fece qualche commento ?
" No niente, tranne quanto scrissi sull'involucro : Lascio ad altri
commentare o decidere ".[2]
" In seguito tornò mai sull'argomento?
" No, mai. Tuttavia la devozione di Fatima rimase viva in lui   "

1. Così detto, perché appartenuto a S.Gregorio Barbari=
go. Il Papa l'ebbe in dono dal Co.Gius. Dalla Torre (1960
2. Vedere allegata nota di agenda Giovanni XXIII, 10 no=
vembre 1959 .

Dalla Agenda 1959
di Giovanni XXIII , 10 novembre , S.Andrea Avellino

[handwritten note]

1. Concistoro 14-17 dicembre con creazione di otto cardinali.

2. João Pereira Venâncio , nato 1904; vescovo tit. di Sursa
di Spirzo 1954 ; vescovo di Leiria 1958

Interessanti i colloqui col C.S.S (Cardinale Segretario
di Stato) in preparazione al Concistoro, e col giovane vescovo di Leiria - il vescovo di Fatima - Mgr J. Pereira Venancio. Parlammo ampiamente della veggente di Fatima, ora
buona religiosa a Coimbra. Il S[anto] O[fficio] si occuperà
di ogni cosa e a buon fine .

L. F. C.

Appendix II

101 Grounds for Doubting
Cardinal Bertone's Account

Among other things, this book has surveyed in detail the evidence that convinced Antonio Socci that it "is certain" Cardinal Bertone and his collaborators are hiding a text of the Third Secret of Fatima containing "the words of the Madonna [which] preannounce an apocalyptic crisis of the faith in the Church starting from the top" and probably "also an explanation of the vision (revealed on June 26, 2000) where there appear the Pope, the bishops and martyred faithful, after having traversed a city in ruins."[324]

This appendix, rather than reviewing the evidence as a whole, focuses on the specific grounds for doubting the veracity of Cardinal Bertone's account, according to which: (a) the vision published in 2000 is the entirety of the Third Secret; (b) the Virgin had nothing to say about the vision's meaning; and (c) Heaven left the "interpretation" of the vision to Bertone and his predecessor, Cardinal Sodano. As the reader will see, many of the grounds for doubt arise from Bertone's own statements and omissions over the past seven years.

Bertone evades the testimony of Archbishop Capovilla and the evidence presented by Antonio Socci.

1. In July 2006 Archbishop Loris Capovilla, the personal secretary to Pope John XXIII reveals to Solideo Paolini:

    - that there are two different envelopes and two different texts pertaining to the Third Secret: the "Capovilla envelope" and the "Bertone envelope";

    - that the "Capovilla envelope" was kept in the papal apartment of John XXIII, in a desk called "Barbarigo," located in the papal bedchamber;

---

[324] Socci, *Fourth Secret*, p. 82.

- that after Pope John read the text of the Secret inside that envelope in August 1959, he placed the text back into the envelope, resealed it, and instructed Capovilla to write on the outside "I give no judgment," along with the names of all those Pope John had asked to read the Secret;

- that Paul VI retrieved the "Capovilla envelope" from the same desk where Pope John left it ("Barbarigo") and read its contents in 1963 — *two years before* the date Bertone says Pope Paul read the Third Secret for the first time — and then resealed the envelope, as had John XXIII.

2. The "Bertone envelope," on the other hand, was always kept in the Holy Office archives, and Pope Paul, according to Bertone's account, read its contents in 1965 — two years *after* Pope Paul had read the contents of the "Capovilla" envelope.

3. In the face of Capovilla's explosive testimony proving the existence of another envelope and text of the Secret, Cardinal Bertone remains silent, even after Antonio Socci publishes that testimony to the world in November 2006 as part of his book *The Fourth Secret of Fatima*.

4. Bertone fails to deny or even to mention Capovilla's testimony *even when Giuseppe De Carli brings it to his attention* while interviewing Bertone for *Last Visionary of Fatima*.

5. *Last Visionary* fails to address a single point Socci raises in *Fourth Secret*, including the testimony of Capovilla, even though *Last Visionary* is supposed to be a rebuttal of *Fourth Secret*, wherein Socci presents massive evidence of a cover-up of a text of the Secret.

6. During his television appearance of May 31, 2007 on the Italian television show *Door to Door*, a few weeks after *Last Visionary* is published, Bertone continues to avoid any discussion of Socci's points, including Capovilla's testimony, even though the very title of the show ("The Fourth Secret of Fatima Does Not Exist") is a direct attack on the title of Socci's book.

7. Although this installment of *Door to Door* is an attack on Socci's book, Socci is not invited to participate in the show or even to submit questions to Bertone.

**Bertone evades, then blatantly misrepresents,
Lucia's telltale "etc" — the gateway to the Third Secret.**

8. For the past seven years of an ongoing controversy, Bertone has refused to answer any questions about the words following Lucia's "etc" in the momentous declaration of the Virgin: "In Portugal, the dogma of the Faith will always be preserved etc.", which Lucia recorded in her Fourth Memoir as part of the integral text of the Great Secret revealed by the Virgin on July 13, 1917, and which Fatima scholars unanimously regarded as the opening words of the Third Secret.

9. Bertone, collaborating in *Message of Fatima* (2000), the Vatican commentary on the vision of "the Bishop dressed in white," falsely describes the Virgin's words ending in Lucia's "etc" as merely "some annotations" by Lucia, when he knows the phrase is part of the integral text of the Great Secret as spoken by the Virgin herself and recorded in the Fourth Memoir.

10. To avoid the momentous words of the Virgin recorded in the Fourth Memoir, which they would have to explain to the faithful, Bertone and his collaborators use the less complete Third Memoir, offering no explanation for this strange decision other than the demonstrably false claim that the Virgin's words in the Fourth Memoir are mere "annotations" by Lucia.

11. Yet, in another context, Bertone himself quotes from the Fourth Memoir *precisely because it is more complete than the Third.*

12. During the press conference of June 26, 2000, at which *Message* was published, Bertone states to the press: "It is difficult to say if it [the "etc"] refers to the second or the third part of the secret [i.e., the Great Secret of July 13, 1917]… it seems to me that it pertains to the second." Hence *Bertone does not deny that the "etc" could in fact be part of the Third Secret*, which would mean that the Third Secret includes the Virgin's *spoken words.*

13. Bertone refuses to address the "etc" issue, even though he himself makes a mocking reference to the issue in *Last Visionary*, only to avoid answering any questions about it.

14. Despite what he claims are ten hours of unrecorded interviews with Lucia concerning the Third Secret and the Message of Fatima in general, Bertone mysteriously fails to ask her whether there are any words of the Virgin following the famous "etc", even though he knows this matter is at the very heart of the

Third Secret controversy. In the alternative, Bertone does ask Lucia about what is contained within the "etc", but he conceals her answer.

15. During the same ten hours of interviews Bertone mysteriously fails to ask Sister Lucia if the Virgin ever explained what *Message* calls the "difficult to decipher" vision of "the Bishop dressed in white," and if so, whether there is a text of the Virgin's explanation. In the alternative, Bertone does ask Lucia if the Virgin ever explained the vision, but conceals her answer.

16. During a radio broadcast on June 6, 2007, Bertone falsely asserts that the Virgin's words in the Fourth Memoir end with ellipses (…), not with "etc", when he knows full well that the "etc" — indicating further words of the Virgin — has been at the heart of the Third Secret controversy for decades, so that he could not have mistaken the "etc" for ellipses, and further knows that it is absurd to suggest that the Message of Fatima ends with the Virgin trailing off in the middle of a thought.

17. During the same broadcast Bertone falsely suggests that the telltale words of the Virgin concerning the preservation of dogma in Portugal (but evidently not elsewhere) are not important because they are merely part of Lucia's "memoir," which he characterizes as "another writing," when he knows that Lucia's memoirs are the source texts of the integral Message of Fatima, and that *he himself used the less complete Third Memoir* to obtain the text of the Great Secret the Vatican published in 2000.

Bertone demolishes his own position on national television.

18. During the appearance on *Door to Door* in May of 2007, Bertone himself finally reveals — after seven years of failing to mention it — that Sister Lucia prepared *two different sealed envelopes* for transmission of the Third Secret, each bearing the notation "By express order of Our Lady, this envelope can only be opened in 1960 by the Cardinal Patriarch of Lisbon or the Bishop of Leiria."

19. Bertone himself thus verifies the "two envelopes, two texts" theory of Socci and the "Fatimists," since it could hardly be the case that Lucia would use two sealed envelopes, with the "1960 order" on each, for one text.

20. Contrary to what he revealed on television, Bertone reports in *Last Visionary* that during his purported interview of Lucia on April 27, 2000, he asked her to identify only *one* sealed envelope as hers.

21. During the same appearance on *Door to Door* Bertone also reveals for the first time that the text of the vision of the bishop in white *is not a letter* to the Bishop of Fatima—which is how Lucia described the text of the Secret she had transmitted to the Bishop—but rather is written *on four contiguous pages of her notebook*, comprising *a single sheet of folio paper*.

22. Bertone himself thus confirms the contention of Socci and the "Fatimists" that, just as Sister Lucia herself revealed, the Secret was contained *both* in her notebooks *and* in her letter to the Bishop of Fatima.

23. Contrary to what he says on television on May 31, 2007, in *Last Visionary*, Bertone asserts that during the meeting of April 27, 2000 Lucia authenticated *sheets* ("fogli" in Italian) of paper pertaining to the Secret, not the single sheet he produced on *Door to Door* and which he described as "the folio (sheet of paper)... the only *authentic* folio ("l'unico foglio autentico"), the only folio in which is contained the Third Secret."

24. During the appearance on *Door to Door*, Bertone makes it a point to display an envelope containing a 1967 translation of a text of the Secret (while failing to display the translation inside), but he does not display or even mention the 1959 translation of a text of the Secret, *specially prepared for John XXIII*, whose existence Archbishop Capovilla himself later reveals during a television broadcast staged by Bertone in September 2007.

25. Bertone inadvertently reveals during his appearance on *Door to Door* that the Third Secret contains "words" and an "interior locution" that Lucia committed indelibly to memory, when the vision of the bishop in white contains no words of the Virgin, only one word spoken by the angel ("Penance," uttered three times) and no interior locution: that is, no address by the Virgin to her.

26. Bertone also finally admits during the *Door to Door* appearance that Cardinal Ottaviani affirmed "categorically" that there is a one-page text of the Secret comprising 25 lines, as opposed to the four-page text of 62 lines setting forth the vision of the bishop in white. Yet, in *Last Visionary*, Bertone claimed that he

did not know what the Cardinal was talking about.

27. Curiously, Bertone says that he is "a little amazed" by Ottaviani's testimony, instead of denying it outright and producing witnesses or documents that could readily disprove the testimony, if such witnesses and documents existed.

28. Bertone further declares to the TV audience that he does not find Ottaviani's testimony about a one-page, 25-line text of the Secret *"so convincing* as to say that there exists a sheet of paper *(foglio)* of 25 lines...", as if the matter were open to debate, when he would not speak this way if he were quite certain Ottaviani was wrong.

29. In a contrived attempt to explain away Cardinal Ottaviani's testimony, which he cannot deny or refute, Bertone falsely suggests on *Door to Door*, and in a radio broadcast during the following week (June 6, 2007), that Ottaviani could have counted 25 lines on two pages of the four-page text of the vision — somehow thinking the two pages were one page! — when Bertone knows very well that the two pages he indicated on both occasions contain 32 lines of text and could not possibly have been mistaken for one page of 25 lines.

Bertone fails to obtain a retraction from Capovilla, finally admitting to the existence of the never-produced "Capovilla envelope."

30. When, at Bertone's request, De Carli finally interviews Capovilla in August 2007, *he fails to obtain a retraction* of any element of Capovilla's testimony to Paolini as recounted by Socci in *Fourth Secret.*

31. An earlier version of De Carli's interview of Capovilla — also devoid of any retraction — is first published in *a women's magazine*, indicating an attempt to "float" an unofficial "trial balloon" that will be passed off as a change of Capovilla's testimony, when no change has in fact occurred.

32. According to De Carli's transcript of his August 2007 interview of Capovilla, Paolini is *not even mentioned* during the interview, nor is Socci's publication of Paolini's account of what Capovilla told him.

33. The deliberate avoidance of any discussion of Paolini's report of what Capovilla told him can only mean that Capovilla is not

willing to deny or even modify what he said to Paolini.

34. During the interview with De Carli, Capovilla not only fails to deny or modify his testimony to Paolini, he *confirms the existence of the "Capovilla envelope"* containing the Third Secret, kept in the papal apartment in the desk called "Barbarigo" and bearing the words Capovilla had written on the outside at the direction of John XXIII.

35. Although his own witness now confirms its existence, *Bertone fails to produce the "Capovilla envelope" or to give any explanation for its non-production*, which he would certainly do if there were an innocent explanation.

36. Having failed to obtain a retraction of Capovilla's testimony, De Carli, at Bertone's behest, tries to supply (during the telecast Bertone stages in September 2007) the conclusion he could not extract from the witness: "I [De Carli!] conclude, therefore, there is not a Capovilla envelope to contrast to a Bertone envelope. The two envelopes are the same document."

37. Yet, Bertone and De Carli both know that Capovilla himself said no such thing to De Carli, but on the contrary — according to De Carli's own transcript of his interview of the Archbishop — Capovilla confirmed there is a "Capovilla envelope" bearing the Archbishop's notations, *which Bertone has never produced*.

38. Bertone thus falsely represents to the public (through his agent De Carli) that there is no distinct "Capovilla envelope," when his *own evidence* now demonstrates that it exists but has not been produced.

39. After seven years of having failed to reveal its existence, Bertone (through De Carli) now concedes that an envelope containing a text of the Third Secret and bearing Capovilla's notations was kept in the papal apartment during the pontificates of John XXIII and Paul VI, even though, in *Last Visionary*, he scoffs at the claim that there was an envelope in the papal apartment as distinct from the Archives of the Holy Office.

**Bertone changes his story on the text
in the papal apartment, thereby creating
many new discrepancies in his account.**

40. Forced by Capovilla's testimony to concede that there was, after all, an envelope containing a text of the Third Secret in the

papal apartment, not the archives, and that Paul VI read this text in 1963, not 1965 as Bertone had claimed, Bertone has De Carli ask Capovilla leading questions during the August 2007 interview which suggest—for the first time in seven years of controversy—that Paul VI read the same text twice, in 1963 and 1965, and that the text Pope Paul read in both years was merely the text of the vision the Vatican published in June 2000. This suggestion is "floated" during the *Telepace* broadcast, staged by Bertone in September 2007.

41. Bertone's attempt to change his account to fit the evidence—evidence whose existence he had previously denied or appeared to deny—creates the following fatal discrepancies:

- If Paul VI read in 1965 the same text he read in 1963, then that text would be the one *inside the "Capovilla envelope", which Bertone has never produced;* for as Capovilla told De Carli, after reading a text of the Secret in 1963, *Paul VI placed it back in the "Capovilla envelope" and resealed the envelope.*

- If there is nothing to hide, then Bertone would have produced the "Capovilla envelope" on television.

- The "official account" has never mentioned that Paul VI read a text of the Secret in 1963, even though that reading was a momentous historical event.

- There would have been no reason for the official account *not* to mention this momentous historical event *unless* the text Pope Paul read in 1963 was (and is) being hidden.

- If Paul VI read in 1965 the *same* text he read in 1963, the official account of the 1965 reading would have mentioned this also—unless, again, there is something to hide.

- As Bertone himself now reveals through Capovilla, Paul VI resealed the envelope containing the text he read in 1963, stating that he would "do as much as" Pope John had, meaning leave it to others to judge the text. Why, then, would Paul VI *reopen* the envelope he had *resealed* in 1963 in order to read the same text again in 1965?

- Even if Paul VI decided to reopen the envelope he had resealed in 1963 in order to give its contents a second reading in 1965, how is it that neither his diaries, nor the records of the members of his staff, nor any Vatican document whatsoever, reflect that the Pope decided to revisit the same text he had previously decided to leave to others to judge?

- According to De Carli's own transcript, Capovilla stated that after the 1963 reading of a text of the Secret by Paul VI "The envelope was resealed *and I don't know if it was spoken of further.*" Thus Capovilla, contrary to what Bertone suggests (via the leading questions posed by De Carli), *could not have known* whether Pope Paul reopened the same envelope and read the same text again in 1965.

Bertone feigns ignorance of whether John Paul II read a text of the Secret in 1978.

42. In *Last Visionary*, Bertone states he is "convinced" and it is his "opinion" that John Paul II did not read the Secret in 1978, within days of his election, even though papal spokesman Navarro-Valls so reported to the press — a report that indicates a text in the papal apartment, not yet disclosed.

43. Confronted with the testimony of Navarro-Valls, Bertone mysteriously declines simply to ask Navarro-Valls, the Pope himself (while he was still alive) or any number of other knowledgeable witnesses if the report is true, even though he had ample time to do so in connection with his written interview in *Last Visionary*. Alternatively, Bertone does verify the report and has hidden the fact that John Paul II did indeed read a text of the Secret in 1978, three years before the date given in Bertone's account.

44. Despite repeated questioning even by De Carli, his handpicked interviewer, Bertone claims that John Paul II, the very "Pope of Fatima," waited until the third year of his pontificate (1981) to read the Third Secret, when Paul VI read it within days of his election.

45. Pressed by De Carli for the third time during the interview in *Last Visionary*, Bertone incredibly suggests John Paul II was too busy "reevangelizing the world" to read the Third Secret in 1978.

46. Nos. 42-45 suggest Bertone's determination not to admit that John Paul II read the Secret in 1978, when there would

be no reason not to admit it unless there is something to hide concerning that earlier reading.

Bertone defends a patently untenable "interpretation" of the vision of the bishop in white.

47. Bertone, following the lead of his predecessor, Cardinal Sodano, insists that the vision of a Pope being executed by soldiers outside a half-ruined city signifies Pope John Paul II escaping death at the hands of a lone assassin in 1981—an "interpretation" even the Vaticanist Marco Politi categorically rejects as untenable during Bertone's appearance on *Door to Door*.

48. Bertone fails to explain why, if that is all the vision signifies, it was kept under lock and key in the Vatican for nearly 20 years after the attempt.

49. Yet, Bertone asserts preposterously that the mere decision to publish the vision in 2000 "brings to an end a period of history marked by tragic human lust for power and evil..."—in which case, why was the decision not made sooner?

50. Bertone's "interpretation" of the vision makes the 1981 assassination attempt the very culmination of the Message of Fatima, even though the Pope recovered from his wounds, resumed an active life of skiing, hiking and swimming for the next twelve years, and died nearly twenty-five years after the attempt from the complications of Parkinson's disease.

51. In 2001, in the communiqué concerning his alleged interview of the seer in November 2001, Bertone claims that Lucia "fully confirms" his interpretation of the vision. But in May 2007, in *Last Visionary*, Bertone says "not in these terms" when asked directly by his own chosen interviewer, De Carli, if Lucia had accepted the interpretation.

52. All told, Bertone has given *six different and inconsistent versions* of Lucia's alleged statement to him that she "accepted" his "interpretation" of the vision.

53. Bertone asks the faithful to believe that the Virgin Mary had no words of explanation concerning a vision he has "interpreted" in a manner plainly at odds with what the vision depicts.

54. Bertone asks the faithful to believe that the Virgin left it to him and his predecessor to explain the meaning of the vision to the

Church and the world, some 83 years after the Virgin confided it to the seers, and that Lucia herself consented to be guided, not by the words of the Virgin delivered from Heaven, but by two Vatican cardinals (Bertone and Sodano) who have no competence in the matter whatsoever.

Bertone accuses Lucia of inventing the Virgin's order that the Secret was not to be revealed before 1960.

55. Over the course of seven years Bertone claims repeatedly — in *Message*, in *Last Visionary*, and during his television appearance on *Door to Door*—that Lucia "confessed" to him during unrecorded interviews that the Virgin never told her the Third Secret was not to be revealed until 1960, and that she (Lucia) arbitrarily selected that year for the revelation of the Secret.

56. Throughout the seven years he makes this claim, however, Bertone fails to reveal (until the appearance on *Door to Door* on May 31, 2007) that he has in his possession not one, but *two*, envelopes on which Lucia had written: "*By express order of Our Lady*, this envelope can only be opened in 1960 by the Cardinal Patriarch of Lisbon or the Bishop of Leiria."

57. Bertone has an obvious motive to obtain Lucia's "confession" that she invented the "express order" of the Virgin regarding 1960: the Virgin's linkage of the Secret to 1960 destroys his ridiculous "interpretation" linking the vision of the bishop in white to the failed 1981 assassination attempt as the culminating Fatima prophecy, and further points to a relation between the Secret and events around 1960, including the Second Vatican Council, which John XXIII had announced in 1959.

58. Bertone gives three different and totally inconsistent versions of the "confession," based on his unrecorded "interviews" of the seer:

   - In the first version Lucia allegedly says: "I had the intuition that before 1960 it would not be understood, but that only later would it be understood."

   - In the second version the "intuition" disappears, and Lucia allegedly says: "I felt that 1960 would be a date very far from the writing of the 'Secret' in 1944 and because I had thought that I would be dead in that year, therefore the last obstacle to the interpretation and to the disclosure of the secret would have been taken away."

- In the third version Lucia allegedly says: "It was I who set that date. It was I who thought that 1960 would be a term sufficient to be able to open the envelope. And I thought that perhaps I would be dead and not be involved in the Secret."

59. All three versions of the "confession" are patently incredible for the following reasons:

- As a child, Lucia would not reveal the Secret without Our Lady's permission, even under threat of death.

- Sister Lucia would never, on her own, make a "decision" when to reveal the Secret Our Lady had ordered her to "tell no one" except Francisco.

- The seer chosen by the Mother of God would not simply invent an "express order" from Mary and then forge it on two envelopes, thus misleading her superiors, the Church and the whole world for over 60 years.

- 1960 was not "very far" from 1944 (the year the Virgin ordered her to write down the text of the Secret); and even if it were, that a date was "very far" from 1944 was not a logical reason for Lucia to "decide" that *this* date, of all dates, would be a good time to reveal the Secret she was (at that time) under heavenly orders *not* to reveal.

- Of all the years that elapsed between 1944 and her death in 2005, Sister Lucia had no reason arbitrarily to "choose" 1960 as the year to reveal the Secret—*sixteen* years from 1944—rather than a round number like ten or twenty years from 1944.

- If, as Bertone himself admits, the Virgin directed Lucia to write down the Secret in 1944, the Virgin could not have failed to direct also the date for its revelation

- Sister Lucia could not have had the premonition that she would be dead in 1960 when she lived to the advanced age of 97, and nowhere in any of her writings do we find the least suggestion that she anticipated dying before her 53rd birthday.

- Sister Lucia could not have thought that she, the very recipient of the Third Secret, the chosen seer of God, was an *obstacle* to its disclosure and "interpretation."

- In *Last Visionary* Bertone claims he was sent to Coimbra to interview Lucia in April 2000, just before publication of the vision and the commentary in *Message*, because the Pope "had need of a definitive interpretation on the part of the religious." Yet, in the same book, Bertone asks us to believe that Sister Lucia viewed her very existence on earth as "the last *obstacle*" to the Secret's interpretation.

60. No independent witness has ever corroborated Bertone's claim that Lucia "confessed" to fabricating the Virgin's "express order," even though witnesses were supposedly in attendance during the "confession."

Bertone relies on unrecorded, uncorroborated "interviews" and ever-changing "quotations" he attributes to the seer.

61. Bertone conducts an alleged ten hours of interviews of the seer in order to substantiate his account, but fails to make a videotape, an audiotape or even a written transcript of these historic encounters, and does not even provide a signed statement by Lucia in her own language (Portuguese).

62. From ten hours of alleged interviews with Lucia, which would comprise thousands of spoken words, Bertone "quotes" exactly *nine words* attributed to Lucia concerning the contents of the Third Secret — the very matter in controversy — and no witness has come forward to corroborate even those nine words, although witnesses were allegedly present.

63. Bertone claims he has signed, edited "minutes" of his meetings with Lucia, but he has never produced them.

64. Bertone has never quoted Sister Lucia the same way twice on the same subject, and the fragmentary "quotations" allegedly drawn from his never-produced "notes" change every time he repeats them. In particular, Bertone has given:

- *Six inconsistent versions* of his claim that Lucia told him she "agrees" with his "interpretation" of the vision of the bishop in white. No independent witness has corroborated this claim.

- *Four inconsistent versions* of his claim that Lucia told him the consecration of Russia was effected by a consecration of the world in 1984. No independent witness has corroborated this claim.

- *Three inconsistent versions* of Lucia's "confession" that she invented the "express order of Our Lady" regarding 1960. No independent witness has corroborated this claim — not even the retired Bishop of Fatima, who attended the meeting of April 27, 2000 at which Lucia allegedly "confessed," yet conspicuously fails to confirm Bertone's account of the "confession" during his appearance on the *Telepace* telecast.

- *Three inconsistent versions* of the configuration of envelopes involved in the transmission of the Third Secret, wherein the following telling discrepancies, among others, appear:

  - o None of the three versions mention the "Capovilla envelope" his own witness (Capovilla, as interviewed by De Carli) identifies, but which Bertone has never produced and whose non-production he fails to explain.

  - o Bertone variously claims that Lucia personally prepared one, two or three envelopes for transmission of the Secret, depending on which version one considers, yet not until the TV appearance of May 31, 2007 does Bertone mention *two* sealed envelopes bearing the "express order of Our Lady" that the envelopes not be opened until 1960.

  - o One of the versions mentions an outer envelope bearing the notation "Third Part of the Secret" — another envelope Bertone has failed to produce, and perhaps a reference to the never-produced "Capovilla envelope."

65. Bertone claims that during the interview of November 2001 Lucia told him she agrees with everything in *Message*, a 44-page document, even though *Message*

- as accurately reported by the *Los Angeles Times*, "gently debunks" Lucia's account of the Third Secret;

- suggests that Lucia concocted the vision of the bishop in white from images she had seen in devotional books;

- accuses her of inventing the "express order of Our Lady" concerning revelation of the Secret in 1960; and

- cites as an eminent expert on Marian apparitions the modernist Jesuit, Edouard Dhanis, who declared that Sister Lucia invented the entire Message of Fatima except for its call to prayer and penance.

66. Bertone claims that during the same November 2001 interview Lucia uttered verbatim as her own statement a 165-word passage from *Message*, written by Cardinal Ratzinger.

67. In May 2007, only after Lucia has died and Capovilla has revealed the existence of a second text of the Third Secret, Bertone suddenly announces — for the first time in seven years of controversy — that during one of his alleged interviews of the seer she declared: "Yes, this is the Third Secret, and I have never written other." Yet Bertone fails to identify which of the interviews contains this never-before-mentioned statement or to provide any transcript or other independent verification of the purported quotation, and no independent witness corroborates it — even though Bertone names Bishop Serafim, the retired Bishop of Fatima, as a witness to the alleged statement.

68. When Bishop Serafim does appear during Bertone's telecast on *Telepace* in September 2007, he conspicuously fails to corroborate Lucia's alleged statement, even though he was brought to Rome for the very purpose of defending Bertone's position.

69. As to all of the contested statements Bertone attributes to Lucia during ten hours of interviews he never recorded, Bertone is literally *the only witness in the world* who claims to have heard the statements.

Bertone suddenly shifts to an emphasis on an "authentic" text and a mere personal "conviction" that all has been revealed.

70. After Socci shows conclusively that there is (or was) a text of

the Secret located in the papal apartment, Bertone, during his appearance on *Door to Door*, begins to harp on an "authentic" text in the Holy Office *archives*, while ignoring or refusing to answer all questions about a text in the *papal apartment*, whose existence he will finally admit (through De Carli) in September 2007.

71. Instead of stating forthrightly on *Door to Door* that he has revealed the entire Third Secret of Fatima and that there are no other texts related to it (whether or not deemed "authentic"), Bertone states only that he and his collaborators "decided to publish *all that actually existed in the archives of the Holy Office...*", when he knows very well that the burning issue in the controversy is precisely the text that was *not* in those archives but in the papal apartment.

72. During the radio broadcast of June 6, 2007, Bertone states he is "firmly convinced" there is no other text pertaining to the Secret, even though *if* he had really asked Sister Lucia, and *if* she had really told him categorically that there is no other text besides the text of the vision, he would hardly have expressed his remark as a mere personal conviction.

73. During the same radio broadcast Bertone states his "conviction" that there is no other text of the Secret is based on "the documentation that was *in the Secret Archive of the Holy Office*" — again focusing on what was in the archives, when, again, he knows very well there was a text in the papal apartment, that being the text contained in the "Capovilla envelope" he has never produced, and whose existence is not recorded in the archives.

74. During the radio broadcast Bertone also purports to base his "firm conviction" on what he calls "explicit declarations of Sister Lucia in the presence of the Bishop of Fatima" — declarations Bertone has never mentioned during the previous seven years; and he fails to quote any such "explicit declarations."

75. During the radio broadcast Bertone fails to mention his earlier claim (suddenly announced in *Last Visionary*, published after Lucia's death) that Lucia told *him* on some unknown date that "Yes, this is the Third Secret, and I have never written other"; Bertone now relies instead on the never-before-mentioned (and still not quoted) "explicit declarations" of Lucia in the

presence of Bishop Serafim.

76. Yet when Serafim appears during the *Telepace* broadcast on September 21, 2007, *he fails to corroborate any "explicit declarations" by Lucia* regarding the alleged non-existence of another text of the Secret; reading from a prepared text, he pointedly remarks that he has "nothing, almost nothing" to say, and carefully notes that he will testify to *"only one fact"*: that Lucia confirmed that the text of the vision is authentic, which is not in dispute.

77. Regarding the existence of another text, Serafim does affirm mysteriously that the Third Secret has been revealed "in an *authentic* and integral way" — thus joining Bertone in emphasizing an "authentic text" rather than simply declaring forthrightly that absolutely no other text pertaining to the Secret exists, either authentic or "inauthentic."

Bertone relies on a bogus "letter from Lucia" that he conspicuously fails to ask her to authenticate.

78. In *Message*, Bertone fails to cite any direct testimony of Lucia that the 1984 consecration of the world sufficed for a consecration of Russia, even though he had just "interviewed" Lucia weeks before *Message* was published (the purported interview of April 27, 2000) and could readily have obtained such testimony if Lucia had been willing to provide it.

79. Instead, *Message* in 2000, and *Last Visionary* in 2007, rely on a computer-generated letter from 1989 to an unnamed addressee, even though that letter is widely known as a patent fabrication because it contains factual errors Lucia could not have made, and because Lucia never used a computer to write letters (especially back in the dawn of the personal computer age).

80. Bertone *never asks Lucia to authenticate this letter* during any of his three alleged interviews of the seer, spanning ten hours. Or, alternatively, he did ask her to authenticate it, she declined to do so, and Bertone has concealed this fact.

81. As if to authenticate the letter, Bertone stated in 2005 that "'at the end Lucia even used the computer," only to state in 2007 (in *Last Visionary*) that Lucia "*never* worked with the computer."

Bertone provides deceptive translations of
Lucia's purported 1982 letter to the Pope.

82. In *Message* Bertone and his collaborators publish a fragment from a purported letter of Lucia to John Paul II in 1982 regarding the content of the Third Secret; nothing in the fragment indicates that it was addressed to the Pope, and neither the salutation nor the signature page is provided.

83. The phrase in the Portuguese original of the fragment "The third part of the secret, *that you are so anxious to know...*" proves that the purported letter could not possibly have been addressed to the Pope, for the Pope could not have been "so anxious to know" the Secret he had already read as of 1982.

84. Knowing this, Bertone and his collaborators systematically delete "that you are so anxious to know" from every translation of the fragment, without using ellipses to indicate the deletion. (*See* Appendix IV.)

85. Nevertheless, the purported letter fragment demolishes Bertone's "interpretation" of the vision of the bishop in white as culminating in the 1981 assassination attempt, because the fragment, written a year *after* the attempt, not only says nothing about the attempt, but informs "the Pope" that "if *we have not yet seen the complete fulfillment of the final part of this prophecy*, we are going towards it little by little..."

Lucia is never allowed to speak in person.

86. Although Bertone claims there has been nothing further to reveal concerning the Third Secret since publication of the vision on June 26, 2000, he and his collaborators never allow Sister Lucia to testify in person on any of the matters at issue at any time.

87. Sister Lucia is not permitted to participate in the press conference at which the vision was published, and is not even permitted to watch it on television.

Lucia's book fails to corroborate
any of Bertone's claims.

88. When Sister Lucia writes an entire book on the Message of

Fatima to "answer multiple questions in a global manner, not being able to answer every person individually," the book fails to answer a single question concerning the Third Secret controversy (or the Consecration of Russia), and does not even mention the Third Secret (or the Consecration).

89. Sister Lucia's book fails to corroborate a single statement attributed to her by Bertone based on his alleged ten hours of unrecorded conversation with the seer.

Bertone speaks often, but avoids all issues and all independent questioners.

90. Despite having written a book and made two television appearances and a radio appearance in an attempt to defend his account, Bertone has never once personally and directly addressed in his own words *any* of the crucial points in the Third Secret controversy, set forth above.

91. Bertone never, in his own words, explicitly denies that there is a text containing the words of the Virgin Mary pertaining to the Third Secret which explain the vision and/or provide what is indicated by Lucia's "etc."

92. Bertone refuses to answer questions on the controversy from *any* independent journalist, even though the Pope himself takes questions from the press.

93. Bertone will not even speak to Socci about the controversy at the time when Socci, his personal acquaintance, was intent on defending Bertone's position.

94. Socci, one of the most prominent and respected Catholics in Italy, is physically removed from the premises of the *Telepace* telecast like a common trespasser, after Bertone literally flees from his question by a side entrance to the auditorium.

95. Having failed for seven years to provide direct answers to any of the major questions in the controversy—and, in fact, having only provided further proof of a cover-up—Bertone maintains that he has laid all questions to rest.

The Holy See and the Pope decline to give
official support to Bertone's account or to criticize Socci.

96. The Holy See offers *no* official response to the testimony of Capovilla, the reported testimony of Cardinal Ottaviani, or the internationally publicized contention of Antonio Socci that there has been a Vatican cover-up of a text of the Third Secret.

97. The Holy See offers *no* official defense of Bertone's position, which he has defended on his own by way of private interventions: his book, his two TV appearances and his radio broadcast.

98. The Pope gives *no* statement, official or otherwise, regarding the testimony of Capovilla, the reported testimony of Cardinal Ottaviani, or Antonio Socci's public accusation of a Vatican cover-up.

99. The Pope does, however, write Socci a personal letter thanking him for his book and "the sentiments which have suggested it" (while also providing a letter introducing Bertone's book but avoiding any details of the Third Secret controversy).

100. The Pope's letter to Socci does not even suggest that Socci has made false accusations, even though Socci has publicly called into question the veracity of Bertone's entire account and charged Bertone and his collaborators with hiding from the Church and the world a text that contains the very words of the Mother of God.

101. Neither the Pope nor the Holy See has provided *any* statement, official or unofficial, declaring that the text Socci contends exists and is being hidden does not exist, or any statement even *mentioning* the controversy between Socci and Bertone.

Appendix III
The Great Secret of Fatima as Recorded in Sister Lucia's Fourth Memoir

The pertinent section of the handwritten integral text of the Message of Fatima from Sister Lucia's Fourth Memoir, which contains the Virgin's words at the beginning of the Third Secret: "In Portugal, the dogma of the Faith will always be preserved etc." Cardinal Bertone avoided this key phrase by using the less complete Third Memoir, which does not contain the phrase, and by falsely characterizing the Virgin's words in the Fourth Memoir as "some annotations" by Lucia.

Appendix IV

A Systematic Deception

> *A terceira parte do segredo, que tanto ansiais por conhecer, é uma revelação simbólica, que se refere a esta parte do Mensagem, condicionado a se, sim ou não, nós aceitarmos ou não, o que a Mensagem nos pede: "Se atenderem a Meus pedidos, a Russia se converterá e terão paz; se não, espalhará seus erros pelo mundo", etc.*

The Vatican's June 26, 2000 commentary on the Third Secret, *The Message of Fatima*, contains this Portuguese text from a fragment of a purported letter from Lucia to the Pope in 1982 concerning the Third Secret. The fragment has no address or closing to indicate it was sent to the Pope, and contains the revealing statement to its recipient "that you are so anxious to know" (*que tanto ansiais por conhecer*) the Secret. As Bertone himself admits, the Pope had already read the Secret in 1981 and thus could not have been "so anxious to know" it in 1982. The Vatican deleted the phrase "that you are so anxious to know" from all translations of the fragment, without using ellipses to indicate the deletion, thereby concealing the whole phrase which proves that the purported letter could not have been addressed to the Pope. The systematic deletion of this phrase from every translation, and even from the Portuguese typeset reproduction of the handwritten fragment, could only have been calculated to deceive.

Set forth below are photographic reproductions from the various language versions of the Vatican commentary, showing deliberate deletion of the key phrase without ellipses to indicate the deletion:

English:

> The third part of the secret is a symbolic revelation, referring to this part of the Message, conditioned by whether we accept or not what the Message itself asks of us: 'If my requests are heeded, Russia will be converted, and there will be peace; if not, she will spread her errors throughout the world, etc.'.

Italian:

> La terza parte del segreto è una rivelazione simbolica, che si riferisce a questa parte del Messaggio, condizionato dal fatto se accettiamo o no ciò che il Messaggio stesso ci chiede: "Se accetteranno le mie richieste, la Russia si convertirà e avranno pace; se no, spargerà i suoi errori per il mondo, ecc.".

Spanish:

> La tercera parte es una revelación simbólica, que se refiere a esta parte del Mensaje, condicionado al hecho de que aceptemos o no lo que el mismo Mensaje pide: "si aceptaren mis peticiones, la Rusia se convertirá y tendrán paz; si no, diseminará sus errores por el mundo, etc.".

French:

> La troisième partie du secret est une révélation symbolique, qui se réfère à cette partie du Message, conditionné par le fait que nous acceptions ou non ce que le Message lui-même nous demande: "si on accepte mes demandes, la Russie se convertira et on aura la paix; sinon elle répandra ses erreurs à travers le monde, etc...".

Incredibly, even the Portuguese version of the Vatican commentary deceptively omits the phrase *"que tanto ansiais por conhecer"* from the typeset reproduction of the handwritten fragment. Compare the highlighted lines below:

A terceira parte do segredo é uma revelação simbólica, que se refere a este trecho da Mensagem, condicionada ao facto de aceitarmos ou não o que a Mensagem nos pede: "Se atenderem a meus pedidos, a Rússia converter-se-á e terão paz; se não, espalhará os seus erros pelo mundo, etc". Porque não temos atendido a este apelo da Mensagem, verificamos que ela se tem cumprido, a Rússia foi invadindo o mundo com os seus erros. E se não vemos ainda, como facto consumado, o final desta profecia, vemos que para aí caminhamos a passos largos. Se não recuarmos no caminho do pecado, do ódio, da vingança, da injustiça atropelando os direitos da pessoa humana, da imoralidade e da violência, etc. E não digamos que é Deus que assim nos castiga; mas, sim, que são os homens que para si mesmos se preparam o castigo. Deus apenas nos adverte e chama ao bom caminho, respeitando a liberdade que nos deu; por isso os homens são responsáveis ».[5]

Texto original da carta:

A terceira parte do segredo: —Refere-se às palavras de Nossa Senhora: "Se não, espalhará seus erros pelo mundo, promovendo guerras e perseguições à Igreja. Os bons serão martirizados, o Santo Padre terá muito que sofrer, várias nações serão aniquiladas." (13–VII–1917)

A terceira parte do segredo, que tanto ansiais por conhecer, é uma revelação simbólica, que se refere a este trecho da Mensagem, condicionado a se, sim ou não, nós aceitarmos ou não, o que a Mensagem nos pede: "Se atenderem a Meus pedidos, a Russia se converterá e terão paz; se não, espalhará seus erros pelo mundo", etc.

Porque não temos atendido a este apelo da Mensagem, verificamos que ela se tem cumprido, a Russia foi invadindo o mundo com os seus erros. E se não vemos ainda, o facto consumado, do final desta profecia, vemos que para aí caminhamos a passos largos. Se não recuamos no caminho do pecado do ódio, da vingança, da injustiça atropelando os direitos da pessoa humana, da imoralidade e da violência etc.

E não digamos que é Deus, que assim nos castiga, mas sim, que são os homens, que para si mesmos se preparam o castigo. Deus, apenas nos adverte e chama ao bom caminho, respeitando a liberdade que nos deu; por isso, os homens são responsaveis.

Appendix V

The Pope Publicly Declares, *After* the 1984 Consecration of the World, That Our Lady is "Still Awaiting" the Consecration of Russia

L'OSSERVATORE ROMANO

GIORNALE QUOTIDIANO — POLITICO RELIGIOSO

UNICUIQUE SUUM — NON PRAEVALEBUNT

Anno CXXIV · N. 72 (37.564)   CITTÀ DEL VATICANO   Lunedì-Martedì 26-27 Marzo 1984

NELLA GIORNATA GIUBILARE DELLE FAMIGLIE IL PAPA AFFIDA ALLA MADONNA GLI UOMINI E LE NAZIONI

Liberaci dalla fame, dalla guerra

Madre della Chiesa! Illumina il Popolo di Dio sulle vie della fede, della speranza e della carità! Illumina specialmente i popoli di cui tu aspetti la nostra consacrazione e il nostro affidamento. Aiutaci a vivere nella verità della consacrazione di Cristo per l'intera famiglia umana del mondo contemporaneo.

Tre eventi

CONTINUAZIONE DALLA PRIMA PAGINA

Liberaci dalla fame, dalla guerra

Photographic reproduction of the March 26, 1984 issue of *L'Osservatore Romano*, with translation, enlarged, of Pope John Paul II's words. On March 25, 1984, the Pope, making the consecration before the statue of Our Lady of Fatima, departed from his prepared text to add the words highlighted above and translated below. The words he added at this point indicate clearly, that the Pope knew then that the consecration of the world done that day did not fulfill the requests of Our Lady of Fatima. After performing the consecration of the world proper, a few paragraphs above, the Pope added the highlighted words which translate: "Enlighten especially the peoples of which you yourself are awaiting our consecration and confiding." This clearly shows he knows Our Lady is awaiting the Pope and bishops to consecrate certain peoples to her, that is the peoples of Russia.

Opponents of the Consecration of Russia have, conveniently, from 1984 until this day, omitted to report that the Pope actually said, in effect, that he had not done the Consecration of Russia as requested by Our Lady of Fatima.

Principal Publications Cited in This Book

Alonso, Father Joaquin, *La verdad sobre el Secreto de Fátima*. Madrid: Centro Mariano, 1976.

Bertone, Cardinal Tarcisio, *L'Ultima Veggente di Fatima* (Last Visionary). Milan: Rai and Eri Rizzoli, 2007.

Congregation for the Doctrine of the Faith, *The Message of Fatima*. (English edition). Vatican City: Libreria Editrice Vaticana, 2000.

Kramer, Father Paul, *The Devil's Final Battle*. Terryville: The Missionary Association, 2002.

Michel de la Sainte Trinité (Frère), *The Whole Truth About Fatima*,
    Volume I   *Science and the Facts*   (1989)
    Volume II   *The Secret and the Church* (1990)
    Volume III   *The Third Secret*   (1990 and 2001)
Buffalo: Immaculate Heart Publications.

Socci, Antonio, *Il Quarto Segreto di Fatima* (Fourth Secret). Milan: Rizzoli, 2006.

Further Suggested Reading

Books

Alonso, Father Joaquin, *Fátima ante la Esfinge*. Madrid: Ediciones "Sol de Fátima," 1979.

----------, *Fátima, escuela de oración*. Madrid: Ediciones "Sol de Fátima," 1980.

----------, *El Mensaje de Fátima en Pontevedra*. Madrid: Ediciones "Sol de Fátima," 1975.

Authors various, *The "Divine Impatience"*. Buffalo: Immaculate Heart Publications, 2000.

Fellows, Mark, *Fatima in Twilight*. Niagara Falls: Marmion Publications, 2003.

----------, *Sister Lucia: Apostle of Mary's Immaculate Heart*. Buffalo: Immaculate Heart Publications, 2007.

Ferrara, Christopher A., *EWTN: A Network Gone Wrong*. Pound Ridge: Good Counsel Publications, 2006. See Chapter 16, "The Assault on Fatima."

François de Marie des Anges (Frère), *Fatima: Intimate Joy, World Event*: Book One, *Fatima: The Astonishing Truth* (1993); Book Two, *Fatima: Mary's Immaculate Heart and Your Salvation* (1993); Book Three, *Fatima: The Only Way to World Peace* (1993); Book Four, *Fatima: Tragedy and Triumph* (1994). Buffalo: Immaculate Heart Publications.

Gruner, Father Nicholas, *World Enslavement or Peace ... It's Up To the Pope*. Fort Erie: The Fatima Crusader, 1989.

Manifold, Deirdre, *Fatima and the Great Conspiracy*. Buffalo: The

Militia of Our Immaculate Mother, 1993.

Mura, Father Gérard, *Fátima Roma Moscú: La Consagración de Rusia al Corazón Inmaculado de María aún está pendiente.* Santiago, Chile: Librería Fátima, 2005.

Periodicals

The Fatima Crusader magazine can be obtained by writing to The Fatima Center, 17000 State Route 30, Constable, New York 12926 USA or 452 Kraft Road, Fort Erie, Ontario, L2A 4M7 Canada; or calling toll-free 1-800-263-8160; or by e-mail to info@fatima.org.

Web Links/Videos/DVDs

I.

Paolini, Solideo, "Report from Italy: My Meetings with Archbishop Capovilla and the Socci-Cardinal Bertone Struggle," address at Fatima conference in Botucatu, Brazil, August 2007—www.fatimapeaceconferences.com/solideo_paolini_2007_en.asp

Socci, Antonio, "Bertone in the 'Wasp's Nest' of Controversy", June 2, 2007—www.fatimacrusader.com/cr86/cr86pg43.asp.

----------, "Dear Cardinal Bertone: Who—Between You and Me—is Deliberately Lying?", May 12, 2007—www.fatima.org/news/newsviews/052907socci.asp

II.

The Fatima Crusader—www.fatimacrusader.com

Gruner, Father Nicholas, *World Enslavement or Peace ... It's Up To the Pope* (Fort Erie, Ontario: The Fatima Crusader, 1989)—www.worldenslavementorpeace.com

Heaven's Key to Peace video/DVD (Fort Erie, Ontario: The Fatima Center, 2006)— www.fatimaondemand.org/media/hkp/hkp-watch.htm

Kramer, Father Paul, *The Devil's Final Battle* (Terryville, Connecticut: The Missionary Association, 2002)—www.devilsfinalbattle.com/content2.htm

"A Prophetic Interview with Sister Lucy of Fatima," *Fatima Priest* (Pound Ridge, New York: Good Counsel Publications, 1997, Second Edition)—www.fatimapriest.com/Appendix3.htm

III.

"Consecration of Russia"—www.fatima.org/consecrussia/default.asp

"Published Testimony: Cardinal Ratzinger (November 1984)"—www.fatima.org/thirdsecret/ratzinger.asp

"The Seers Kidnapped (August 13-15, 1917)"—www.fatima.org/essentials/opposed/seerkidn.asp

"Silencing of the Messengers: Father Fuentes (1959 - 1965)"—www.fatima.org/essentials/opposed/frfuentes.asp